GET THE LOOT
AND RUN

GET THE LOOT AND RUN

FIND MONEY FOR YOUR BUSINESS

ANTHONY PRICE

Whether you're a startup or billion-dollar business, *Get the Loot and Run* will show you how to source capital while building an extraordinary business focused on solving problems for customers.

A portion of the sale price supports the Ucal McKenzie Breakaway Foundation. Visit ucalbreakaway.com.

To Donovan,

Face up. Make yourself big. Shoot.

Risk is a challenge to those who are brave.

—Charlie Murphy

CONTENTS

PART III – MONEY: THE MAIN INGREDIENT

PART IV – SIDE A: MOSTLY DEBT

PART V – SIDE B: MOSTLY EQUITY

FOREWORD

SUCCESSFUL ENTREPRENEURS ARE THE NEW LEGENDS of the American dream. Bill Gates at Microsoft, Elon Musk at Tesla, Oprah Winfrey, Larry Page and Sergey Brin at Google, the late Steve Jobs at Apple, Brian Chesky, Joe Gebbia and Nathan Blecharczyk at Airbnb, Dr. Dre at Beats Electronics and others have all solved, or are solving large problems, attracting vast amounts of capital, and have become wealthy beyond even their dreams. These and many cases that are works in progress are stories of the power entrepreneurs have to change society, here in the United States and in the world.

However, these are the exceptions, not only in their success, but in how they solved the inherent problems associated with being an entrepreneur. The problems facing all entrepreneurs are either overcome or lead to the demise of that particular dream. Some entrepreneurs, like the ones listed above, acquired the knowledge to overcome these problems. Most entrepreneurs do not have the knowledge or the access to knowledge to turn their dreams into reality. This new book by Anthony Price is a welcome addition to the body of entrepreneurial literature that provides a basic understanding of the challenges entrepreneurs must overcome.

The breadth and completeness of this work makes it a must-read for any entrepreneur in the midst of trying to start, fund, and launch their business. This book is a road map that can be read from beginning to end or from end to beginning, depending on where you are in your entrepreneurial journey. But no matter where you start, this book will assist you in getting to where you are going faster.

Entrepreneurship is a difficult road to navigate. It is often said among economists and others who study entrepreneurship, that time is the most valuable asset you don't own. In entrepreneurship, time is often in a race with money.

It sometimes feels like time spent reading is inimical in this struggle, but your time is well spent reading and absorbing the wisdom in these pages. You can learn the hard way through the hard lessons of uninformed experience, or you can learn the smart way by learning from the experiences of others. I don't know about you, but I prefer the smart way.

Dr. Fred McKinney
Carlton Highsmith Chair of Innovation & Entrepreneurship
Quinnipiac University

ACKNOWLEDGMENTS

I DREAMED OF WRITING A BOOK for a long time, but my dream slept like a hibernating bear. In 2015, my excuses vanished when I left the world of steady paychecks to start LootScout. In the beginning, my fledging business ate up all my time and resources. In 2017, during a slow time for the business, I put an end to excuses and awakened the sleeping bear in me. I launched a Kickstarter campaign to fund this book.

This book is a coordinated effort. I am fortunate that I have two amazing people who turned my dream into a reality. Kathy Worthington is the best editor a writer could have. She is a lover of words and is an inquisitive person. Kathy was patient with me and provided a critical eye when my thoughts and grammar came off the tracks. Her attention to detail makes every sentence better. Thank you for editing this book. May your days be filled with fun and sun—and plenty of mischief with your grandchildren.

Design matters. Suzanne McKenzie is a business owner, creative director, lover of art, all things Andy Warhol and New York City. Over the years, she has worked on countless projects for me and has delivered every time. Suzanne gave this book its personality. I appreciate her thoughtfulness, patience, and desire for perfection. Thank you for pushing me to get this project done.

A special thank-you message goes to Michael Ciaburri, Everett Cook, Mark Cousineau, Michael Duncan, Evan S. Goldstein, Jay J. Rasmus, Gert McCarthy, and Cecilia Molinari for all of their help. I send my gratitude to John Katovich and his team at Cutting Edge Capital in Oakland, California. John is a securities lawyer and pioneer in the growing movement to democratize capital for entrepreneurs and small-business owners.

No one achieves by himself. I am thankful to the people who helped me focus on the prize: a book to help entrepreneurs build better businesses and source capital. I was never alone on this journey because of the people who inspired me—and the shoulders of a nation of people whom I stand on today who paved the road for me. Their triumphs and struggles allowed me to keep my eyes focused on the prize.

George Eliot, the English novelist, said, "It's never too late to be what you might have been."[1] What's your dream? What are you waiting for? The difference between success and failure is starting. You can do it. You must do it!

A SPECIAL THANK YOU TO MY SUPPORTERS

I received financial assistance from family, friends and strangers on Kickstarter. I am thankful for every dollar received. The names that follow are supporters who went the extra mile: Access Rehab Centers (I serve on the Board of Directors), Andrew Woods, Eric C. Hampton, John E. Robinson, KC Ward, Normando Moquette Jr., Suzanne McKenzie, Tony Jorgensen, Tricia and Wendell Price. Writing this book has been the experience of a lifetime. To all my supporters, I offer a big thank you. See the appendix for more about the wonderful people who supported me.

INTRODUCTION

I DEDICATE THIS BOOK to people like you—aspiring entrepreneurs and business owners—focused on solving real problems for customers, like a firefighter rushing toward a burning building. My goal is to show you why your business model and customers, not capital, are the primary drivers of success. Fix your business model and capital will follow.

As a former economic development executive and business owner, I have met people who thought finding capital was like solving Rubik's Cube. I wrote this book to help you find capital and to provide must-have information to grow your business. But don't lose sight of the bigger picture: Capital is a conduit for you to live your dream—your best life. Your business is how you deliver that dream. Take care of your business and it will take care of you.

William Shakespeare, the English playwright, actor and poet, wrote, "Brevity is the soul of wit."[1] In your hands, you have concise instructions to source capital, along with practical wisdom to grow your business. I want to help you build the best business the world has ever seen by cutting through the noise, hype, and confusing information. This book is your Swiss Army knife to get to the truth.

MONEY

Money has as many nicknames as there are dishes on The Cheesecake Factory menu: loot, moolah, dough, bread, cheddar, capital, bucks, cake, CREAM (Cash Rules Everything Around Me, made famous by Wu-Tang Clan), Benjamins, paper, chips, bank, band, gaup or C-note.[2] While the names may be interchangeable, know your audience. I prefer "capital," which is used by bankers, financial types, and professionals—people who have a say in whether you get money. When you find capital, use it wisely.

If you are like most business owners, there is never enough capital. It seems mysterious and elusive, especially when one doesn't have the proper credit score, collateral, or a multimillion dollar business that bankers want to fund. This book will help put capital in your hands, but only when you understand its message: **You don't have a capital problem. You have a business model problem.** Repeat the previous two sentences three times. Let it sink into the dark recesses of your subconscious mind.

I discuss numerous types of capital and where to find it. However, make no mistake, my preferred source of capital is from community lenders, who typically are community banks, credit unions and nonprofit lenders throughout the country. I focus on community lenders because they have deep roots and a rich tradition of serving their customers face-to-face in their communities—not by algorithms.

FOOD FOR THOUGHT

Before we get started, think of capital as food at your favorite buffet restaurant. Imagine all the different colors, textures, and aromas dancing with your olfactory receptors. The thought of mouth-watering flavors is enough to make you hungry. Food serves the purpose of nourishing us, just like capital is the fuel for business. However, all food is not good for your long-term health—or waistline. You must decide what you value most when it comes to eating; the same holds true for sourcing "patient" (slower) capital. Find capital that makes your long-term business health a priority.

I discuss the capital phenomena: good, cheap or fast. In reality, it's hard to find capital that is simultaneously good, cheap and fast. You must choose which two you value most. If you accept fast capital with higher interest rates and onerous terms, you may be asking for trouble—it's the fast food of capital. Focus on patient capital, reasonable interest rates—

WHEN YOU FIX YOUR BUSINESS MODEL,
YOU FIX YOUR CAPITAL ISSUES
BECAUSE THE TWO ARE INTERWOVEN.

given the risk—with generous terms that are good for your business health and community.

Some people can't wait to get to the end of a book. If that's you, here's a spoiler-alert summary:

1. Declare yourself an entrepreneur or small-business owner.
2. Create your business model.
3. Build your team.
4. Delight customers.
5. Find capital.

That's the essence of any successful business.

YOUR PERSONAL SOUNDTRACK

I have sprinkled music throughout the book to document my journey. My soul craves music. It has the ability to inspire and motivate me to new heights. When all else fails, music, art and nature are a respite from the rigors of making a living. I turn to music to pick me up, when inspiration wanes. Make a soundtrack for your life.

Your journey will be difficult and rewarding, but don't stop. May your family, friends and the world be the beneficiaries of your dedication, hard work, and brilliance. You are part of the chain of humanity that stretches back to the beginning of time. You were put on this earth to do great things. Now is your time to shine.

You must do something. Napoleon Hill, author of the book, *The Law of Success*, wrote, "Books and lessons, in themselves, are of but little value; their real value, if any, lies not in their printed pages, but in the possible action which they may arouse in the reader."[3] The power is in your hands to build a better business. This is your time. I wish you luck on your odyssey called life.

PART I
Start Here:
Keep It Simple

"My Shot," featuring Busta Rhymes, Joell Ortiz & Nate Ruess (Rise Up Remix), *The Hamilton Mixtape*

1

WHAT ARE YOU: ENTREPRENEUR OR SMALL-BUSINESS OWNER?

MY UNIVERSE WAS SHAKEN TO ITS FOUNDATION, like a building crumbling to the ground under the force of a 9.0 earthquake, after reading Ben Lamm's guest column in *Entrepreneur* magazine: "Stop Calling Everyone an Entrepreneur—They Aren't."[1]

I thought this was typical Silicon Valley propaganda, from a hotshot in a hoodie and jeans. But after my less-skeptical self emerged, I began to think there was merit to what Ben was espousing. Ben, the founder of several companies and CEO of a startup, believes that the "entrepreneur" label has become as ubiquitous as Nikes on NBA-wannabes. He says that a lot more people are qualified to manage a "Jamba Juice than take companies from inception, through market traction (paying customers), funding, growth and eventual IPO or exit."[2] I full-heartedly agree. Ben comes from a world where solving big "hair-on-fire" problems and scaling a

I THOUGHT THIS WAS TYPICAL SILICON VALLEY PROPOGANDA, **FROM A HOTSHOT IN A HOODIE AND JEANS.**

business as fast as possible are crucial to owning a market and attracting OPM: Other People's Money. This business template requires a steady stream of capital to be pumped into the business as fuel, which most businesses don't have. The money that your small business burns through is yours, or if you are lucky, your family's, friend's or the bank's. In reality, a startup business has a limited amount of time to build a business with paying customers, or it will fail. Think of Chobani yogurt in your refrigerator—it's expiration date is a constant reminder that it will not last forever.

The pressure comes from investors. When you play with OPM, investors are the house, they make the rules, and they want to make lots of money (10, 20, or 30x return or more) from a liquidity event (an exit from your business within five to seven years as a result of selling or going public). In Ben's view, the mission is the domination of an industry from the playbooks of Facebook, Google and Amazon.

ENTREPRENEURS TAKE BIG RISKS

Entrepreneurs view problems from a unique perspective. George Bernard Shaw, the playwright, said, "The reasonable man adapts himself to the world: the unreasonable one persists in trying to adapt the world to himself. Therefore all progress depends on the unreasonable man."[3] Entrepreneurs are the unreasonable men (and women), risk-takers, but not gamblers. To them, gambling is working at a job they don't like, with no future for advancement, for a boss who doesn't value them. Entrepreneurs are confident in their abilities to solve big problems, assemble a team and scale. They are a special group of people who believe in their vision, talent, version of reality and work ethic.

Blaze Pizza, a restaurant concept started five years ago with two stores in Southern California, plans to open 100 to 150 stores a year, starting in 2018.[4] Blaze creates made-to-order pizzas in an assembly-line style, similar to Chipotle or Subway, and cooks pizzas in three minutes. Its cooking innovation is the "secret sauce" that opened the lunch-crowd market to pizza. Blaze makes its own dough, fresh, and from scratch. The company has attracted a lot of attention on its social media channels. LeBron James, the perennial NBA all-star, is a spokesperson and early investor in the company, choosing an equity deal over a multimillion-dollar deal from McDonald's.

The biggest differentiator between an entrepreneur and a small-business owner is that the former wants to solve big problems, grow quickly and takes huge risks. Think Facebook, Google, and Tesla. Facebook has over two billion monthly users, and its mission is: "Give people the power to build community and bring the world closer together."[5] Google is the most visited website on the Internet. Its mission is: "To organize the world's information and make it universally accessible and useful."[6] Founded in 2003, Tesla Motor's mission is: "To accelerate the advent of sustainable transport by bringing compelling mass market electric cars to market as soon as possible."[7]

SMALL AND POWERFUL

A business consists of coordinated activities that deliver value to customers with the intent of generating a profit to its owners. There are twenty-nine million small businesses in the U.S., which represent 99.9 percent of all businesses.[8] The U.S. Small Business Administration (SBA) defines a small business as having fewer than 500 employees; organized for profit; has a place of business in the U.S.; operates primarily in the U.S.; is independently owned and operated, and is not dominant in its field on a national basis.[9]

Michael Gerber, the author of *The E-Myth* states, "There is a myth in this country—I call it the E-Myth—which says that small businesses are started by entrepreneurs risking capital to make a profit. This is simply not so."[10] Most small business owners make the misguided assumption that because they know the technical work of the business, they understand the business that does the technical work.[11] These are two different things, just as being a home baker doesn't make one competent to run a neighborhood bakery or a corporate chain of bakeries.

Small business owner does not equal entrepreneur. Gene Marks, a *Forbes.com* contributor and proud small-business owner, said it best in his piece, "The Difference Between An Entrepreneur And A Small Business Owner": "Entrepreneurs take risks."[12] Gene goes on to say that they take much bigger risks than business owners do. Marks' dad was an entrepreneur in the mid-nineties who dreamed of delivering his proprietary bookkeeping software to the world. At the time, Gene and his dad were both certified public accountants (CPAs), who took on Intuit's QuickBooks and the Year 2000 bug. Unfortunately, they lost.

Gene is not afraid to say he is a small-business owner. He likes stability and is satisfied with knowing what the future holds. Gene says that in contrast, entrepreneurs are never satisfied with the status quo. The typical pizza store owner is content making a good living with one store.

Compare Ben Lamm's vision of a startup business on steroids with how most small businesses start. Look at your favorite small business. For example, the guy (Jim) who owns the automobile repair garage down the street probably started because he either worked in the family business or got tired of working for someone else. Jim doesn't have a grand vision to be as ubiquitous as Pep Boys. Sure, he wants to make money, but the love of his craft, freedom from a boss, quality of life, and a sense that he can shape his destiny are all reasons that usually motivate someone to start or buy a business.

JUST DO IT

Customers determine winners in business. But a decisive factor for your future success comes down to how you answer this question: Will you be an entrepreneur or a small-business owner? Entrepreneurs take big risks to create something new, while small-business owners provide goods and services that the market needs right now. Each has its own value.

Life as a small-business owner is appealing. There's no disputing its impact on the American psyche. In our winner-take-all society, we need balance between big-risk takers and steady small businesses. Ben states, "Entrepreneurs, at their core, are rare, transformative and risky. They are going to propel the society forward with big leaps of creative disruption. Small-business owners give us a stable base that de-risks the moonshots and protects us from the fallout of failures."[13] Our economy needs both the entrepreneur and the small-business owner.

To succeed in business, you have to know whether you're playing as an entrepreneur who is ready to change the game, the industry, the world, or as a small-business owner seeking to make an impact on a smaller scale. If you're trying to change the game, put on a pair of Shaquille O'Neal's size 22, because that's what changing the game feels like. Your choice whether to be an entrepreneur or small-business owner will affect how you start, fund, manage, and grow your business.

TAKEAWAY: Decide what you will be. Choose one.

2

BUILT TO LAST: YOUR VISION, MISSION & CULTURE

SOME STARTUP BUSINESSES TRIP OVER THEMSELVES to source capital before they articulate their value proposition to customers. They skip building a strong and safe foundation for the business. Big mistake! A foundation protects a home from shifting, the elements, or collapsing. A business also needs a foundation to tether it to something and to support the structure above it. Your vision, mission statement and culture form the support structure and are part and parcel of your business model.

A motivating vision and concise mission statement become a competitive advantage, especially when you hire staff and introduce your brand to the world. The vision, mission statement and culture are a flag waving high in the air that symbolizes your position. Not only must customers know what the business stands for, employees also want to know the company's values and beliefs.

LEAD WITH A VISION STATEMENT

Your vision statement expresses a higher purpose of what the organization aspires to be. Simply put, the vision statement is an inspirational roadmap of where the business is going in a warm and fuzzy, feel-good wrapper. Think of the vision statement as a light shining from a lighthouse. It shines during good and bad times.

The Walt Disney Company is the world's largest media company with 95,000 employees and $55.6 billion in revenue in 2016.[1] Kids of all ages from around the world have been captivated by the company's stories. Disney's iconic brands and businesses include ESPN, Disney Channel, ABC, Disneyland, Walt Disney World, Shanghai Disney Resort, Disneyland Paris, Tokyo Disney Resort, Disney Cruise Lines, The Walt Disney Studios, Pixar Animation Studios, Marvel Studios, Lucas Studio LTD (the creator of Star Wars), and the Disney Store. At this time, its acquisition of 20th Century Fox is pending.

A vision statement is the "why" of a company. Saying that there are a lot of moving parts to Disney is an understatement. Yet, its vision is simple: "To make people happy."[2] Warren Buffet says business owners should "delight" their customers, which Disney has been doing since 1923.[3]

IKEA is the world's largest furniture company. In 2017, the company had 936 million store visits and 2.3 billion website visits to Ikea.com.[4] With operations stretching around the world, the company has 194,000 employees. Its vision is as succinct and simple as its product packaging: "To create a better everyday life for the many people."[5]

Walmart is the largest retailer in the world with over 2.3 million associates (parlance for employees) and serves over 260 million customers per week.[6] Globally, Walmart operates 11,695 stores in 28 countries. The company generated $485.9 billion in revenue during its 2017 fiscal year. Walmart's vision is succinct: "To be the best retailer in the hearts and minds of consumers and employees."[7]

THE MISSION STATEMENT

A mission statement is a brief description of the business or organization's purpose. It's the nuts and bolts of "how" it will do it.

A business must have a higher purpose than making money. In fact, a good mission statement will not mention money because the financial reward comes from delivering something of value to customers. Delighting customers should be the driving force of the business.

The Walt Disney Company's website states its mission is to be one of the world's leading producers and providers of entertainment and information. "Using our portfolio of brands to differentiate our content, services and consumer products, we seek to develop the most creative, innovative and profitable entertainment experiences and related products in the world."[8]

IKEA's mission is "offering a wide range of well-designed, functional home furnishing products at prices so low that as many people as possible will be able to afford them."[9] One of the ways the company keeps its prices low is by packing its unassembled products in flat boxes. Another way is by constantly looking at better materials and methods to produce its products with fewer pieces, lowering the cost.

Walmart's mission states that it "helps people around the world save money and live better - anytime and anywhere - in retail stores, online and through their mobile devices."[10] Whether operating a grocery store in Maine or a surf shop in California, a concise mission statement is powerful for both big and small businesses.

CULTURE: THE "IT" FACTOR

Have you wondered what holds a company together? No, it's not glue. The magic ingredient to a business is its culture. You can't put your finger on culture, but you can describe it. The Merriam-Webster dictionary defines culture as "The set of shared attitudes, values, goals, and practices that characterizes an institution or organization."[11] Napoleon Hill, author of the book, *Think and Grow Rich*, said, "Every business and every place of employment has also a distinctive atmosphere that consists of the combined personalities of those who work there."[12] That's culture.

Culture is the invisible hand that guides your company in good and bad times. It is what people do when the boss is not looking. Culture is what you do and don't do. It is how employees answer the telephones, treat customers, dress and speak. A business should never leave culture to happenstance. Companies invest billions in training employees, developing systems, writing employee manuals, and conducting employee reviews; they model appropriate behaviors, and implement reward systems for desired behaviors, outcomes and performance.

Culture can go wrong. In 2017, Uber was an example of a company culture spinning out of control. Travis Kalanick was the CEO of Uber, the ride-hailing company he founded in 2009. Uber revolutionized the transportation industry with its mobile app. But in its efforts to grow—using OPM—something went terribly wrong with its hard-driving culture.

The New York Times reported that Kalanick's resignation "caps months of questions over the leadership of Uber, which has become a prime example of Silicon Valley startup culture gone awry."[13] At the time of his resignation in June 2017, the company was valued at almost $70 billion. The story reported that Uber had a "workplace culture that included sexual harassment and discrimination, and it has pushed the envelope in dealing with law enforcement." Other companies have had issues that seem to speak to their poor culture, including Fidelity, Wells Fargo and The Weinstein Company (TWC).

Whether you are a startup, in business five years, or the CEO of Walmart, culture matters. James Allen states in his book, *As a Man Thinketh*, "Good thoughts and actions can never produce bad results; bad thoughts and actions can never produce good results."[14] Lead by positive example and you'll have a winning culture.

The long-term value of your business rests on the foundation you build. You can't build a sustainable business until you create value, which is what customers covet and buy. Invest the time to create a vision, mission statement and culture you can be proud of, which will separate you from the competition.

TAKEAWAY: Your business needs a foundation.

"Aston Martin Music," Rick Ross, featuring Drake
& Chrisette Michele, *Teflon Don*

3

REV YOUR ENGINE:
THE BUSINESS MODEL

THE WEBSITE INVESTOPEDIA explains that a business model "lays out a step by step plan of action for profitably operating the business in a specific marketplace."[1] In other words, your business model spells out how you plan to compete. It's your competitive advantage of how you differentiate yourself from competitors, and make money.

The business model is the engine that makes your business go. When you look under the hood of your business, what do you see? What is it that you do that makes the competition irrelevant? Your business model is often the key to winning over skeptical investors, friends, family, banks, and customers.

Joan Magretta, the author of *Why Business Models Matter*, states that the business model answers the question, "What is the underlying economic logic that explains how we can deliver value to customers at an appropriate cost?"[2] A business model must solve a pain point for customers and create value, at a desirable price point.

14

Every business has a story and the business model is a starting point. Magretta suggests having "at heart, stories—stories that explain how enterprises work."[3] A good story attracts attention and may lead to media mentions and interviews, which will lead to more coverage and interest. None of this is possible for a business model that is poorly conceived.

BUSINESS MODELS COME IN MANY FLAVORS

Ice cream is a fun business, an impulse purchase that is irresistible to both young and old. You may remember your parents rewarding you with ice cream. This is not just an occasional treat—it might be considered a fifth food group. It's big business.

Statista, the online business statistics portal, reports that ice cream sales were over $6.6 billion in 2017.[4] The average American eats 20 quarts of ice cream a year, and 87 percent have ice cream in their freezers.[5] The popularity hasn't been lost on business. These days, everyone seems to be selling ice cream, from mom-and-pop stores, franchises, and truck vendors to supermarket chains. The concoction may be sold as ice cream, soft serve, gelato, or frozen yogurt. Stores have made it a must-see experience to watch it being crafted and piled high like skyscrapers teetering on wobbling cone foundations, with all types of delicious toppings. Baskin-Robbins bills itself as the "world's largest chain of ice cream specialty shops." The company has over 1,300 ice creams in its library of flavors, which means you could eat one flavor a day for three and half years.[6] With over 7,800 stores in 50 countries, there's plenty of ice cream to go around.[7] Ben & Jerry's, Carvel, Cold Stone Creamery, Dairy Queen, Dippin' Dots, Friendly's, Häagen-Dazs, and Rita's Italian Ice compete in the space. The industry has had to overcome negative trends as Americans reach for healthy foods and locally sourced ingredients.

THE BUSINESS MODEL IS THE ENGINE THAT
MAKES YOUR BUSINESS GO.

There seem to be as many business models as flavors—one size doesn't fit all when it comes to the ice cream business. Large manufacturers sell to distributors who sell to stores that sell to the final consumer. Some companies make and sell their product directly to customers, similar to craft beer manufacturers with their tap rooms.

TRANSPORTATION: CARS

Tesla Motors is an automobile manufacturer that sells electric cars, with semis and pickup trucks coming soon. Its competitors are much bigger. Founded in 1908, General Motors (GM) is an automobile manufacturer of gas and diesel-powered vehicles and the electric Chevy Bolt. General Motors sold roughly 10 million cars in 2016 compared to Tesla's 76,000.[8] GM earned $9 billion in profit in 2016 and Tesla has had only two profitable quarters in its history.[9] Despite GM's huge advantage as an automobile manufacturer, Tesla's market capitalization was $58.7 billion compared to GM's $51 billion and Ford at $41.4 billion in August, 2017.[10] Tesla is valued for its future and as a technology company, not as a traditional automobile manufacturer—it's the iPhone of electric vehicles.

Both companies compete in the market for consumers who want electric vehicles. But General Motors has a business-to-business (B2B) model and sells through a dealer network, whereas Tesla Motors' business model is business-to-consumer (B2C) and they sell direct to consumers, which is illegal in some states. Two companies with different cultures, strategies, results, revenue and business models.

SELECT THE RIGHT BUSINESS MODEL

One size doesn't fit all when it comes to business models. Mark Johnson wrote the book, *Seizing the White Space*, to provide a map for companies to innovate through their business models.[11] Companies also need to modify their business plan to match changes in the market. For example, the movie business has changed and so has the DVD rental space.

Netflix charges a subscription fee to provide access to watch an unlimited number of movies. While Netflix continues to send DVDs through the mail, they have reduced costs by encouraging subscribers to forgo DVDs and to stream videos instead.

Redbox rents DVDs at its video kiosks. At one time, Blockbuster dominated the video rental market. In the early 1990s, there were over 9000 Blockbuster videos stores.[12] Blockbuster filed for bankruptcy in 2010.[13] Today there is one store left in the United States. Blockbuster had the opportunity to purchased Netflix but passed.

Companies try to lock you into their business model. Buy a Gillette razor at a low price and pay for expensive disposable blades for the rest of your life. The same strategy is employed by computer printer manufacturers like HP and Epson. Buy a printer at a reasonable price and pay for high-priced ink forever. That's a business model that generates billions for both companies.

• Walmart and IKEA have business models described as low-touch, where the prices are kept low by decreasing levels of service.

• Leasing is a business model where you pay for what you use. Car and equipment companies use this approach.

• LinkedIn uses "freemium" to provide free services and charges for premium services.

• Net Jets and time-shares sell partial use of their products, where many people buy access to units of time on airplanes or at vacation condominiums.

• Disintermediation is another business model in which the middleman is eliminated, a method adopted by Dell Computer and WebMD.

- The HuffPost recently eliminated its contributor's program that allowed nonprofessionals to post directly on the platform. Its contributors provided free content and advertising was sold to generate revenue.

- Wikipedia and YouTube also get their users to develop content for free. YouTube charges advertisers a fee and splits revenue with top content producers.

- Bundling is a strategy to package a number of products for one price. McDonald's has meals that include a burger, fries and drink for one price, which is lower than if all the items were purchased separately.

- Electric utilities companies have a pay-as-you-go business model that charges customers for the amount of energy consumed.

- Angie's List required consumers to pay a fee to access the website's reviews, and service providers to pay to advertise—a two-sided market. (HomeAdvisor purchased Angie's List in 2017 for over $500 million, and homeowners no longer pay a fee to access the website.)[14]

- Airbnb and Uber are considered two-sided marketplaces, where both customers and product providers are needed.

- Daymond John, of Shark Tank fame, is an advocate of licensing agreements as a business model, especially when a company is taking on well-established industry players. This strategy generates revenue for the licensor with little risk and much upside.

Recurring revenue is a business model in which software companies charge a yearly fee for use of the product. Adobe produces the popular design software Photoshop. Back in the 1980s, the business model was to design software and sell a CD with the program on it. Customers would install the software on their computers, and everybody was happy.

But customers would buy the software once and wouldn't upgrade for three or four years, which eliminated selling opportunities for the company. Today, software as a service (SaaS) companies are able to keep their digital products updated for productivity and security, increasing customer satisfaction while generating stable revenue streams.

A business model is how the pieces of the business come together to compete. When you fix your business model, you fix your capital issues because the two are interwoven. You can't talk about your business model without discussing how you generate revenue and when it is received.

There is not a shortage of capital, only a shortage of management teams who can execute their business models. Look at your business model before searching for capital.

TAKEAWAY: One size doesn't fit all.

4

YOUR MAP:
FROM BUSINESS PLAN
TO PITCH DECK

INNOVATORS ARE CONSTANTLY CHANGING THE RULES for business with their bright ideas and fresh solutions to nagging problems—often before industries, the public, and laws can catch up. Investors, with their deep pockets, are lurking in wait for the next big opportunity. Uber harnessed the power of a hungry, on-call workforce into a mobile-phone app sensation, bypassing the traditional taxi model. Uber, a private company, is valued at over $60 billion.[1] Starting in Hartford, Connecticut in 1981, Alan Lazowski and his childhood friends improved parking and built the global company Laz Parking, the third largest parking company in America.[2]

What may have worked yesterday is usually the prompt for entrepreneurs to ask, "Is there a better way?" When an entrepreneur finds a novel solution to a problem, it's time to create a business around that solution. In the past, a voluminous business plan was the first tangible document that entrepreneurs would share with outsiders. If you wanted to open up the bank vault to get capital, bankers demanded to see your business plan before they would take your business seriously.

Anyone can start a business, but to succeed, you have to have your stuff together. So, flying by the seat of your pants is not an acceptable way to start a business. The old adage is still true: If you fail to plan, you're planning to fail.

BUSINESS PLAN HISTORY

Business plans became popular with military contractors such as DuPont and GM during World War II. But the business plan fell out of favor a long time ago with funders and professionals who create businesses. "In many circles, it's a fairly antiquated term," says Bill Kenney, CEO of Test My Pitch.[3] Investors want a document that is a quick read and answers salient questions. Using Microsoft PowerPoint, presentations morphed into what is now called the pitch deck. Kenney states, "It's not your granddad's business plan."[4] He sees over 100 pitch decks a year.

Evan Baehr and Evan Loomis are entrepreneurs and authors of the book, *Get Backed.*[5] Their book condenses the building blocks of a pitch deck into 10 sections: overview, opportunity, problem, solution, traction, customer or market, competition, business model, team and use of funds. The pitch deck is presented in 11 to 12 succinct pages designed to get attention and save time for the readers, who are often the investors in the room.

The transition from business plan to pitch deck is complete. Loomis says, "Business plans are not that bad, but what is happening is a major shift. You're not going to get funded with a business plan. Investors won't take you seriously if you give that to them. It's not a funding document—20 years ago, it was a legit document. If you're knocking on doors for investors' money, don't bring a business plan."[6]

PITCH DECK ADVANTAGES

No longer is the business plan the essential document you need to start a business or raise capital. Pitch decks have the advantage over a business plan because they are concise and can be updated quickly. According to Loomis, once you create one, the second and third are really easy. He has personally created about 50 decks. Loomis states, "Investors have insane ADD [Attention Deficit Disorder] because they are hit up every day."[7] So, a pitch deck will help you get to the point, fast.

The pitch deck is practical because at some point you will have to pitch your idea to an audience, whether that be family, friends or angel investors. Kenney states, "The pitch is one moment of how you can connect and build relationships."[8] His tips for a successful pitch are:

1. Know your audience.
2. Have something worth talking about—from the audience perspective.
3. Communicate simply and directly.

Get Backed offers insight into the investors mindset with the three questions they ask themselves during a pitch:

1. Do I like you?
2. Do I trust you?
3. Do I want to do business with you?

During your pitch, Loomis observes, "The best investor meetings are great conversations, not pitches. Better to be interrupted than to finish your sentence."[9]

While the business plan may live on with bankers, universities, the Small Business Administration and other service providers, it is no longer the be-all for business. Times change, and you should too. Put the pitch deck into your lexicon and create one.

SUPPORTING DOCUMENTATION

While the pitch deck is short and to the point, it should not be a substitute for doing the research required to build the business. Your pitch deck will not have your complete marketing plan, customer research, financials with assumptions, location analysis and other supporting documentation.

Develop an appendix section that can go in-depth into the key areas that need more attention. For example, the pitch deck will have a brief overview of the management team's background. An appendix document can provide more detail by adding a bio with career highlights. This document can be sent as a separate document, if the investors are looking for additional information. Another option is to make this information password protected on a website, which would eliminate the need to send separate documents and emails.

If the new business is a retail store, you should have ample research that demonstrates that customers will come to your store. You can provide a Google map of the area with photographs of competitors or complementary businesses in the area. A document with the traffic counts in the area could be part of this package. Your package should include a layout of your store and other particulars about the physical experience. You are doing all you can to make something intangible, tangible to a potential investor or in support of the business.

The appendix can have best-case, most-likely, and worst-case scenarios of your financials. This is not a useless exercise because most startups present the best-case scenario. What happens if you don't meet the best-case numbers? What happens if the local, regional or national economy takes a dip or a major competitor decides to enter the marketplace? You know that there will be bumps in the road. It's good to do several different financial models to show you have done your homework and to be prepared. If an investor asks tough questions about what you would do in a down market, you can send them your numbers. Being prepared is always a positive sign for any investor.

TAKEAWAY: Commit your plan to paper.

"Say Something," Timbaland, featuring Drake, *Shock Value II*

5

SATISFY NEEDS & WANTS:
YOUR VALUE PROPOSITION

CUSTOMERS ARE NOT MYSTERIOUS ALIENS: They are living and breathing humans. In aggregate, customers form a market. Markets are composed of people who have similar wants and needs, which are problems masquerading as opportunities for business. Your job as a business owner is to translate those needs and wants into specific products. With so many competing products, customers seek a clear message with your brand on it that addresses their pain point.

Your value proposition is a secret weapon that gives you an unfair advantage over the competition. The Kissmetrics blog describes a value proposition as "a believable collection of the most persuasive reasons people should notice you and take the action you're asking for."[1] Companies spend fortunes to develop brands that communicate their value propositions. When a customer doesn't notice the difference between value propositions, they will naturally gravitate to the lowest price, making all solutions a commodity. The goal of your value proposition is to be so strong that it lives in the customer's head as the only solution. Kleenex, Xerox, and Velcro created value propositions so strong they defined their categories.

The value of your offering is equal to the benefits (real or perceived) that customers receive. A diner that is open twenty-four hours a day is catering to convenience, whether people are working the third shift, traveling through the state, or coming home late. Enterprise Rent-A-Car positioned itself as the rental car company that will pick you up. Customers don't have to worry about getting to and from Enterprise, which can be a huge pain point if their car has broken down or was in an accident. Uber caters to people who need a vehicle to get from point A to B.

CUSTOMERS ARE UNIQUE

Not all customers are looking for the same solution; they have different ideas of value, based on location, convenience, cost and more. Segmenting customers is a way to provide further value to those who are part of the larger market, but with different needs. A market can be segmented based on geography (e.g., region or urban vs suburban), demographics (age, gender, income), behavior (loyalty, rate of usage or benefits sought), and psychographics (personality, lifestyles, attitudes or class). The soft drink market in the U.S. is controlled by the Coca-Cola Company and PepsiCo. They segment the markets for carbonated soft drinks, fruit beverages, bottled water, functional beverages, sports drinks and more.

Major companies such as Subway, Sprint and Staples constantly solicit feedback from customers. Observe your customers. Talk to them and get their feedback. When it comes to developing your value proposition, data is king. In order to understand what customers want, you have to have data.

YOUR VALUE PROPOSITION IS A SECRET WEAPON THAT GIVES YOU AN UNFAIR ADVANTAGE OVER THE COMPETITION.

Find out what customers like about your business and the competition. Look for pain points they want solved. Develop an online or in-store survey. Encourage participation by giving customers an incentive (discount on a future purchase) to complete the survey.

The goal is to learn as much about your customers as possible. Some customers may be willing to pay for a first-class seat on an airplane. Others may prefer Southwest and its first-come, first-served policy for seating. Focus your limited resources on the customers you can serve best because you can't be all things to everyone. Products should be focused on customers who will provide a decent return. New customers may be different from existing customers and may be willing to pay more for additional benefits. And make sure your price covers your cost and allows you to make money on each unit. The higher the cost, the better margins you will have.

No company owns a customer; in fact, some of your customers may go frequently to the competition. Build a moat around your business, where the competition cannot get to your customers because of your value proposition. Your challenge is to find a way where your business can meet all of your customers' needs, all the time. Ask yourself this question: Why should anybody care about my product? The answer is the key to unlock the customer market.

UNTAPPED CAPITAL

When your value proposition registers with customers, they will reward you with their business. Over time, customers are an unlimited source of revenue. Customers are the ultimate investors—they don't ask for equity, they buy your products and market them to their friends through word of mouth and social media. That's loyalty.

To increase sales, it is as simple as getting your customers to frequent your business more often. Many businesses have developed reward programs to offer incentives for customers to frequent their business more often. A reward card keeps customers coming back. With today's technology and the ubiquity of smartphones, it's easier than ever to start a rewards program. The big businesses have them, why not you? Starbucks' loyal fans love flashing their smartphones to order ahead of their store visits and earn reward points, increasing loyalty. There is nothing stopping your business from cashing in, with your local touch.

On the backend, businesses receive valuable purchase habit data that can be used in segmenting and marketing. You can capture customers' email addresses to send a monthly newsletter with offerings and specials—but don't carpet bomb customers with daily messages. The more you engage customers, the more opportunities to generate revenue. Develop a long-term relationship, not a one-way transaction with customers.

There are clever ways to keep customers focused on your business, and to get customers to promote your business, thus reducing your marketing spend, and driving more business to you. The holiday season from Thanksgiving to New Year's Day, is a time of year when customers spend—it's the Olympics of shopping. Let customers know you have gifts cards available. Make creative and wacky gift cards with your logo on them. Promote gift cards throughout the year and incentivize workers to sell them. This strategy alone can generate tens of thousands of dollars in sales, a source of capital that may be going untapped.

A VIP sale for your top customers is another option to tap into your customers' passion, while generating cash for your business. Set aside a week or a few days a year, where customers can come into your place of business and receive a discount off of a purchase or some special reward for staying loyal to your business. Keep it hush-hush and the word will travel. People will be lining up to be a VIP member. This is a win-win strategy. What's stopping you from trying something new?

Whatever you do, make your marketing social-media friendly. You can rent a giant inflatable animal to put in front of your business. Customers love taking pictures and sharing on social media. Before you know it, your business could be trending in your area on Twitter, Facebook, or Instagram, which could lead to local media featuring your business in their print and digital media assets. The more creative and wacky you get, the better your story will generate buzz and attention.

Don't pass up the opportunity to better serve your customers. It's about communicating your value proposition and connecting with customers. You're in the driver's seat. Take your customers along for the ride.

TAKEAWAY: Customers fund growth.

6

DELIGHT CUSTOMERS:
HAPPY CUSTOMERS SPEND

HAVE YOU BEEN to a Starbucks lately? Customers come in the door and their beverages are waiting at the pickup counter with names in black marker on the cup. This choreographed ballet takes just seconds and is performed hundreds of thousands of times a day. Starbucks, the coffee behemoth with almost 28,000 locations, and 170,000 ways to "customize beverages" has turbo-charged the customer experience, and, at the same time, sent a warning shot across the bow of mom-and-pop coffee shops: delight customers or fail.[1]

With the Starbucks app, customers are now in control when it comes to interacting with the company. No longer do they wait in long lines staring at their smartphones while the thought of their first sip makes their mouth salivate. Starbucks found a way to make their happy customers even happier. Delighting customers is the new rule. Are your customers excited to come to your business? If not, you need to find a way to release their excitement by giving them what they want, when they want it. If you don't, another business will.

MAKE IT EASY

Start with life's little annoyances, called friction—the stuff that slows us down and makes life difficult. You know, things like putting stamps on envelopes, feeding parking meters, going to the grocery store, waiting in line at the motor vehicle, or trying to send large files via email. Companies are finding ways to make those everyday experiences less painful and easier to handle. Now you can buy postage on Stamps.com, feed the parking meter with an app, get your groceries delivered, renew your vehicle registration online and send large files using services such as Dropbox, which recently filed confidentially for an IPO. Life is getting easier.

The more friction you remove, the more likely you are to earn repeat customers. Friendly's, a Northeast restaurant chain, empowers customers to pay their bills at the table without a server. Warby Parker found a way to reduce friction by making the purchase of eyeglasses easy and at a much lower price point than the dominant companies in the industry. To up the ante, Warby Parker is working on developing an eye exam that people can do at home—they are seeing green.

Illiano's, a Middletown, Connecticut restaurant, gives every customer who walks in the door a small slice of pizza as they wait for their takeout orders or their sit-down meals. It's a small gesture that sends the message that the business cares about the customer experience—no one complains when they receive free pizza. When repeat business is calculated, the cost to give out the pizza slices is minuscule compared to the word-of-mouth advertising and increased customer satisfaction.

Keep improving by putting yourself in your customers' shoes. Observe what competitors are doing to improve the experience. Customers view friction as a pain in the derrière, but as a business owner you should see opportunities.

WHEN THINGS GO WRONG

In business, it is not whether things will go wrong, it is only a matter of when. Here's my story. I produce the LootScout Capital Summit, an annual event to educate entrepreneurs about capital. The past two years, I rented a video projector. In 2017, I decided to buy my own projector. After researching projectors, I went to Amazon and a found a brand with wireless Wi-Fi at a reasonable price. I purchased it.

The projector arrived as promised in two days—Prime membership delivers again. I opened the box and all was fine. I tested it. I knew it would take some time to learn how to use the remote and other features but that could wait. Fast forward to the morning of my event, I had stayed up all night working on the last-minute details. The DJ arrived on time that morning to set up. Hosting an event is like juggling knives, tap dancing and smiling, all at the same time. The room was arranged properly and hotel staff was getting the food ready.

Murphy's Law strikes—I should have known it was all going too well. I couldn't get the projector to display on the screen. My heart was beating fast—as if I had chugged three cups of coffee—because there was no backup plan. The closest rental location was about 20 minutes away, which would result in at least an hour delay. I couldn't afford a delay, not with people and sponsors in the room. My friend Ed, the owner of a video production company, saved the day. He got the projector to work but the screen was fuzzy. Despite the minor annoyance of the projector, the event went well.

The plan was to return the video projector, even though the return policy had expired by a few days. I contacted Amazon support via online chat and told the person my problem. They accepted my return and to my surprise issued a refund on the spot—talk about eliminating friction. I couldn't help but smile. The only stipulation was that Amazon would charge my card if the projector wasn't received. I was delighted. It's no small wonder Jeff Bezos is one of the richest people on earth. Amazon delighted me.

SAVING PENNIES, LOSING A CUSTOMER

Eliminating fat is what savvy business owners do. It's a balancing act to reduce costs without sacrificing the customer experience. Merchant processing provides value to customers because everyone uses plastic cards. Processors are the companies that provide the point-of-sale terminals to accept and process credit cards. Many companies provide this service, so it is up to the business owner to get the best deal. Card processors charge a fee per transaction and for the equipment.

I used to frequent an independent coffee shop (I'll call it Good Coffee) next to my office, run by a husband and wife team. Good Coffee has a great central location, pleasant environment, nice staff and a loyal following. Starbucks, Dunkin' Donuts and a number of mom-and-pop coffee shops are competitors, but this busy store seems to have found a winning runner's stride.

One morning, I went to the counter to pay for my morning tea, and to my surprise, the friendly cashier informed me that I had to spend a minimum of $5 to use my debit card. This made me mad, since I was worth one tea a day, not including other purchases. The company was ruining my experience. (A merchant may establish a minimum purchase up to ten dollars on credit cards, under Dodd-Frank. However, a minimum purchase cannot be applied to transactions that are processed with a debit card.) I imagine the business owners ran the numbers and assumed that if a minimum order is $5, it would be worth the transaction fees for processing credit cards. But is a .25 fee worth losing the lifetime value of a loyal customer? Starbucks proved that convenient, high-margin items purchased regularly produce big business. The moral is, don't alienate customers for short-term gain.

TAKEAWAY: It's all about customers.

"All I Do Is Win," DJ Khaled featuring T-Pain, Ludacris, Snoop Dogg & Rick Ross, *Victory*

7

FOCUS:
EXCEL AT ONE THING

TIME IS PRECIOUS, and everyone has just 24 hours a day. The challenge is figuring out what to do to maximize your potential and productivity. To paraphrase Jim Croce's classic song, "Time in a Bottle":

There's never enough time
For the things you want to do
When you find them.[1]

His poignant song would portend his future. Jim died at 30 years old.

An entrepreneur has to make every minute count before the business clock expires. The movie, *In Time*, is a twist on time and age, where people never look older than 25.[2] The character Will Salas, played by Justin Timberlake, sees his time literally counting down digitally on his arm—like the giant U.S. debt clock in Times Square. He rushes to get money to buy enough time to live longer, before it is too late. This movie compels you to look at time differently. Imagine if your time left was displayed on your arm. Would it change how you live your life?

DO ONE THING

Dave Hieatt, the founder of the "The Do Lectures" in West Wales and the jeans company, Hiut Denim, says "Do one thing well." As a business owner, there are many things your business could do today. However, to get the attention of customers, do only one thing you can do well. Trying to be all things to everyone is a losing battle. Focus on doing one thing well that will generate value. Make the best cupcake, build a better office chair than Herman Miller, paint a masterpiece, or be the best baby photographer. Find your one thing, and focus on doing it well, like a heat-seeking missile locked in on success.

Conventional wisdom would say multitasking is the solution because one can accomplish more in less time. However, research has shown that multitasking doesn't work. In fact, the word multitasking is a misnomer because we can do only one task well at a time, says Susan Weinschenk in her blog post, The True Cost of Multi-Tasking.[3] Researchers use the words "task switching", not multitasking. Switching back and forth to different tasks can reduce productivity by 40 percent, if done frequently over the course of a day. Og Mandino, author of the book, *The Greatest Salesman in the World, Part II: The End of the Story*, says, "It is those who concentrate on but one thing at a time who advance in this world. The master of a single trade can support a family. The master of seven trades cannot support himself."[4]

Cal Newport wrote the book, *Deep Work*. Deep work is defined as "professional activities performed in a state of distraction-free concentration that push your cognitive capabilities to their limit."[5] His hypothesis is that deep work

AN ENTREPRENEUR HAS TO MAKE EVERY MINUTE COUNT
BEFORE THE BUSINESS CLOCK EXPIRES.

is becoming increasingly valuable at the same time that it is becoming increasingly rare. Therefore, if you cultivate this skill, you'll thrive.

In contrast, Newport defines shallow work as "noncognitively demanding, logistical-style tasks, often performed while distracted. These efforts tend to not create much new value in the world and are easy to replicate."[6] Learning how to get into deep work while avoiding shallow work will help business owners.

The one thing your business does well will propel it to new heights. Focus is how you get there by aligning your effort, resources, energy, and thoughts into a goal. With the right strategy, team, and focus, you can reach the goal you have in your mind's eye. What you focus on is what drives you, day in, and day out. The one thing you want to do well must be paired with deep work.

Apple CEO Tim Cook explained that one of the core principles Steve Jobs instilled in the company is the need to stay focused on doing only what you do best. "It's easy to add... it's hard to stay focused," he said.[7] "And so the hardest decisions we make are all the things not to work on."[8] Steve Jobs said, "People think focus means saying yes to the thing you've got to focus on. But that's not what it means at all. It means saying no to the hundred other good ideas that there are."[9] Cook added, "But in the scheme of things versus our revenue, we're doing very few things. I mean, you could put every product we're making on this table, to put it in perspective."[10] Few companies in the world near the magnitude of Apple's size could say the same.

DISTRACTIONS

Facebook, Google, LinkedIn, Amazon and every internet company develop metrics to show how many people are coming to their digital properties, and how long they stay, or if they open emails. Data is information waiting to be mined in a modern-day gold rush. Companies are fighting for your attention. Why? Because your attention is the new currency. Companies spend billions of dollars for your fleeting attention. They have all types of tricks to get you to fall for their time-wasting activities, emails, cute bells alerting you on your smartphone, and "like" buttons to push.

But distractions keep us from being our most productive selves. They take us away from the essential things a business must do well. Your smartphone can be a productivity tool or the number one time-waster—and make you dumber, not smarter. Most mobile phone notifications are attention killers! Stealing your time, second by second.

Customers are the prize; they can make or break a business. Doing one thing well should be customer-focused. You must focus on anything that impacts customer experience and sales—that's the bottom line. Investors and lenders are important, but customers hold the power to create successful businesses.

VISUALIZE SUCCESS

Usain Bolt, the eight-time Olympic gold medalist sprinter, found his one thing and eliminated distractions along the way. Sports psychologists help elite athletes to achieve peak success. In track, one-hundredth of a second is the difference between being second or being the next Usain Bolt, worth tens of millions of dollars. When time is so precious, one has to gain a competitive advantage.

Jack Canfield is the driving force behind the *Chicken Soup for the Soul*® series, which has sold over 500 million copies.[11] Canfield believes in utilizing visualization techniques to achieve a single purpose.[12]

When you apply visualization techniques to your goal, it accomplishes four indispensable things:

1. Your subconscious mind is activated to begin the process of generating solutions or pathways to achieve the goal.

2. Your brain is programmed to act like computer software to be conscious and recognize the resources you will need to achieve the goal.

3. Your mind empowers the law of attraction, where you become a giant magnet bringing the people, resources and ideas to reach the goal.

4. Your internal motivation is fired up to achieve the goal, like a football player before the Super Bowl.

Decide to do one thing well because distractions eat away at your time—like flesh-eating bacteria. You are the master of your time. There's no end in sight to what you can achieve in business and your personal life if you focus on your one thing and eliminate distractions.

TAKEAWAY: Do one thing well.

"Part II (On the Run)," Jay Z featuring Beyoncé, *Magna Carta...Holy Grail*

8

CHANGE THE GAME: MEET LAVAR BALL

WHEN PEOPLE CHANGE THE GAME, the competition is doomed. They do this because it gives them a competitive advantage against the established players, increasing the odds of success—that's how David beat Goliath. LaVar Ball, the father of three sons who aspire to basketball greatness, threw out the rule book. And traditional media, social platforms, and just about everyone, has had something to say.

LaVar made a bold prediction that his son would play for the Lakers. "All I said was that my boy is going to play for the Lakers," he said. "I'm going to speak it into existence. I want him to be a Laker, but I wasn't saying he's only going to play for the Lakers."[1] Turns out, his eldest son, Lonzo Ball, was the first pick by the Los Angeles Lakers in the 2017 NBA Draft, after only one season at UCLA. Judging by Magic Johnson's smile, Lonzo may be the building block that ignites Showtime 2.0.

Speak it into an existence is a clever mantra—I see tee shirts for sale in the future. LaVar's goal is to get his other two sons on the Lakers. LaVar pulled his son LiAngelo out of UCLA during his freshman year (after he and several teammates were caught stealing sunglasses in China); he did the same to LaMelo Ball. LaMelo was a high school junior. LiAngelo and LaMelo signed professional contracts to play basketball in the Lithuanian League—a bold and most unusual destination to start chasing NBA dreams.

THE RULES

The business model for an NBA first-round draft pick is to sign their lucrative contact, which is governed by the Collective Bargaining Agreement (CBA). The CBA spells out what salaries draft picks will receive, based on where they were selected in the draft. To increase their earning potential, players seek endorsement deals to pitch a host of products— some familiar, and others not so. Players can pocket millions of dollars from brands like Nike, Adidas and Reebok.

LaVar is a master self-promoter. Lonzo spurned a potentially lucrative deal with Nike, Reebok and Adidas to go it alone to create the Big Baller Brand (BBB), which took Twitter by storm when it came out with a $499 basketball sneaker.[2] Not since Tanya Harding got her comeuppance—she is forever associated with former Olympian Nancy Kerrigan—has there been a villain scorned by so many.

In the movie, *Jerry McGuire*, Marcee Tidwell, the wife of Rod Tidwell, a professional football player, says to Rod's agent (played by Tom Cruise), "you're giving him waterbed warehouse when he deserves the big four—shoes, car, clothing-line, soft drink."[3] The four jewels of the celebrity endorsement dollar. A conservative estimate is Lonzo Ball lost millions of dollars that a major sneaker company would have offered. But on the other end of the spectrum, Lonzo is building his brand, BBB.

NEW MEDIA, NEW MESSAGE

LaVar is rewriting the rules for launching a brand. His brash moves—and mouth—have generated millions of dollars' worth of media, reaching tens of millions of people. His name has been in the headlines and continues to attract attention. To generate future interest, the family is part of a reality series on Facebook, *Ball in the Family*, which is scheduled for a second season.[4]

All great companies use the media as a surrogate to deliver their messages. Apple broadcasts its new product launches as if the products were blockbuster movies, with their own trailers and public relation teams. Invites go only to top media and influencers. Elon Musk uses Twitter to engage his nearly 20 million followers. His Tesla presentations are must-see events as well. LaVar's moves will continue to be questioned, but if the big companies can do it, why shouldn't LaVar—or you?

LaVar will continue to use the media to deliver his message. For example, he claimed he could beat Michael Jordan in a one-on-one. He stated that Lonzo, prior to playing in the NBA, was better than Stephen Curry, the three-time NBA champion and arguably, the most exciting player under 6'-3" to watch in sports. BBB receives publicity every time the media mentions the sneakers, even when they speak negatively about the product. The price of the sneakers is in the stratosphere, which is part of the marketing strategy to get attention. Stay tuned, there will be more from the Ball family.

MAKE YOUR MARK

You can change the game for your business. Entrepreneurs create paths where paths didn't exist. They leave jobs with steady paychecks to start risky ventures that are one move away from tumbling like Jenga blocks. If the business fails, it could lead the owners to financial ruin. It seems all the greats in business are as close to bankruptcy as success, at some time.

Entrepreneurs display passion, perseverance and resourcefulness. Ray Kroc was not the founder of McDonald's, but he had an entrepreneurial mind. What Kroc did was introduce America to fast food through the concept created by the McDonald brothers. Ray Kroc saw the genius in speed, service, and systems. Kroc said, "The two most important requirements for major success are: first, being in the right place at the right time, and second, doing something about it."[5] He did both.

Rule breakers are not confined to business. Dr. Martin Luther King entered college at 15; he skipped grades 9 and 12.[6] He protested for civil rights and quality. According to the King Center, the civil rights leader went to jail 29 times.[7] Susan B. Anthony led the women's suffrage movement. From the time of the American Revolution to 1920, women fought for the same social, political and economic status that men had. Women would eventually earn their right to vote through the passage of the 19th Amendment.[8]

You can make your mark in business, sports or whatever you desire. While there is no secret formula, say these sentences over and over in your head and act upon your thoughts:

1. You are amazing!

2. You will do great things!

3. You must start now. Speak it into existence.

In the end, you can change the game and at the same time be authentic. Make a product that customers want and benefits humanity. Perhaps in LaVar's mind he is making the world more entertaining.

TAKEAWAY: Do it your way.

9

WHEN IT DOESN'T WORK:
PIVOT

NEW AUTOMOBILES ARE TECHNOLOGICAL MARVELS that can alert you before problems surface, for things like low tire pressure, when to change the oil or the Dark Vader of warnings, the check engine light. In the future, you will be able to press autonomous driving mode and read your favorite book while the car drives itself. There is no autonomous mode to avoid hazards in business. The most relevant low-tech indicator is your bank account balance. You have a major problem when cash is low and the cash register is not recording transactions. Now is the time to take decisive and corrective action. Cue the music for "Lose Yourself" by Eminem.[1]

As an entrepreneur, you have one chance—sometimes two chances—to put the business on solid ground. When plan "A" is not working, it's time to pivot to plan "B." Changing direction means the assumptions you had in the planning stages are not working. The market has spoken. Sales are the measuring stick that matters. When your product solves customers' hair-on-fire problems, they will spread the word, which will lead to greater sales—all while lowering your marketing spend.

Your business is a tiny speedboat, not a battleship, which means you can change direction relatively quickly, again and again. The advantage of being small is that you can receive feedback from customers and make the necessary changes, without bureaucracy creating red tape. Some of the biggest companies didn't realize it was time for them to pivot until it was too late. Their corporate tombstones are visual reminders for all. Big companies do pivot too, and must, but smaller companies have an advantage.

SAY CHEESE

Long before Google, Apple, Microsoft, Amazon and Facebook, Eastman Kodak dominated the photo film business. The company accounted for 90 percent of the film and 85 percent of camera sales in America by 1976.[2] It was one of the world's five most valuable brands. The company's slogan was, "You press the button, we do the rest."

Times have changed—may film rest in peace. Digital photography, a transformational technology that comes along perhaps once in a generation, replaced film, and the smartphone replaced cameras. Few people could have predicted such a dramatic fall from grace as Kodak would encounter. In 1996, Kodak had $16 billion in revenue and $2.5 billion in profits.[3] Today, the company is a shell of its former self, as it struggles to remain relevant.

Eastman Kodak is not the only giant to fall after squandering a huge advantage. Many other large companies failed to make the turn toward greener pastures. Well-known companies like Borders, Toys "R" Us, Sears, RIM (Research in Motion, better known as BlackBerry), Motorola, Nokia, Yahoo, Sony and Blockbuster all faced similar challenges. Those companies had all the advantages: brand recognition, employees, and access to capital. Hubris and poor decision-making can change the prospects for any business—as easily as an entrepreneur tinkering with new technology.

SEARCH FOR TAILWINDS

Heraclitus of Ephesus, a Greek philosopher, born in 500 B.C., said "Everything changes and nothing stands still."[4] Adaptability is the skill that will help a business most. One cannot predict the future with 100 percent certainty, but bank on change. Whether you're a big company, mom and pop, or startup, you have to be able to read the tea leaves.

Success is not guaranteed tomorrow. Shrewd leaders have a special ability to look into the future and see things others cannot, which allows them to prepare for change long before the incumbents. Looking back provides clues to the future. Since many once-great companies have not been able to stay around forever, entrepreneurs should take heed that they too will not dominate forever.

It has been said entrepreneurs have a reality distortion field. They look at an industry leader and see change coming. Apple entered the smartphone business when BlackBerry had a stranglehold on the industry—people called it "CrackBerry" for a reason. The smartphone continues to disrupt industries from watches, GPS, cameras, to music—and health, in the future. Netflix took on Blockbuster. Airbnb reimagined how ordinary people could monetize their homes for travelers. Uber took on the transportation industry. Eventbrite changed how people manage event registration. WeWork presents a different plan for how we work, play, live and socialize. This shared working space company, which started only eight years ago, is valued at $20 billion.[5] It's cofounder, Adam Neumann, says "Once you choose to enter a WeWork, you choose to be part of something more 'we' than 'me.'"[6]

SEARCH FOR TAILWINDS
TO CARRY YOUR BUSINESS
TO WHERE THE MARKET IS GOING.

Business and technology change. Companies can, and do, get outmaneuvered. "Getting disrupted is the defining characteristic of this industry," said Aaron Levie, the chief executive of Box, an online data storage company.[7] Microsoft replaced Digital Equipment Corporation, Wang and Novell. "You can even have a near monopoly like Microsoft did, and then everything gets redefined."[8]

Warren Buffet is known as the world's greatest investor. For every $1,000 an investor put into Berkshire Hathaway in 1964, they would have $45 million today.[9] His company, Berkshire Hathaway, owns a portfolio of companies such as Burlington Northern Santa Fe, See's Candies, Geico, Precision Castparts and others. Buffet says, "With few exceptions, when a manager with a reputation for brilliance tackles a business with a reputation for poor fundamental economics, it is the reputation of the business that remains intact."[10]

Apple is considered by some as the greatest corporate comeback story of all time. In August 1997, Apple was on life-support, with 12 years of financial losses, Gil Amelio was fired as the CEO, and Steve Jobs was anointed interim CEO. With Steve Jobs back in the cockpit, Apple would soar to new heights—the back story is that leadership matters. Without Steve Jobs leading the company, some of the world's best products would not have seen the light of day: iPads, iPods, iMacs, iPhones and the App store. You can pivot under the right leadership. If you're facing headwinds, it may be time to pivot before it's too late. Search for tailwinds to carry your business to where the market is going.

TAKEAWAY: Stay nimble.

10

IT TAKES A TEAM:
PLAY TO WIN

PROFESSIONAL ATHLETES HAVE THEIR OWN TEAM to assure they perform on and off the court. They may have a personal assistant, manager, publicist, personal trainer, massage therapist, chef, nutritionist, sport psychologist, financial advisor, agent, accountant, and attorney. So, when you watch NBA superstar Stephen Curry nailing a winning jump shot—from what appears to be the parking lot—think about his personal team.

From a practical point, a one-person business is hard to scale, but not impossible. As the saying goes, "two hands are better than one." But every business must start somewhere. In the beginning, you will do everything to get the job done. You will make and sell the product, talk to suppliers, appease unhappy customers, develop strategy, and sweep the floor. In business for yourself, that's the way it is.

With the cost of technology decreasing, and productivity gains increasing, it doesn't take a million-dollar budget to change the algorithm of the company. You will need to build your team. It's a process to go from just you to a ten-person team. The herculean task is finding and identifying people with skills, experience, and the right attitude who will mesh with the business. Marla Malcolm Beck, CEO of Bluemercury, a makeup, skincare and spa business, has a framework for assessing people: skill (prospect has the talent), will (hunger and passion to succeed) and fit (compatible with company culture and size).[1] Use skill, will and fit to assess potential talent.

HIRE THE BEST

Start by determining your immediate needs. Do you need a technician to do the work or a manager to keep the business organized? You will be responsible for evaluating talent, training and indoctrinating people into your culture. Hire people who will generate revenue or free you up to generate revenue. Independent contractors are one way to get talent on a budget. Developing a specific project for the contractor will make it easier to evaluate their skill, will and fit. Bring onboard the best people you can afford. A number of websites will help you find independent contractors such as Freelancer.com, Upwork.com, Outsourcely.com, Guru.com and others.

An independent contractor is someone who is self-employed (often called a "1099" after the tax form reporting their earnings). The Internal Revenue Service states, "The general rule is that an individual is an independent contractor if the payer has the right to control or direct only the result of the work and not what will be done and how it will be done.[2]

An individual is not an independent contractor if he or she performs services that can be controlled by an employer (what will be done and how it will be done). This applies even if the contractor is given freedom of action. What matters is whether the employer has the legal right to control the details of how the services are performed. If an employer-employee relationship exists, an individual is not an independent contractor and the earnings are generally not subject to the Self-Employment Tax. However, persons who work as independent contractors are responsible for reporting and paying their own taxes.

TEAM DYNAMICS

People work for a paycheck but also for the challenge, intellectual stimulation, to be part of a team and personal accomplishments. Money is not always first on the list for employees. A number of studies have borne this fact out. An understanding of rewards systems and group dynamics is essential. Bruce Tuckman developed a team development model in 1965.[3] The life cycle of a group consists of Tuckman's four stages:

1. Forming
2. Storming
3. Norming
4. Performing.
5. A fifth step was added years later: Adjourning.

The forming stage is characterized by uncertainty about roles, thus the group seeks outside guidance. Storming is when the groups starts becoming confident in its members and rejects outside authority. Norming is where rules about fitting into the group are established. Members want to be a team at this stage. Performing is focused on the task and larger goal. Each member has responsibilities and is concerned with getting the job done. The adjourning stage is when the team has met its goals and objectives and then dissolves. Humans have feelings and emotions—they are not robots. This stage can be difficult for members to accept, and is consistent with the feelings of loss.

Teams often don't reach the productive stage. Kevin Garnett, the former Celtic and future NBA Hall of Famer, states, "Timing is everything, and chemistry is something that you just don't throw in the frying pan and mix it up with another something, and throw something on top of that, and they fry it up, put it in a tortilla, put it in the microwave, heat it up and give it to you, and expect it to taste good."[4] Tuckman states that there are three issues that will impact team performance: content, process and feelings. Content refers to what the group does. Process deals with how the team works toward its objectives. Feelings means how the team members relate to one another. All groups are different and may go through the phases differently. The goal is for the group to become self-reliant as it seeks to achieve its objective.

Think about the best team you have been a part of—a work group, sports team or volunteer project. What were the qualities the team had that you admired? What didn't work about the team? What would you change? As the owner, your job is to set the direction of the group. Learn from mistakes. Take corrective action as necessary. If you let bad or inappropriate behavior become the norm, the long-term consequences for the business could be dire. Groups are opportunities to accelerate growth and learning.

ADVISORY GROUP

Think about adding more brain power by forming an advisory group. This is a team with the sole purpose of providing the owners and management with advice, guidance, and counsel to grow the business. An advisory group can foster growth for the business without adding costs. Your advisors should meet at least four times a year. However, it is recommended that the group meet as often as necessary to develop a good working rapport and to build a strong bond. Initially, an advisory group of up to five is encouraged. Seek expertise in the following areas: accounting, business law, marketing, human resource, and finance. Add people based on business needs. Use your advisory team to get outside feedback to build your business.

TAKEAWAY: You need a team.

PART II
Essentials: The Stuff that Matters

11

EMPLOYEES WANT MEANING: TREAT 'EM RIGHT

YOUR BUSINESS NEEDS TALENTED and committed people, and they need you. In the past, workers wanted only a paycheck; whereas, today, they want more because work is no longer only about work. "Work is more than what people do to make ends meet. For many, work is central to their identity and sense of self", says Jim Emerman, a contributor to *Next Avenue*, part of the PBS system and a media service for America's booming older population.[1]

The prospect of doing something good is a driving force for today's Millennial workforce, and companies are taking notice. Employees want to feel connected to the company's mission. They have aspirations, emotions and desires. The best companies tap into their employees' motivations because the competition for labor is tight. Companies have to put their best foot forward. "If one wanted to crush and destroy a man entirely, to mete out to him the most terrible punishment," wrote Russian novelist Fyodor Dostoyevsky, "all one would have to do would be to make him do work that was completely and utterly devoid of usefulness and meaning."[2]

FOOSBALL AT WORK

Roman Krznaric, in his book, *How to Find Fulfilling Work*, lists five dimensions of meaningful work:

1. Earning money

2. Achieving status

3. Following your passions

4. Making a difference

5. Using your talents[3]

Krznaric says, "choosing a career for its monetary rewards is the oldest and most powerful motivation in the world of work."[4] We all exchange our time for money. But happiness is important. "The pursuit of wealth is an unlikely path to achieving personal well-being, says Krznaric."[5] At some point, money, an extrinsic motivator, is no longer the determining factor in meaningful work.

Like money, social status is an extrinsic motivator when it comes to meaningful work. A doctor or CEO is a prestigious job that comes with status based on how society views these positions. People sometimes choose positions that have status, but may not be personally fulfilling, and as the eighteenth-century philosopher, Jean-Jacques Rousseau warned, "this universal desire for reputation, in which we judge ourselves through other people's eyes, is fraught with dangers."[6] Napoleon Hill, the self-help author, said, "Performing labor that one does not like is one of the great tragedies of civilization."[7]

Krznaric's next three dimensions of meaningful work are intrinsic in nature, where the work is valued for itself, not simply as a means to achieve money or status. A passion is something that is developed—you can't buy it. Contrary to what you read or hear, people don't have ingrained or pre-existing passions. They develop over time. So, the rule to follow your passion is not the solution for the masses when it comes to work. Cal Newport, a professor and author of the book, *Deep Work*, says, "Long-term career satisfaction requires traits like a real sense of autonomy, a real sense of impact on the world, a sense of mastery that you're good at what you do, and a sense of connection in relation to other people."[8]

Your interest in getting better at your craft will drive you. It's not your passions that make work meaningful, it's doing work that you are good at after honing your skills over time that releases your passion. In the end, being good at something brings satisfaction, which leads you to continue to learn about your craft. The top professional athletes work hard to be the best at their craft. If pushing yourself physically, for hours a day, does not suit you, you won't be a professional athlete.

Teachers, firefighters, clergy, physical therapists, and psychologists tend to be the happiest in their jobs, but not the best paid. These jobs are about helping people and making a difference. Companies have social missions because customers and employees want to make a difference in the world. Businesses are building social missions into their business models and this trend is growing. Companies like Kickstarter, TOMS Shoes and Ben & Jerry's Ice Cream all have social missions.

"Where the needs of the world and your talents cross, there lies your vocation," said Aristotle.[9] Use your strengths for meaningful work and it will benefit you in many ways.

For example, a Gallup study indicates that the more American workers use their strengths, the less likely they are to report feeling worry, stress, anger, sadness, or physical pain.[10] When people are worrying, stressing, sad or in pain, their work suffers, which can lead to reduced productivity or worse.

UNDERSTANDING HUMAN NEEDS

No two humans are the same; we are complex creatures. Yet, we all have needs. Abraham Maslow developed his conceptual framework to explain humans' hierarchy of needs as they relate to motivation.[11] Maslow's pyramid attempts to explain the varying needs that people have at different times of life, from low to high-level needs:

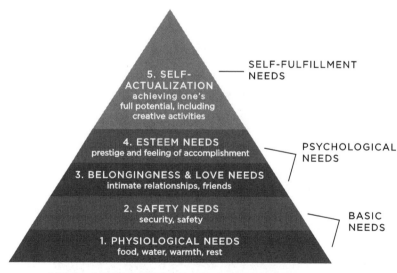

MASLOW'S HIERARCHY OF NEEDS

Physiological needs are the basics such as food, water, shelter. Safety needs include personal safety, financial security, health, and well-being. Once the basic needs have been met, interpersonal relationships and a sense of belongingness follow, which can be achieved through friendships, family, organizations or volunteering. Esteem needs relate to our desire to be accepted and valued by others. Self-actualization reflects people's desire to reach their full potential, without worrying about the trials and tribulations of making a living. People don't want to wait until retirement to get to this stage in life.

Maslow's pyramid is important in explaining employees' needs. As the boss, you should be asking yourself whether the wages paid allow for your employees to meet their basic needs at the physiological and safety levels. Working two jobs and worrying about making ends meet can have a negative effect on both the employee and the business. The company should look at how it can help employees to meet their social belonging and esteem needs. Helping employees get to the self-actualization stage may not be possible at work, but it is worth the effort to understand what each employee wants out of work and life.

You're the boss, but your success depends on employees. Create a place where employees want to come and achieve organizational and personal growth goals. Embrace your role as the leader because the culture you create will be the guiding hand that steers your business. Create a workplace employees want to come to.

TAKEAWAY: Your advantage is people.

12

THE ENTREPRENEURIAL UNIVERSE: KNOW YOUR ECOSYSTEM

WORKING OUT ALONE is not smart. A workout partner is there just in case you need support or motivation. No business should have to go it alone—lifting the heavy weight of business. Fortunately, it doesn't have to. There's a support system in every town, city, county and state waiting to help businesses. The entrepreneurial ecosystem is designed to harness the power of the private and public sectors to support economic development.

The ecosystem is a living and breathing thing run by people. Each ecosystem is different, but taps the history, culture, dreams, aspirations and hopes of the place. What Worcester, Massachusetts needs is different from Beeville, Texas; the same holds true for Portland, Maine and Portland, Oregon; and Arkansas. If a business or industry can compete on uniqueness, so too can an ecosystem. Showcasing a community's strengths is a differentiator. Every community has a personality—despite the constant push for globalization. Uniqueness is an advantage worth investing in because personality is the spice that adds flavor to a community.

GET HELP NOW

The door to enter the entrepreneurial ecosystem is in your community. Chambers of commerce are great starting points. They will encourage you to join, but most will not turn you away from assistance or a referral to free technical assistance. Every state has a Service Corps of Retired Executives (SCORE) office, which is a free resource for business help supported by the U.S. Small Business Administration (SBA). Small Business Development Centers (SBDC) and Women's Business Development Centers (WBDC) are located across the country. Community colleges, nonprofits, colleges and universities provide small-business services throughout the country. Trade associations are great resources for your industry and offer business services and referrals.

When an entrepreneur is initiating the planning phase to start a business, whether it be writing a business plan or a pitch deck, she should spend a few hours learning about the entrepreneurial ecosystem in her community. The investment in time pales in comparison to the long-term return. Knowing the key players in the entrepreneurial ecosystem will pay dividends immediately, from learning about low-cost capital, local, state and federal programs, to workshops and seminars. The burden is on you to know your entrepreneurial ecosystem as well as you know your customers.

Many communities have business incubators or accelerator programs. Incubators help get ideas off the ground by offering reduced-rate office space in a communal environment, access to a support network, training services and other bundled services. The goal of an incubator is to achieve milestones and move out. On the other hand, accelerators have formal application processes to vet companies before accepting them into a program. Accelerators assist with growing startups and existing businesses. The top accelerators in the country require an equity stake of up to 10 percent from the company upon acceptance into the program. These accelerators are connected to top-rate networks and businesses.

A business should never fail because it didn't know where to get free and low-cost help. Entrepreneurs should view their entrepreneurial ecosystems as their personal pit crew. A NASCAR pit crew can change four tires and fuel a vehicle in about 16 seconds, which puts the driver back on the track to chase the checkered flag and prize money. The sooner you know where to get support in your community, the better off you will be. The resources available are advice, technical assistance, access to business strategy, as well as training in many business topical areas from social media, marketing, accounting, human resources, to taxes and more.

BUILDING THE BUSINESS

Nothing is more important than the three rules of business:

1. Delight customers with products they can't resist.

2. Serve and love the communities you operate in.

3. Take care of your employees.

When times get tough—as they always do—these rules should never be deserted. Your brand—or company name—is all you have. Make sure you build a brand that is results-oriented and focused on the rules.

You will make mistakes in starting your business, from not understanding who is in your target market, their likes, dislikes and more. Your estimates for revenue and profitability will take longer than you plan—because no one has ever been able to predict the future with 100 percent accuracy. You may not have as much capital as you need. These are all common mistakes.

A BUSINESS SHOULD NEVER FAIL BECAUSE IT DIDN'T KNOW WHERE TO GET FREE AND LOW-COST HELP.

Competition will be tough. However, if you offer a superior product, customers may be willing to try your offering. Give them an incentive to try your product for the first time. Compete on your value proposition, not price. Make your brand mean something that differentiates it from the competition.

"A man may rise to high success in the world, and even to lofty altitudes in the spiritual realm, and again descend into weakness and wretchedness by allowing arrogance, selfish, and corrupt thoughts to take possession of him," said James Allen, author of *As a Man Thinketh*.[1] When times are tough, the easiest thing to believe is that the business will not work. Remember, it's about customers, not you. Don't be afraid to adjust your offering to what the market wants. Your willingness to let go of your ego, may be the best advantage you have over the competition.

You are special. Your story is unique. Mokhtar Alkhanshali, who is the subject of the book, *The Monk of Mokha* by Dave Eggers, says, "Your story is the most personal asset you have."[2] You are part of the most important community of all: humanity. As you build your business, serve customers with dignity, respect, and they will take care of you. Value the community where you do business not as a place to extract dollars, but also to invest, because the entrepreneurial ecosystem will have your back.

TAKEAWAY: Know what's in your backyard.

13

MARKETING:
JUST DO IT

WHEN IT COMES TO MARKETING, business owners want to be the DC Comics character, The Flash. They are in a hurry to turn on the revenue spigot. But they should pump their brakes to understand the problem they solve and differentiate themselves first. Marketing doesn't begin when you hit the send button on an email blast or an advertisement drops in a print publication. Marketing begins when you identify the problem your business will solve for a specific group of customers (a market).

Your value proposition is the secret sauce and key to your marketing strategy. Diana Kander's book, *All in Startup*, is a novel that helps startup businesses understand their value proposition by identifying the core problem and the solution they solve.[1] The novel format drives home the central message of knowing the problem your business solves before it is too late.

Let's take a look at how an entrepreneur (Jane) might approach a new business venture. Jane sees a potential restaurant location that is off of a busy thoroughfare. She says, "This area needs a steakhouse because there is not one here." Her logic is flawed and may lead to an expensive mistake. The better way of figuring out what customers want is to use the eight-step process that follows:

1. My business serves customers who are _____.

2. The customer's hair-on-fire problem is _____.

3. Customers use _____ to solve their problem.

4. Competitors in the marketplace are _____.

5. I know this is a hair-on-fire problem because _____.

6. Based on research, customers would pay _____ to solve this problem.

7. Given the unit cost of _____, I can sell _____units.

8. Total revenue will be _____, minus expenses of _____ will yield a profit or loss of

_____.

TAKE A ROAD TRIP

The best way to develop a product to solve a problem is to understand what the market needs. Observing customers' shopping patterns at brick-and-mortar stores is an easy and inexpensive way to glean market intelligence. Examining what days and time the location is busy, the number of customers frequenting the store and the number of cars in the parking lot. Estimate the age of the patrons.

When researching competitors, the owner should visit the physical locations. Just by visiting a few stores, a clear picture will emerge of the opportunity. Leave no stone unturned. The exterior and interior is part of the overall evaluation. This is a great way to evaluate the interior of the store (lighting, color scheme, layout of the store, its product offering, and whether music is playing) and can go a long way to evaluate the competition.

Track where competitors are located. How many competitors are within a few miles of the business? After ascertaining the competitors in the area, you can visit the website to learn how the business is positioned. Much can be gleaned from a website. For example, does the business come across as customer-friendly by putting telephone numbers, contact people and the owner's name on the website? Is it easy to navigate and find product? What products does the business offer and at what price points? What's the business story?

THE 6 P's

Once you know the hair-on-fire problem that you solve for customers, it's all about telling your story through the brand experience. The story will be encapsulated in the way the business operates, which includes all the details of the business, from the how the telephone is answered, the appearance and functionality of the website, and employees' demeanor. That's your brand.

Edmund Jerome McCarthy introduced the world to the four P's of the marketing mix in 1960. His book, *Basic Marketing: A Managerial Approach*, has been a top selling textbook on college campuses.[2] The marketing mix is the combination of strategies and tactics a company uses to execute its marketing plan. The 4 P's are product, price, promotion and place. McCarthy's original four P's were expanded to six: people and process.

The product can be a physical good or service. The product solves the pain point for the target customer. Price is the cost customers pay for the product. New business owners tend to want to have the lowest prices like Walmart; whereas, Apple charges a premium. Few businesses should compete only on price. Promotion is how the company positions the product, communicates its message and promotes the product to its target market, which could be on TV, radio, direct mail or social media, to name some ways. Place is the location where the product is sold. Many businesses have multiple distribution points including physical stores, online, and pickup/drop-off points. People are key to your product. A company's personnel must have the appropriate skills and experience. Process refers to systems and methods to deliver a consistent product every time. Franchises are good at creating processes to deliver the same product across large geographic areas.

BE UNIQUE

Solving a pain point and differentiating the business from competitors are the aim of your marketing. A distinguishable value proposition can lead to premium pricing. At the other end of price is a commodity business where customers cannot tell the difference between competitors. Insurance, gasoline, meat and boxed pasta are examples of commodities. However, companies spend billions of dollars to convince customers there is a difference. GEICO positions itself as the low-price automobile insurance company with the gecko. You're in good hands with Allstate when mayhem strikes. Two different approaches for a commodity. Get your story out in a unique way.

Customers will give you a second chance if you treat them right. When something falls through the cracks, admit your mistake. Dirty bathrooms, poor service, and bad food will not be tolerated. That's a recipe for disaster and failure. The cable show *Bar Rescue* hosted by Jon Taffer, helps rescue failing bars and night club establishments—similar to Gordon Ramsay's *Kitchen Nightmares*. The common problems Taffer discovers are poor food quality, service, cleanliness, tired decor, and owners and employees who seem not to care. All can be fatal to a business, regardless of your marketing message.

Satisfied customers are your number one source for positive word-of-mouth. Take control of your brand experience. If you don't serve your customers, and they are not delighted, they will go elsewhere. In the end, you don't own your customers. Provide a positive, and unforgettable experience that differentiates you from the competition, and you will have loyal customers.

TAKEAWAY: Be unique.

"I Got 5 on It," Luniz featuring Michael Marshall, *Operation Stackola*

14

LISTENING IS SELLING: SOLVE PROBLEMS

MENTION SELLING TO YOUR NEXT-DOOR NEIGHBOR, and she will think you said a four-letter word. Selling is not a daily annoyance; it is an essential skill that everyone should have. When you think about it, we are all selling something. Napoleon Hill, an early convert to the self-help field and author of *How to Sell Your Way Through Life*, wrote, "We are all salesmen [and saleswomen] regardless of our calling."[1]

When done right, selling is a "win-win" for all parties. At its core, selling is listening to a problem and communicating how your product will solve the pain point. Whether it be a vendor at a stadium concert, yelling, "Get your exclusive Beyoncé merchandise"; a politician asking for your vote; or your significant other talking you into going out to dinner— with your money, it's all selling.

Invest the time to listen for problems. Frank Bettger, the author of the book, *How I Raised Myself from Failure to Success in Selling*, says, "Try to find out what people want, and then help them get it."[2] Once you know the problem, you can introduce your solution as the superhero to save the day. Dale Carnegie once said, "There is only one way under high heaven to get anybody to do anything. And that is by making the other person want to do it... Remember, there is no other way."[3]

Customers don't buy drills, dentists or plumbers, they buy solutions that create a hole, a beautiful smile, or a hot shower. "When you show a man what he wants, he'll move heaven and earth to get it," says Bettger.[4] People buy solutions, not features. Mention features of your product, but tie them to how it will make the customer's life better—not yours. Connect on an emotional level.

Imagine a salesperson in a big box store talking to a married couple with two kids. Donovan, the salesperson, says, "The TechWizard oven has the latest technology to cook food evenly and comes with a ten-year warranty. Donovan focuses on how the oven turns itself off, so the couple won't ever have to worry about leaving the oven on again, which is what had happened and led to the fire department coming to their house to put out what turned out to be a minor fire. The customers bought Donovan's solution: a safe home.

EMOTIONS SELL

Geoffrey James, a contributing editor to *Inc.com*, says that "Buying decisions are always the result of a change in the customer's emotional state."[5] Men or women who are single and looking to attract a mate may buy cologne because of how it makes them feel, perhaps making them more confident. So, it's not the cologne that attracts the mate, it is the new-found confidence that one feels, and projects, when wearing the cologne.

James identifies six emotions that play out when making a buying decision:

1. Greed

2. Fear

3. Altruism

4. Envy

5. Pride

6. Shame

If I make a decision now, I will be rewarded: that is greed. If I don't make a decision now, it will impact me in a negative way: that is fear. If I make this decision, it will help others: altruism. If I don't make the decision, my competitors will: envy. If I make the decision now, I will look good: pride. If I don't make the decision, I will look dumb: shame.

The key is to make your product fit into an emotional state. State lotteries tap into our desire for the good life. Life insurance taps into the fear that a loved one will die, leaving a spouse without enough money to pay the mortgage, raise a family, or pay for a child's college education. Volvo, ADT (home security) and Michelin tires all play on the fear of personal safety. The thought of a burglar breaking into your home may motivate you to purchase a security system and monthly monitoring from ADT (recurring revenue is good for business).

Emotions are used in many different ways in selling. TOMS provides a free pair of shoes to someone in need in another country, after each purchase. This is altruism at work. When a neighbor buys a new car, adds solar panels to their home, or goes on an expensive vacation, only to keep up with their neighbors, this is envy, also known as keeping up with the Joneses. Several home cleaning products allude to shame if a customer doesn't use their product and guests see a dirty toilet—oh, the shame!

SELLING IS LISTENING TO A PROBLEM **AND COMMUNICATING** *HOW YOUR PRODUCT WILL SOLVE THE PAIN POINT.*

DON'T FEAR "NO" WHEN SELLING

The word "no" is one of the most powerful words in the English language—it's an automatic braking system (ABS) for a conversation. Parents have been telling kids "no" since the beginning of time. In fact, you probably have strong memories, emotions and feelings linked to "no", from your childhood. Think about your negative feelings associated with the word "no." Let them go. As a business owner selling, think of "no" as way to reclaim your time from prospects.

"No" is an important word every entrepreneur should embrace because it comes with the territory of selling. The trick is to turn "no" into a positive. When you hear "no", it means you don't have to invest more time waiting for a response. You are free to move on to the next prospect that is waiting to say "yes."

Get familiar with hearing the word "no." Don't internalize "no" as something you did wrong. People say "no" for all types of reasons that often have nothing to do with you. If we said "yes" every time a telemarketer called, an ad appeared on TV, or one appeared in our email, we would be broke. Richard Fenton and Andrea Waltz wrote the book, *Go for No! Yes is the Destination, No Is How You Get There*, which is a good read to help business people get comfortable with hearing "no."[6]

"No" has the single purpose to help you reclaim your time, faster. The good thing about hearing "no" is that you don't have to waste any more time going down a rabbit hole. Learn from it. Move on. The "no" you hear will eventually lead to "yes." Bankers may say "no" to your credit request. Potential partners may say "no" to working with you. Employee prospects may say "no" to your offer of employment. The more you hear "no", the more successful you will be.

To turbo charge your business, learn to love listening, which is the quickest way to grow your business. Don't target every person in the world for your solution; find the segment that has the problem you solve and the money to pay for it. When you discover customers who need your solution, listen and a sale will follow.

TAKEAWAY: Problems lead to customers.

15

ACCOUNTING:
THE NUMBERS ARE THE BUSINESS

PEOPLE VIEW ACCOUNTING as the worst thing about a business. If accounting was a character in a movie, he (or she) would be down on his luck, drinking in a dark bar, wondering why no one wants to be around him. Accounting should be the superstar, a blockbuster movie for any business. But it doesn't get the attention it deserves until last-minute—if at all. Accounting is not something that should be put off for a rainy day like dirty laundry.

Accounting is a language the business owner should get familiar with. You don't have to know every minute detail, but you should be conversational in accounting—the same holds true for visiting a foreign country and knowing a few words in the native tongue. One of the best ways to improve your business immediately is to hire a bookkeeper. Say "hire a bookkeeper" three times until it becomes part of your subconscious mind. The sooner you hire a bookkeeper, the quicker your financial house will be in order.

Entrepreneurs don't start businesses to do accounting. Be that as it may, the numbers are the business. The more you know and understand about accounting, the better off you and your business will be. Accounting is the organization of numbers according to generally accepted standards and principals. Accounting is like your favorite selfie, a snapshot of the numbers at a specific moment. Your best or worst selfie shouldn't define you, because tomorrow is a new day full of promise.

A man described as a "monk, magician and lover of numbers," changed forever how we look at numbers.[1] That man, Luca Pacioli, we have to thank for popularizing double-entry accounting, the system for recording transactions twice, which still is used all over the world. Each entry is either a debit or credit entry.

In double-entry accounting, the accounts must remain in balance, so a change in one account will correspond with a change in another account, whether it be an asset (debit is equal to an increase and credit is equal to a decrease), liability (debit is equal to a decrease and credit is equal to an increase), income or revenue (debit is equal to a decrease and credit is equal to an increase), expense (debit is equal to an increase and credit is equal to a decrease) or capital (debit is equal to a decrease and credit is equal to an increase).[2] See the image below.

DEBIT OR CREDIT

KIND OF ACCOUNT	DEBIT	CREDIT
ASSET	INCREASE	DECREASE
LIABILITY	DECREASE	INCREASE
INCOME/REVENUE	DECREASE	INCREASE
EXPENSE/COST/DIVIDEND	INCREASE	DECREASE
EQUITY/CAPITAL	DECREASE	INCREASE

In 1494, Pacioli, who taught math to and collaborated with Leonardo da Vinci, published a math encyclopedia and included an instructional section on double-entry accounting. Pacioli didn't create double-entry accounting, he spread the idea and it took off. "Before double-entry, people just kept diaries and counted their money at the end of the day," according to David Kestenbaum, who wrote, "The Accountant Who Changed the World."[3] Pacioli made capitalists all over the world love, or hate, numbers.

REPORTS

Some business owners use their monthly bank statements as a proxy for their financial health—this is not recommended. They often put off producing financial reports until tax time. But should the need come to access bank credit, the owner is left scrambling to produce financial statements, reports, and other documents needed for the bank to evaluate credit worthiness. Hire a bookkeeper to do your monthly statements before it is too late. You will learn that a competent bookkeeper or accountant is worth every dollar.

At a minimum, the owner should generate the following reports at least once a month: 1) Income Statement (known as Profit and Loss or P&L), 2) Balance Sheet, 3) Cash Flow. With these three reports, you will have a snapshot of your business at any given moment. While your bookkeeper or accountant may produce the reports, it is imperative for you to understand how to interpret them.

Add accounts receivable (A/R is money owed to the business) and accounts payable (A/P is money that must be paid out) aging report and the picture will be crystal clear. The owner's role is to interpret the reports to make decisions that will impact the business. Let's talk about the purpose of the three reports and provide an overview of why these reports are vital to business success.

INCOME STATEMENT

The income statement is often referred to as the Profit and Loss (P&L) statement. The Income Statement reflects the operations of the business. The income statement has five key lines: Sales (also known as Revenue) is the amount of money the business generated. This part of the report will have top-line revenue for the business, minus your costs of goods sold to get to your gross profit (also called gross margin), which can be a positive or negative number. Costs of goods sold (COGS) is the cost of materials and labor to make the goods sold. See Income Statement in the appendix, courtesy of Zions Bank.[4]

Next, the business will deduct its operating expenses (also known as Selling, Administrative & General or SGA). This is where all your expenses for operating the business will be located such as labor, rent, office supplies and utilities. The gross margin number minus expenses will lead to a number called Profit from Operations. After taxes have been accounted for, you will arrive at Net Profit After Income Tax. It's that simple. In the appendix example, the profit margin is 10.80 percent (Net Profit After Tax of $21,600 divided by $200,000) for the business. With a little bit of practice, over time, you will become a leading expert at interpreting your Income Statement.

To arrive at the gross margin (also known as gross profit), take net sales of $200,000 minus costs of goods sold, to get to $70,000. Then take $70,000 and divide it by $200,000, which equals a gross margin of 35 percent. The higher the margin, the better likelihood the business will be profitable, once all expenses have been deducted. All industries have different margins. High margins are good. Low margins may be a sign of a commodity business, which means you are competing on price alone.

The higher the gross profit, the more likely you will attract competition. Let's look at the margins of a local restaurant. Sales minus costs of goods sold (food & alcohol) costs will generate the gross profit. Restaurants want to keep their food costs around 30 percent, which will lead to gross margins of 70 percent. The gross margins on alcohol are higher. Make sure your numbers are consistent with industry standards. Here is an article from The Balance.com about calculating margins: thebalance.com/calculating-gross-profit-margin-357577.

Divide Net Income After Income Tax by Net sales of $200,000 to get your Net Profit Margin. In this case, the number is 10.80. Check this number with your industry to get a better understanding of where your business stacks up. A healthy business will have a positive number for the net income. The Zions Bank guide to creating a Profit & Loss Statement can be found here: zionsbank.com/pdfs/biz_resources_book-3.pdf.

BALANCE SHEET

"The purpose of financial statements is to communicate. Financial statements tell you and others the state of your business," according to Zions Bank, "How to Prepare and Analyze a Balance Sheet."[5] A balance sheet statement is the quickest way to assess the health of a business by looking at its assets, liabilities and owner's equity. Every balance sheet must balance: Assets are equal to liabilities plus owner's equity. See image below.

BALANCE SHEET

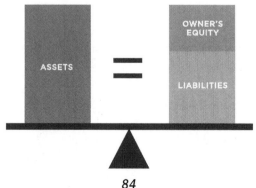

On the asset side, in the appendix example, Current Assets are cash on hand, cash in the bank, accounts receivable (money owed to the business), merchandise inventory, and prepaid expenses (such as rent or insurance). The value of equipment and commercial real estate would be reflected on the asset side—the debt on the building would appear on the liabilities side. Prepaid expenses such as insurance often are paid in advance, but are used over a period of months. Total current assets are $10,800. Add fixed assets, and total assets are $12,000.

On the liability side, you will include accounts payable (bills you owe others), lines of credit or loans. The total current liabilities in this example are $3,800. Long-term liabilities are $5,500, which are notes payable (loans owed by the business). Total liabilities are $9,300. Total liabilities and Net Worth are $12,000. Your assets will always equal liabilities and owner's equity, which is why they call it a balance sheet. Here's a link to Zions Bank, "How to Prepare and Analyze a Balance Sheet": zionsbank.com/pdfs/biz_resources_book-2.pdf.

CASH FLOW

The Zions Bank's "How to Prepare a Cash Flow Statement" says, "A cash flow statement can answer the questions, 'Where did the money come from?' and 'Where did it go?'[6] Your business is a cash machine and a cash flow statement shows how money flows into and out of your business. The old saying "cash is king", is true. The cash flow statement should be generated weekly, especially for a small business. A weekly cash flow will help the owner understand the cash needs of the business. Without cash, the business is in peril. Cash can come into the business in three ways:

1. Operations
2. Investing activities
3. Financing activities

At all times, you should know how much cash the business has available to operate.

On the operations side, the cash flow shows how much money comes into the business and goes out. In the appendix example, the business has a Net Cash Flow from Operations of $165. Cash Flow from Investing Activities is ($400) (the parentheses show this is a negative number). Cash Flow Associated with Financing is $30. The Net Change in Cash Flow has decreased by ($205). If the business has a negative amount of money going out of the business, cash will have to come from investment and financing activities. Investments are activities that generate positive or negative cash from the gain or sale of investments. Financing is the amount of capital that comes into the business from borrowing capital. Here is the Zions Bank document, "How to Prepare A Cash Flow Statement": zionsbank.com/pdfs/biz_resources_book-4.pdf.

Get familiar with the Income Statement, Balance Sheet and Cash Flow Statement. You may not want to be an accountant, but don't fall asleep at the wheel because the numbers are the business. Without a firm grasp on what is happening, a business is waiting for an accident to happen. In the end, the numbers are the vital signs of your business health.

TAKEAWAY: Hire a bookkeeper.

16

FIND AN ATTORNEY:
PROTECT YOUR BUSINESS

BEING PREPARED AND PROACTIVE is indispensable when starting a business. Still things can go wrong. Business relies on trust and mutual interest, but when one or both break down, the court system may be necessary. Law is complex and the stakes are high. Lawsuits can spring up from legitimate misunderstandings, corporate malfeasance, or blatant disregard for an agreement. These legal hit-and-runs are not rare. In fact, the new troika should be death, taxes and lawsuits.

By hiring an attorney early in the startup process, an entrepreneur may avoid the financial ramifications, enormous distractions and reputational risk of a legal action. Attorneys are like taxi drivers because their legal meters are perpetually in motion. Nevertheless, in the long run, your attorney will save you money. They have developed customer-focused fee arrangements from hourly rates, capped, fixed, flat and contingency or success fees. But all attorneys are not created equal, so you will need to get a referral to avoid the time-consuming process of screening for competent attorneys. Your attorney should be an expert in the area in which you have a need, whether it be general business transactions, securities law, commercial real estate, employee law, environmental issues or intellectual property (IP)—there should be a Tinder for attorneys and entrepreneurs.

A company's legal structure is important to the overall health of the business and how it will function in the future. Most first-time business owners will not understand the differences in corporate structures and the effect on governance, liability and tax benefits. Your attorney can help evaluate whether a limited liability company (LLC), C-corporation, S-corporation, or partnership is best. Protecting the business, its employees, IP, and the owners are top priorities. At a minimum, meet with an attorney for an initial consultation to discuss legal issues. Get an estimate, and compare prices and expertise. The attorney-client fit is key for a good working relationship.

SETTING UP THE BUSINESS

When setting up your company, various documents must be completed and filed with the Secretary of State. For example, an LLC will have an operating agreement that spells out who is authorized to sign on behalf of the company, what the business does and its office location. In addition, LLCs must file annual reports in the states where they do business. Your attorney can help think through the potential issues going forward. For example, should the business be incorporated in Delaware? Most venture-back companies are incorporated there.

Depending on the nature of the business, it may have to be licensed to conduct business by all the states in which it does business or by the federal government. Restaurants have to get local, county and state approvals for construction, renovations, food handling, and permits to sell liquor. Local government officials must sign off before the business receives its Certificate of Occupancy (CO) and can open. The business must be in compliance with employment law when hiring staff.

No one wants to go to court. The time to avoid a legal action is before it happens. Know what you're signing when entering into a legal agreement. Every time you sign a document, you are entering into a legal agreement. Read the fine print.

LEGAL ISSUES

Restaurants can run into challenges in relationship to contracts, leases, employment issues, sales tax, insurance and regulatory hurdles such as health and department of consumer protection. Sometimes these can be surprising. For example, gift cards can be a bomb waiting to explode. In some states, including Connecticut, gift cards do not expire, which is a liability on the balance sheet until used. Another area where restaurants or bars get into trouble is copyrighted music.[1] Customers take music for granted because it creates the perfect ambience. But music has a real cost, which is passed on to the consumer in the price of the meal. Any establishment that plays copyrighted music must pay a licensing fee. Many restaurants and bar owners often ignore the rules around music.

BMI, one of the companies that represent the interest of musicians, song writers, and other copyright holders, goes after businesses aggressively when they are not in compliance with the law. The company seeks to work with the establishments. But the best way to avoid a legal action from BMI is to select one of their payment plans to play copyrighted material. Spotify and Pandora have plans to keep businesses on the right side of the law when it comes to music. In the long run, you'll save money.

LAW IS LIKE A GIANT UMBILICAL CORD CONNECTING EVERY ASPECT OF YOUR **BUSINESS AND HUMAN LIFE.**

Employee law is another area ripe for litigation. Companies run afoul of the law pertaining to employees (W-2) and independent contractors (1099). The main difference between an employee and contractor is that the employer has control over the employees' hours, work locations and work product. An independent contractor is not an employee. Contractors provide their own equipment, may work from home, and are responsible for handling their taxes.

Some companies have hired independent contractors and treated them as employees. This is an area where the IRS will review whether the person was an employee or contractor, which could end up costing the business a considerable amount in taxes, penalties and interest. Consult with an attorney to understand the laws.

PROTECT THE BUSINESS

Law is like a giant umbilical cord connecting every aspect of your business and human life. Your business will interact with the law if you have partners, investors, employees, customers, you rent a commercial space, you buy products from vendors, you own intellectual property or you have a website.

One area where you don't want to get into legal issues involves local, state and federal taxes. Work with your attorney and accountant to make sure you know what documents and filings must be completed monthly, quarterly and annually. It is easy to overlook a deadline that could be costly. Many companies hire a payroll company to handle employment withholdings and taxes. This is a smart decision.

There is no way to completely eliminate the possibility of a legal action. The best way to reduce potential legal action is to hire an attorney early in the business formation process. Hire the best attorney you can afford who has the credentials to help your business. The business that decides not to retain an attorney is making a risky bet.

TAKEAWAY: Get it in writing.

17

WHERE TO FIND HELP:
CONSULTANTS ARE EVERYWHERE

I REMEMBER BEING BETWEEN BUSINESS VENTURES, when I saw an ad on Craigslist for an independent sales contractor (1099) position. I interviewed for the sales position, and presto, I was a newly-minted sales representative selling a rewards program to small businesses. I had little sales experience but believed in the product. To get up to speed, I read every book on selling I could get my hands on. The owner of the company (I will call him Jim) provided the basics in a three-ring binder and at weekly meetings. Within days, I was cold-calling small businesses in person.

One day, I called Jim, after a terrible week filled with rejection and no sales. Sensing the seriousness in my voice, he swooped in, driving his American-made sedan over 50 miles to see me. On that day, Jim gave me precious advice. Jim was a tall guy with a stocky build, in his early sixties. On that day, he wore jeans, black dress shoes and a V-neck sweater, no tee shirt. His head full of white hair was neatly groomed to match his white goatee. Jim said, "Everyone needs a pep talk, now and then." This was coming from a guy who spent decades in the sales business. Jim's advice helped me become a better sales person. In less than a few months of having that conversation, he passed away. I still cherish his advice today.

We all need help at some point, whether you're a doctor, master carpenter, designer or business owner. At some point, our enthusiasm, energy, or skill level will need updating. No one can achieve, or maintain, success forever. Atul Gawande, a surgeon, wrote the piece, "Personal Best," in the *New Yorker*.[1] Gawande worked with a coach to improve his surgery outcomes after being a doctor for years. He says, "Coaching may prove essential to the success of modern society."[2]

Never stop improving your craft. It has never in history been easier to access experts. Help can come from a YouTube video in the comfort of your home or from a book. Some people take online classes or continuing education classes. But meeting in person will never go out of style. Most industry have get-togethers once a year at regional or national conferences to learn the latest thinking, methods, procedures, products.

FREE HELP

Growing a business can be lonely, but it doesn't have to be that way. Business owners have limited resources and time. With the internet, you're always a few clicks from finding answers to your questions. The challenge is knowing how to find the right resources in a timely manner—consulting the internet is like turning on a fire hydrant, when all you want is a cup of water. Don't fret. A number of reputable organizations provide free in-person services available to business owners throughout the United States.

Founded in 1964, the Service Corps of Retired Executives (SCORE) is the largest volunteer organization assisting entrepreneurs. With over 300 offices across the country, the organization's goal is to help one million clients by 2020. Its mission is to "foster vibrant small business communities through mentoring and education." SCORE has helped over 10 million entrepreneurs and may be a godsend for your business.

Another program supported by the federal government is the Small Business Development Center (SBDC). President Carter signed into law the SBDC network in 1980. SBDCs combine the resources of higher education institutions and the private sector to grow small businesses. The nearly 1,000 SBDCs provide free face-to-face consulting and low-cost training. They offer help with writing a business plan, accessing capital, marketing, regulatory compliance, technology development and international trade. Women's Business Development Centers (WBDCs) are designed specifically to help female entrepreneurs, with locations all over the country. The Women's Business Development Council in Stamford, CT is "dedicated to providing the tools and resources to help women thrive in business." In 20 years, the organization has helped 18,000 women in Connecticut. There are similar organizations across the country.

Universities, colleges, community development financial institutions (CDFIs), incubators and accelerators all offer assistance to businesses. Not all advice is created equal. Do your homework to assure the free advice is worth it. Review the provider's website and read about their expertise and testimonials.

HIRE A CONSULTANT

At some point, free help could be costing your business in lost opportunities, delays and uncertainty. When speed and a specific expertise are important, consider hiring a consultant. The saying, "you get what you pay for" has never been truer. Expertise is readily available and affordable. A person with expertise who can help you get to your goal is an asset and a valuable member of your team. Hiring the right consultant is a time saver and will move your business forward quickly, and help you avoid going down a dead-end road. Trading someone's skill and knowledge for money could be your best decision.

The consulting business is a $200 billion industry.[3] Depending on the nature of your project, you can hire an experienced professional at Catalant.com, formerly known as HourlyNerd, before rebranding to Catalant. The company's website indicates that it "connects the world's leading companies with over 40,000 experts and firms to meet on-demand business needs." Just Answer, formerly Pearl, and Toptal are competitors in this growing space. Catalant has raised $73 million to date from investors.

Consulting platforms have top talent available. The key is to hire a consultant who will get the job done. Once you complete your due diligence, talk to an attorney before signing a contract. You are responsible for managing the process and driving results. Periodically check to ensure the consultant is on the right path and the work meets your expectations. If the consultant is not producing the work product in a timely manner, that is the time to take corrective action, before the project is over or you are hit with additional fees.

Your consultant may work out so well, you consider hiring or using him/her for additional projects. Weigh all the costs of hiring versus a continued contractual relationship. You want the best work product without getting locked into a weekly salary and benefits. Develop a pro forma with the person as an employee or consultant. Evaluate the pros and cons, including the added expense.

The best way to find a consultant is through a referral, which comes with a recommendation from someone who can substantiate past work. Tell people in your network what type of skill set you need. Call references and ask them about the consultant's demeanor and work product. It's up to you to do your homework to make sure you will get exactly what you need and on schedule.

TAKEAWAY: Everybody needs a pep talk.

18

PRODUCTIVITY TOOLS:
WORK SMARTER

INNOVATION HAS PROPELLED the human race forward with new, better and faster ways to do just about everything. Society is changing at breakneck speed through the use of technology. Doctors operate miles away from patients with robotic devices. Communication devices connected to the internet provide GPS to the most remote places on the planet. Technology is churning out better products in a continuous cycle, reducing cost while utility increases. Customers are the biggest beneficiaries of the technological revolution.

Work smarter, not harder, is the mantra because technology is the equalizer for small businesses. Large, powerful companies are worried about their survival, especially when all one needs to succeed is talent, a computer, access to the Internet, and a smartphone. Your smartphone is a powerful tool—it's the modern Swiss Army knife. With an app, your phone can scan and sign documents, plan your schedule or launch a massive email campaign. Productivity gained from apps allows you to do more in less time, so you can focus on providing value to your customers.

Don't get left behind. Stay abreast of the latest technology through business colleagues, suppliers, trade associations, websites, blogs, magazines or newspaper. To make your life easier, here are some technology tools that may boost your productivity.

ESSENTIALS

GSUITE
Intelligent apps to improve your business: email, word-processing, spreadsheets creating and sharing in the cloud. gsuite.google.com

BOOMERANG FOR GMAIL
Take control of Gmail and send and receive emails when you want. boomeranggmail.com

UPWORK
Find freelancers to help get work done. upwork.com

SLACK
Brings a team's communications together with shared workspaces to organize communications and keep them accessible. slack.com

GOODHIRE
Get background screening for future employees. goodhire.com

INTERCOM
Messaging products for sales, marketing and customer service are on one platform. intercom.com

INNOVATION HAS PROPELLED THE HUMAN RACE FORWARD WITH NEW, BETTER AND FASTER WAYS TO DO JUST ABOUT EVERYTHING.

LEARNING

YOUTUBE
Learn how to create spreadsheets to developing a winning presentation to woo customers. youtu.be/rwbho0CgEAE

KHAN ACADEMY
Learn anything you want for free from this nonprofit organization. khanacademy.org

EDX
Free online courses from major universities and companies such as Harvard, Oxford and Microsoft. edx.org

MIT OPEN COURSE
Here is an entrepreneurship course from a top university. ocw.mit.edu/courses/entrepreneurship/

CODEACADEMY
Learn to code interactively, for free. codecademy.com

MOBILE OFFICE

GENIUS SCAN & SIGN
Put a scanner in your pocket. Sign Documents. Available in the Apple App Store & Google Play

BASE CAMP
Organize your communications, projects, and client work together. basecamp.com

DROPBOX
Share large files and more with this file hosting service. dropbox.com

BOX
Share and edit files in the cloud. box.com

APPOINTY
All-in-one online scheduling software. appointy.com

TEAMWAVE
Platform for collaboration of sales, marketing and HR. teamwave.com

WEWORK
Rent a room or office suite. wework.com

ACCOUNTING/FINANCIAL

FRESHBOOKS
Small business accounting software that makes billing easy. freshbooks.com

QUICKBOOKS
Bookkeeping software for any business. quickbooks.com

FREE AGENTS
Accounting software for freelancers, small-business owners and their accountants. freeagent.com

EMAIL MARKETING

MAIL CHIMP
Create, send and manage email campaigns. mailchimp.com

CONSTANT CONTACT
The place to manage email marketing. constantcontact.com

COMMUNICATIONS/VIDEO CONFERENCING

SKYPE
Video conferencing made easy. skype.com/en/

GOOGLE HANGOUTS
Video conference from Google. hangouts.google.com

GO-TO-MEETING
Video conferencing, webinar & training. gotomeeting.com

E-COMMERCE

SHOPIFY
Commerce platform for any company. shopify.com

PAYPAL
Send and receive cash anywhere. paypal.com/us/home

NETWORKING

LINKEDIN
The world's social network for business professionals.
linkedlin.com

MEETUP
Connect with people with similar interests. meetup.com

HOOTSUITE
Mange all your social media in one place. hootsuite.com

CALCULATORS

CALCULATE STUFF
calculatestuff.com/financial

CREDIT KARMA: AMORTIZATION CALCULATOR
creditkarma.com/calculators/amortization

TAKEAWAY: Tools work for you.

19

EXPANSION MODE: GROWTH BY ACQUISITION

A FOCUS ON THE FUTURE is invigorating because new markets are opportunities. Maintaining the status quo is not a realistic option. In business, you're either growing or dying. A year of flat growth is data, but two years is a trend—like snowflakes announcing a storm. The bleeding of sales may be your competitor's diabolical plan in action—the proverbial death by shrinking sales. Management can never take its eyes off the ball. A bad economy, losing a major customer, or increased competition, are all valid explanations. As the owner, your job is to understand the "why' and map out a new direction. Once a logical explanation of what happened is supported by data, it's time to rearm the business to take back growth.

Growth is positive when it is aligned with the organization's vision, mission and culture. Growth can occur two ways: organically or through acquisitions. Organic growth requires a business plan and resources to implement the plan. In the beginning, companies can grow quickly by organic means. This type of growth requires an investment to support the growth through training, human resources, technology and processes. Not all growth is good, if the cost of growth doesn't yield better margins, economies of scale, quality products, as well as customer satisfaction and a positive culture.

GROWTH BY ACQUISITION

Acquisitions are attractive when organic growth will not achieve comparable results based on resources and time invested. The math for an acquisition follows: $1 + 1 = 3$. Assuming the appropriate due diligence has taken place, an acquisition can be the rocket fuel the business needs. A business' external environment shapes the competitive landscape. Acquiring a competitor can eliminate competition, increase revenues and assure profitability over the long run. Large technology companies frequently purchase small startups for synergistic reasons: talent and technology. The underlining technology may play a role in the acquirer's future.

When a business is pushing up against industry challenges of better, cheaper and faster, an acquisition may be the right opportunity to pursue. Given various economic factors and opportunities, an acquisition can be the quickest way to move forward in both the short and long term. An acquisition, or merger, may require you to take on financing from a bank or inventors. Most payback periods are five years or longer. As the owner, you want to align your commitment to future obligations going forward. Prior to moving into any planning for the long-term future of the business, it's best to do a self-assessment to make sure you want to lead the business over the next five years.

If your interest in the business is waning, it may be time to begin the process of exploring a sale. The decision to sell the business starts with the owner's decision. Once the decision is made, the owner must begin the process of getting the business ready for sale. Owners believe they can slap a for sale sign on the business and make a quick sale. Wrong. Few businesses are ready to be sold in one day. In fact, to maximize the sales price, it can take as much as a year to get the business ready for sale. Depending on the nature of the business, the industry and overall economy, some businesses will sell faster than others. For example, retailers competing with Amazon may have a hard time selling.

BUSINESS BROKERS

A business broker can be crucial to buying or selling a business. Much like a real estate broker, a business broker will help you sell your business or find qualified companies to buy. A knowledgeable business broker and legal team can save you time and money when it comes to consummating a deal. Bizbuysell.com is one of the more popular website to buy or sell a business. In 2017, over 9900 businesses were sold on the platform, a 27 percent increase from 2016.[1] Other competitors are: BizQuest.com, BusinessBroker.net, MergerNetwork.com, BusinessforSale.com and LoopNet.com. However, there are many business brokers throughout the United States. Find a broker with whom you feel you can work. Successful brokers get referred often and stay busy.

A business broker will do the lion's share of the work. Be discrete to whom you mention the business is for sale. You don't want to spook key customers or employees. Potential buyers will be under a nondisclosure agreement (NDA) to protect your privacy. The broker will confirm that the buyer has the financial wherewithal to complete the sale.

Your broker will help you put a fair price on the business. You may have a hard time letting go and not agree with the broker's suggested price range. A business valuation expert may help. The appropriate sales price reflects the market conditions and will generate attention. If the business is overpriced, it will sit for a longer time—just as a home would under similar circumstances. The longer the business is on the market, the more room the buyer will have to negotiate a lower sales prices. Price the business right in the beginning, and the business will sell.

An owner who cares about the business will want to sell it to someone who plans to operate the business long into the future and treat employees fairly. This type of ownership will provide stability to the current employees, customers, vendors and the local community. Make sure the buyer's intent aligns with your culture. Your reputation is on the line as the owner of the business. People want to know that you have selected the appropriate new owner.

Here are some steps to take before the sale:

1. Make sure there are no liens or pending lawsuits.

2. Keep key employees with the business.

3. Focus on the profitability of the business and cut unnecessary expenses.

4. Know the business' competitive advantage in the marketplace.

5. Start early and put together the team: broker, accountant, lawyer.

TAKEAWAY: Buy or sell a business.

20

CELEBRATE SMALL VICTORIES:
TAKE A VICTORY LAP

IN A CBS NEWS PIECE by Anna Robaton, "Why So Many Americans Hate Their Jobs," a Gallup poll reported that 51 percent of America's nearly 100 million full-time employees are not engaged at work, which means they do the minimum because they do not feel a connection to their job.[1] That's a major problem for businesses across the country. Robaton states, "Not surprisingly, companies with lots of unhappy employees pay a price in terms of absenteeism, turnover, productivity, customer service and even internal theft, otherwise known as shrinkage."[2] No company can survive this type of apathy for long.

Happiness trumps money. Perhaps being unhappy working for someone is what drives entrepreneurs to set out on their own. Or maybe it's their knowledge that everything on the material plane was created by humans. The buildings in New York City were all ideas that an architect put on paper, just like the Egyptian pyramids, double-entry accounting, the Space Shuttle operated by NASA, the clothes you are wearing, the pen you write with, the couch you sit on, and the gadgets you love.

NOT YOUR TYPICAL BUILDING

At a City Council meeting in Cupertino, California on June 11, 2011, Steve Jobs proposed his vision for a new Apple headquarters.[3] Steve received roaring applause when introduced by the City Council. No stranger to giving presentations, Jobs went on to describe the project in detail—as if he were on stage unveiling a new Apple device to the world.

Buildings have limitations, whether it be technology, materials, or the laws of physics. Steve understood limitations but choose to focus on possibilities and willed his vision into reality. His flying-saucer themed building seems like it was, well, from another galaxy. Steve commented, "It's pretty cool", in reference to the building that would hold 12,000 employees.[4]

Steve didn't seem to make business his life. He was guided by a higher purpose to make people's lives better through design, intuitiveness and functionality. "I think we do have a shot at building the best office building in the world. I really do think architecture students will come here to see this. I think it could be that good," said Jobs.[5] He was correct. The new campus opened in 2017 to rave media reviews. Perhaps the legacy of the new campus will be measured by the interactions of people and what they create.

SERVE OTHERS

Our time is limited. In the grand scheme of things, our greatest accomplishments pale in comparison to the age of the universe, which is 13.8 billion years old.[6] Serving humanity should be the goal of living a successful life. Giving back is a higher order. Having a purpose helps to make sense of a world made perilous and chaotic by humans. Serving our fellow human beings promotes the connection we share on earth. What do you want to be remembered for? What will be your contribution to making the world a better place?

We are not here on earth only to consume. A purpose in life is just as important as having food, water, shelter, clothing, love and a feeling of belonging, as illustrated in Maslow's hierarchy of needs. People are hungry to incorporate what they believe into how they make a living. There's a movement of nonprofits and B corporations to imbed a social mission into their companies.

The "Millennial Impact" report released in June, 2014, stated that 94 percent of millennials (demographic born between 1981 and 1996) in the study want to use their skills to benefit a cause.[7] "Millennial employees want to be able, through their workplace, to make a tangible difference outside of the workplace," the study reported.[8] Companies are looking for ways to capture their workforce's ideals. Companies that don't find a way to channel such energy may be left behind. The report is proof that leveraging millennials' passion "is crucial" to building a culture they want to be a part of.

SMELL THE ROSES

Starting a business is difficult. There will be times when you want to give up from the constant barrage of challenges—and bottomless well of disappointments. Too often we are waiting for the big success milestones: reaching $1, $5 or $10 million in sales. While sales accomplishments should be celebrated, don't overlook the daily, weekly or monthly successes.

TAKE A VICTORY LAP
TO CELEBRATE.

Money is fleeting. But if you focus on solving problems, your vision will appear closer each day. Each customer you serve is a victory, putting you closer to your vision. "Find something you love to do and you'll never have to work a day in your life," is a popular quote.[9] You were put on earth to achieve your unique purpose. Find it. Love it.

And stop comparing yourself to the entrepreneur who turned computer code into a billion-dollar wonder company. Yes, some people will make an ungodly sum of money (See Jeff Bezos)—some will even flaunt it. But as the hackneyed saying goes, "You can't take it with you." Make your time worthy of the talents, skills and abilities you have. Of the billions of people in this world, there is only one you. Make your life an amazing one by plugging into your interest, which will only blossom like a flower in May when the hard work is put in developing your craft. Work is fertilizer.

Make sure you pamper yourself along the journey they call life. Release your digital tether and walk barefoot on the beach. Get a massage. Go out with friends. Do something nice for someone, just because. Take a loved one out to dinner. Give your employees a bonus. Donate to charity. Work in a homeless soup kitchen. Reconnect with all things nondigital.

Starting a business is risky. Going against the grain and hanging your name on a shingle—is like trying to enter an office building as everyone leaves: it can be done but not easily. Success isn't guaranteed, but freedom is a reward in itself. You are free to create, build, improve, and introduce something to the world. The biggest risk is working at a job to which you feel no connection.

Take a victory lap to celebrate. And when you do, remember these sentences: You are amazing. You will do great things. You must start now because as Nelson Mandela said, "After climbing a great hill, one only finds that there are many more hills to climb."[10]

TAKEAWAY: You will do great things.

PART III
Money: The Main Ingredient

21

CREDIT:
YOU NEED IT

THE WORLD RUNS ON CREDIT, not coffee. Credit is a modern reality. It is the grease that keeps the wheels of commerce moving. Whether you are a consumer paying for your morning joe fix, or a business purchasing goods, credit makes it all work. In 2014, *Bloomberg Businessweek* published "The 85 Most Disruptive Ideas in Our History." Credit was ranked number 19 because we all covet it to live.

American consumers have almost $1 trillion in credit card debt—we are up to our eyeballs in debt.[1] According to a report by Tamara Holmes, "There were some 14.5 billion U.S. general purpose credit card transactions in the first six months of 2015, accounting for more than $1.4 trillion in purchase volume."[2]

Credit was once known as debt, which was something to be avoided—like a person sneezing during the flu season—because unpaid debt could land you in prison. Rapper the

Notorious B.I.G. warned about the dangers of credit in his rap, "Ten Crack Commandments."[3] "Number 6: that goddam credit?[4] With the wave of a marketer's pen and the word Abracadabra, debt was rebranded credit. In 1950, Frank McNamara, the founder of the Diners Club Card, charged dinner at Major's Cabin Grill in New York.[5] It was the first transaction with a credit card. The credit genie was let out of the bottle to forever change American life.

PERSONAL CREDIT

Equifax, Experian and TransUnion are the three credit bureaus (known as credit reporting agencies) that control the market for consumer credit data. These companies collectively make up the Big Three, and are publicly-traded companies. The Big Three provide your credit file to companies that seek to evaluate your credit worthiness, whether it be a mobile phone carrier, automobile dealer or banker—even landlords may request your credit file when you're seeking housing. No part of our lives are safe from massive data collection.

The Big Three's business is to keep your credit file up-to-date, accurate and safe. However, the companies have fallen down on the job regarding security. On September 7, 2017, The *Washington Post* reported "that hackers gained access to sensitive personal data—Social Security numbers, birth dates and home addresses—for up to 143 million Americans."[6] Nothing is safe.

It's important for you to check your credit report annually to make sure that the information is accurate. You may pull a free copy of your credit report from each of the credit bureaus once a year. Visit AnnualCreditReport.com to learn how to get your credit report. A fee is charged to receive your three-digit numerical score. Each of the bureaus have their own proprietary scoring system. The higher the score, the more credit worthy you are deemed. With hacking and identity theft common, you need to ensure that your file has not been compromised and the information is accurate. If you find a mistake, you can dispute the information with the bureaus through a formal process by completing a form.

The Fair Isaac Corporation created the FICO score, the most popular credit scoring model. Its website states that 90 percent of all lending decisions in the United States are made using their scores. On a daily basis, 27 million scores are sold. FICO uses an algorithm to generate a score. Personal credit scores have a range from 350 to 850. The higher the score the better. Many banks and credit card companies now offer free access to your FICO score.

The FICO score is a combination of five factors:

1. Your payment history is 35 percent of your credit score. The frequency, recency and severity of missed payments are critical.

2. Credit utilization is 30 percent of your score and is the percentage of credit available that has been borrowed.

3. Length of credit history is 15 percent of your score and relates to how long you have had credit accounts open and the length of time from recent action.

4. New credit is 10 percent of your score.

5. Credit mix is 10 percent of your score. Opening up too many new accounts can lower your score. The credit mix is the variety of credit used, from revolving to installment loans, which demonstrates you can handle credit responsibly.

BUSINESS CREDIT

Business credit differs from consumer credit. Dun & Bradstreet (known as D&B), Equifax and Experian each assess credit

THE WORLD RUNS ON
CREDIT, NOT COFFEE.

worthiness differently. The bureaus use the information they have in your file to create a score. For new businesses, your personal credit score will be your primary means of determining your credit worthiness. The scores range from 0 to 100; higher scores will help you access credit. A low credit score can be justification to decline credit or increase business insurance rates and other products.

According to the D&B website, there are over 280 million businesses in the world. The company encourages business owners to sign up for a free D&B number to create a credit file. A D-U-N-S (data universal numbering system) number is a nine-digit, unique identifier for every business that D&B has in its files. The Federal government requires a D-U-N-S number for businesses seeking to do business with many government agencies. Commercial banks use the D&B number to learn about your business. D&B's Paydex score is the de facto credit scoring system for business. The SBA uses the Paydex scoring system for loans. A D&B number is required to get a Paydex score.

Equifax has a proprietary business credit scoring system. The company has three different assessments for businesses: the payment index, the credit risk score, and the business failure score. Like D&B's Paydex score, Equifax's payment index ranges from 0 to 100. This score is derived from the number of payments that were made on time, based on data from vendors and creditors. This score does not predict future behavior, which is what its other scores attempt to do.

Equifax's "business credit risk score" measures whether you are likely to be severely delinquent on payments in the future, with scores ranging from 101 to 982. This score measures the available credit limit on credit accounts, the length of the oldest account opened, company size and any documentation of non-financial transactions that have been delinquent or charged off for two or more billing cycles.

A "business failure score" predicts the likelihood the business will close within a 12-month period. Scores range from 1,000 to 1,610, lower scores equal a higher probability of failure. The business failure score measures how much of your credit has been used over the past three months, delinquent accounts or late payments in the prior 24 months, age of oldest financial accounts, any evidence of non-financial transactions, like invoices, that are delinquent or charged off for two or more billing cycles. A zero rating indicates bankruptcy for both the credit risk and business failure score.

Experian has its CreditScore, which includes a business credit score, payment trends, public records and payment trends. Different from D&B's Paydex and Equifax's payment index, it utilizes additional information, not just payment histories. The score ranges from zero to 100. Experian collects credit information from your suppliers, lenders, legal filings from courts, and information from public records and collection agencies. The score weighs business credit history, outstanding loans, payment history, liens, judgements, bankruptcies against the business, and age and size of the business.

Get familiar with both consumer and business credit scoring systems because your credit can affect your access to credit. Correct derogatory information that is not accurate because in the end, creditors will judge you on your creditworthiness.

TAKEAWAY: Business runs on credit.

22

CAPITAL:
GOOD, CHEAP OR FAST

THE BUSINESS OWNER'S DREAM is access to capital that is good for the business, cheap and fast—the trinity of capital. Capital to grow and get through rough spots is essential. But the dilemma businesses face is that they can have only two of the three on their wish list. Which two would you select?

Capital that is good for the business is defined as the right product, conditions, terms, and cost, which doesn't harm the business in the short or long term. The right product could be a line of credit, credit card, term loan, equipment financing or equity. Capital has to fit the business like a comfortable pair of jeans. In the end, the product can't be detrimental to your business health—choking off your blood circulation.

Capital from a community-based lender will usually have the lowest rates and best terms, due to where the source of money comes from. A community-based lender may be a community bank, credit union or nonbank lender with the mission of serving the community. A bank's cost of capital is lowest because it uses depositor's money. Credit unions and nonprofit lenders are also able to provide affordable capital. These sources of capital are, bar none, the best.

Capital is priced relative to current economic conditions in the United States and the globe. Risk is a key component of the price of capital because it can be invested in other places. In theory, the greater the risk, the higher the return, but also the higher the cost. Capital from investors, private equity, venture capital or hedge funds are costlier than banks funds because of various risk factors and the return sought.

The federal funds rate is a key rate that banks use to determine how much interest you pay on consumer or business loans. Prime is the rate that banks will charge their best customers to borrow money, which affects auto loans, personal loans, credit cards, home equity loans and lines of credit. Dictionary.com defines the prime rate as "the lowest rate of interest at which money may be borrowed commercially." Compare the prime rate with various financial products. When evaluating whether an interest rate is fair, start by looking at the prime rate. Visit Bankrate.com to find out the *Wall Street Journal* prime rate.

Lending to small businesses became an asset class when the Great Recession hit and the Fed lowered interest rates. During this difficult time, banks reduced their lending to small businesses. Investors were looking for an asset class that could generate rates substantially higher than government and equity markets. They gravitated to small-business lending and pumped billions into online lenders. Capital from venture capital, hedge funds and lending companies drove up the borrowing cost of lending to businesses not able to procure traditional bank funds, sending huge returns back to investors.

COST OF CAPITAL

The real cost of capital is relative to how the funds are used and the return generated. An owner that uses high-cost capital has to juggle needing capital now with how that capital will help the business in the long term. Cheap debt is a gateway drug. Getting hooked on expensive capital could put the business on the brink of a catastrophe, jeopardizing the business. Businesses have to figure out what is best for them outside of the pressure of the moment.

Business owners have convinced themselves that fast doesn't have a cost, which couldn't be further from the truth. When it comes to fast capital, there is a cost. Most businesses charge a premium for fast. For example, the cost of UPS's next-day delivery is more expensive than three-day delivery. But if the business needs it in a hurry, they have to weigh the cost-benefits of good, cheap or fast.

Online lenders market themselves as fast and make capital available in days, not months. A business that is desperate for cash must ponder the true cost: reduced cash flow, less profit and an unstable future. Lenders may require daily withdrawals from a bank account using an automated clearing house (ACH). When the actual annual percentage rate (APR) is calculated, the real cost may horrify you. Many lenders in this space don't use APR as the standard, they use confusing methods that may sound logical and cheap. APR is the standard when comparing financial products.

EVALUATING EXPECTATIONS: GOOD, CHEAP OR FAST

Applying for capital is an arduous process, especially when it comes to bank financing. A Federal Reserve Bank study indicated that businesses spend over 24 hours completing loan applications.[1] For any business, that's a considerable amount of time. Banks want three years of personal and

THE BUSINESS OWNER'S DREAM IS ACCESS TO CAPITAL THAT IS GOOD FOR THE BUSINESS, **CHEAP AND FAST–** *THE TRINITY OF CAPITAL.*

business tax returns, a personal financial statement (PFS), accounts receivable, accounts payable aging report and more. Start the process at least 90 days before needing capital. Planning ahead will give the business owner ample time to find the best capital for the business, given its unique circumstances. In addition, the firm's bookkeeper or accountant will have time to put together financial documents. An organized business owner will gain the lender's confidence.

The most valuable company in the world, Apple, has made the decision between good, cheap or fast. Apple creates good products (some would argue the best in class) and fast, in the sense of the processing chips inside its products. But when it comes to its pricing, Apple is at the top of the pecking-order with some of the most expensive smartphones on the market, generating the lion's share of smartphone profits in the industry. During a new iPhone launch, Apple lowered prices on older model iPhones to get business from the lower end of the market. Apple's less expensive phones are not the cheapest, but it found a way to be some-what accessible to price-sensitive customers. The company found a way to be good, cheap and fast.

KNOW YOUR CAPITAL OPTIONS

Banks have gotten the message from businesses and are tweaking their underwriting process for speed. For example, an SBA Express lender can approve a loan application up to $350,000 in 36 hours. Make sure your lender is an SBA preferred or certified lender. These lenders are experienced with the SBA's process and have the authority to approve loans. See chapter 44 for more about SBA lenders.

Underwriting of loans takes time and is costly. For loans of $1 million or more, banks will compete for your business. Large loans are profitable, versus loans under $200,000, which is the sweet spot for smaller businesses. Banks require the business to move their operating account to the bank, giving way to cross-selling opportunities, making the relationship more synergistic. The business gets the lowest cost of capital, on reasonable terms, while the banks gets a desirable customer in the community—it's win-win.

Internet lenders look largely at the cash flow of the business; they can provide quick financing. But the APR will be expensive. If that's your only source of capital, then you have to weigh the pros and cons. Given the capital options available to you, make the choice that will give you the best opportunity to grow your business over the long term:

1. Good

2. Cheap

3. Fast

Capital should not be a pill that cures one problem but kills the patient with its side effects. In the end, think before you sign—or hit enter.

TAKEAWAY: Capital must be a "good" fit.

"Congratulations," Post Malone featuring Quavo, *Stoney (Deluxe)*

23

DEBT OR EQUITY:
THE FORK IN THE ROAD

LONG BEFORE AN IDEA is thoroughly vetted, entrepreneurs are off to the races to raise capital, like a greyhound chasing the elusive mechanical rabbit at a race track. Entrepreneurs don't start a business to become capital experts. Nonetheless, if a business owner wants a chance at success, she must be a master at sourcing capital. The capital-raising process is complicated, time-consuming and frustrating, leading to dead ends. Your challenge is to find the right fit.

Early in the capital-raising process, the owner will come to the debt or equity fork. Each type of capital will have profound consequences for the viability of the business. When you come to the debt or equity dilemma, remember the fairytale, *The Story of Goldilocks and the Three Bears*, published in 1837. Goldilocks is walking in the forest and stumbles upon the three bears' house. She opens the door and sees three bowls of porridge (think capital) on the table. She's hungry and sits down to eat. The first bowl of porridge is too hot. The second too cold. And the third porridge is just right—that's the capital you want.

DEBT = PRINCIPAL + INTEREST

Debt has a dreadful reputation; it's the guy in the alley waiting to hit you in the knee caps with a bat. Perhaps this view harkens back to when debt was seen as immoral or seedy. In the 1800s, people who couldn't pay their debts were put in debtor prisons. Generations grew up avoiding debt, as if it were an unsavory character in a dark alley. And when money was tight, loan sharks were the lenders of last resort for the unbankable. If a business owner didn't make his weekly payments, at skyrocketing interest rates, he was threatened with bodily harm. Those fears burned an indelible image in our minds, like the grooves of a worn album.

Times have changed. Rebranding debt as credit was brilliant, and fueled unprecedented growth in America. Debt is borrowing money and paying over time, with interest tacked on. You get what you want now and pay it back in installments. Interest is the cost for using someone else's money. The interest rate is a combination of factors:

1. The cost of capital for the lender

2. The perceived risk

3. The expected return or profit.

For the pure capitalist out there, the people who pay on time actually subsidize the people who don't pay their loans.

Your debt is paid back by amortizing (equal payments) over a specific time. In the beginning, a larger portion of the payment is applied to interest, and a smaller portion to principal (the amount originally borrowed). Eventually, the portion applied toward principal increases, while the amount toward interest decreases—picture a seesaw, with principal on the ground and interest in the air. Monthly payments remain the same, unless additional items are charged on a credit card. Visit bretwhissel. net/cgi-bin/amortize to create a loan amortization schedule.

Debt is not the enemy. For most owners, the advantages of debt far outweigh the disadvantages.

The advantages of taking on debt are numerous:

1. You get something now and pay for it later
2. Your relationship with the lender ends when the loan is paid back
3. Loan interest is tax deductible. (Talk to your accountant.)
4. Loan maturities vary based on how funds are used
5. Your monthly payment will stay the same, unless the loan has a variable interest rate
6. You run your business the way you want, with few covenants (legal restrictions) placed on the business.

There are disadvantages:

1. Scheduled monthly payments must be made on time, if they are not, the loan could be put in default, jeopardizing the business

2. The monthly payments can adversely impact cash flow

3. Too much leverage (debt) can put the business close to insolvency when times get tough

4. Should sales decrease, the business could face uncertainty

5. A personal guarantee and your collateral will secure the debt, usually with a personal residence and business assets

6. Due to interest, the use of the funds must generate a return higher than the interest and opportunity costs.

LONG BEFORE AN IDEA IS
THOROUGHLY VETTED,
ENTREPRENEURS ARE OFF TO THE
RACES TO RAISE CAPITAL,
LIKE A GREYHOUND CHASING
THE ELUSIVE MECHANICAL
RABBIT AT A RACE TRACK.

Banks rarely lend to startups because they lack a track record as well as collateral. Debt financing can come in many forms from credit cards, term loans or lines of credit. **Never use long-term capital for short-term needs; that is the formula for disaster.** If you receive a loan, make sure the capital is deployed in a manner that strengthens the business. And make sure to balance the right amount of debt with other capital raising tools, such as equity, which follows.

EXCHANGING EQUITY FOR CASH

On the popular television show *Shark Tank*, entrepreneurs pitch their ideas and businesses to wealthy investors. In exchange for the capital, the entrepreneur must give up a certain ownership stake in the business, commonly known as equity. The entrepreneurs receive capital, expertise, access to a network, and national exposure for their business.

Equity investments should not be viewed as a game of Monopoly.® Only a select group of startups and fast-growing companies in multi-billion-dollar markets are suitable for investors who seek gigantic returns. If you are looking to solve big problems, then equity may be the right fit. When an equity deal is consummated, you are no longer the only owner of the business. Your investors become owners of the business, governed by ironclad legal agreements. For entrepreneurs, adding new partners can be like a shotgun marriage.

Equity has advantages:
1. The money doesn't have to be paid back monthly or at all, should the business fail.
2. You get access to an investor and their network to build your business.
3. Investors don't expect to get a return for three to seven years, which gives you time to build a real business.

4. Once the business gains traction, additional rounds of capital are available.

5. Equity doesn't have an effect on cash flow.

Of course, there are disadvantages to equity:

1. You give up a percentage of ownership in the business.

2. Growth may drive business decisions.

3. Per the terms of the agreement, the investors may have a major say in decision-making.

4. Based on how the equity agreement is structured, investors may have set up a way to get additional ownership at lower prices, may be able to force a sale in the future, or fire you.

5. Raising money is a full-time job that will take you away from the business of delighting customers.

6. Over time, investors may differ with your long-term goals.

Make sure you consult an attorney when raising capital because securities law is complex. One mistake and you could face legal action from investors, state or federal regulators. Talk with your attorney regarding what types of individuals can invest in your business. Accredited investors, as defined by the SEC, may be preferred because they are considered sophisticated investors and have the wherewithal to sustain a loss, and receive less protection from the regulators. They are individuals who make $200,000 or more ($300,000 as a couple) a year for the past two years, or have a $1 million in assets, excluding their home. Investopedia *states*, "An entity is an accredited investor if it is a private business development company or an organization with assets exceeding $5 million."

HYBRIDS

Mezzanine financing is hybrid capital, which is debt that gives the lender the right to convert the note into equity (ownership) if the loan is not paid back according to the terms of the loan. Some mezzanine financing comes with warrants (the ability to buy shares at a specific price) as part of the financing. See image.

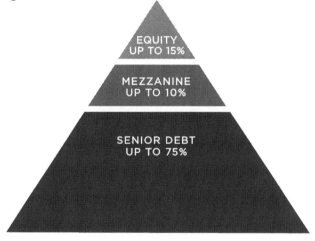

MEZZANINE FINANCING % OF DEAL

This type of financing is expensive and lenders seek up to a 20 percent return on their capital. Private equity firms use mezzanine financing when buying out companies.

Mezzanine financing is subordinate to senior lenders, which means this financing sits behind the primary lender on commercial real estate or other types of financing. On the balance sheet, mezzanine financing is considered equity. Investors may offer you a loan that converts to equity if the business defaults on the loan. For this type of loan, the interest is quarterly or annual. If the interest can't be paid during a specific period, it accrues. At some point, the loan converts to equity, which is spelled out in the agreement. Know the difference between debt, equity and the various hybrid products. Make every penny count toward building your business. Find the right capital fit.

TAKEAWAY: Watch out for capital dead-ends.

24

BE ALL IN:
COLLATERAL & YOUR PERSONAL GUARANTEE

THE CLOUDS OF FAILURE are constantly swirling overhead. Business is personal because your livelihood—and assets—are on the line. According to the SBA Office of Advocacy, "About two-thirds of businesses with employees survive at least 2 years, and about half survive at least 5 years."[1] The competition wants your customers. And they will do just about anything, from copying your marketing and pricing, or worse, badmouthing your business. To succeed, you must own your customer experience. When you serve an unmet need, customers will be your prize.

Times get tough in business, and your spirits may get low. When this happens, you need inspiration that only music can provide. Music is all around us: at the dentist's office, auto repair shop, your favorite restaurant and at the supermarket. In major league baseball (MLB), the batter walks up to the plate accompanied by his favorite music, which is enough to psyche him up to get a hit in pressure-filled situation. For a pick-me-up, listen to Big Daddy Kane's "Ain't No Half-Steppin'". To paraphrase Big Daddy Kane, he's like a pit bull and you're a Chihuahua. It's going to take an act of god to beat him.[2]

BE ALL IN

In the beginning, you must nurture your business. Think of a business as a newborn baby, who requires all your attention. To be all in means everything has to take a backseat to getting your business on firm ground. It's amazing how often entrepreneurs say they will do anything to build their business. They will work long hours, eat Ramen noodles daily, and go with minimal sleep. However, their tune changes when a banker asks for a personal guarantee and collateral in the form of a mortgage on their home to secure the loan. For some, this thought is scarier than a Stephen King novel.

Owners hem and haw when asked to pledge their home as collateral. No one wants to pledge their home as collateral because a home is more than an asset. For a banker, collateral is a prerequisite. They will not lend without something to secure the loan. If you want your business to support you in the future, you have to be all in—there's no other way.

ONBOARDING A SPOUSE

The difficult conversation is the one an owner has to have to convince the spouse to use their home as collateral. It's not an easy conversation, but an essential one, if you plan to get your business off the starting block. A bank will not lend you money without collateral. When a spouse is not willing to go along, it sends a loud message to a banker that you are not 100 percent committed to the business. Your options are few and far between for capital as a startup business. Be prepared to have this conversation.

From a practical point of view, most home owners have a first mortgage on their home. To secure a business loan, a banker will want to put a second mortgage on the home. For example, let's assume Jill, an entrepreneur is seeking a $100,000 business loan to start her business. Her home is worth $350,000 and her first mortgage balance is $100,000. The home has $250,000 available for equity to secure the loan. That second mortgage will secure the loan because there is adequate collateral.

The first source of repayment for a loan is the cash flow from the business. In the event the business fails, the secondary source (or second way out as Arnold Ziegel says in his book, *Fundamentals of Credit and Credit Analysis*) is the collateral.[3]

Typically, a lender cannot foreclose (check the laws in your state) on a home because they are in second position. However, they could buyout the first mortgage lien holder, but that's unlikely because now they have to put another $100,000 into the deal. But if Jill decides she wants to move to Alaska and sell the home, the bank will recoup the remaining balance of the loan from the proceeds of the sale. Jill is obligated to repay the loan, even if she defaults on it.

Being all in is knowing that all your time and assets are pledged as collateral. For most business owners, there are not many alternatives, unless they can get a personal loan from a family member. That's the reality of starting a business.

IT'S PERSONAL

Collateral is only the first step. Next, a banker will want your personal guarantee. Many entrepreneurs don't want to personally guarantee a loan, but a loan will not be forthcoming without one. A confident business owner will do whatever is necessary to get the funds. Do your homework to make sure you are betting on yourself with the best information possible.

THINK OF A BUSINESS AS A **NEWBORN BABY, WHO REQUIRES** ALL YOUR ATTENTION.

Knowing your customers and the market is indispensable. The ultimate sign that the market will support your offering is based on satisfying needs. Spend your time satisfying customers, not worrying about the competition.

TAKEAWAY: Business is personal.

25

CREDITWORTHINESS: ARE YOU BANKABLE?

THE PRIMARY DECISION A BANK MAKES is whether to extend credit. Lending is based on character, and your character is the key to open the bank vault. The late J.P. Morgan, the American icon of finance and banking in the late 19th and early 20th Century, said, "Lending is not based primarily on money or property. No sir, the first thing is character."[1] A bank is a business. Regardless of their cute ads that entice you to apply for credit, your relationship is strictly business.

Arnold Ziegel, a former banker at Citibank and author of the book, *Fundamentals of Credit and Credit Analysis*, states that a lender wants to know the answers to three questions:

1. Who's the borrower?

2. What's the purpose of the loan?

3. When and how it will be paid back?

Your job as an entrepreneur is to convince the banker you are worthy of credit. The reality test is whether your best friend would lend you money to invest in your business. If yes, you probably have good character.

UNDERWRITING

Bank underwriting is shrouded in secrecy—like the formula for Coca Cola—but need not be. Underwriting is a bank's process of evaluating an applicant's creditworthiness by crunching the numbers and comparing the results to established criteria. Each lender has its own process and approval standards. For example, First Connecticut Bancorp Inc. d/b/a/ Farmington Bank is a community bank in Central Connecticut. It rates commercial-related loans on a nine-point grading system based on the loan officer's and management's assessment of risk.[2]

Credit analysis looks at money, property and character, when it comes to lending. For large banks with over $50 billion in assets, algorithms (software) increasingly play a role in making loan decisions, with the goal of maximizing return on investment (ROI). Banks charge a borrower rent (interest) for using their capital. Interest income must generate a return that covers the costs associated with lending and a fair return on the bank's capital—in banker parlance, this is called the spread.

Increasingly, lenders are accepting loan applications online to speed up the process and to better utilize resources. People still play a role in commercial lending. The job of a credit analyst (also known as an underwriter) is to assess the degree of risk associated with a business, its future cash flows, the industry, and the economy.

Once an applicant is approved, a lender knows there are only two ways out of a loan:

1. Payments received from business cash flow.
2. Sale of the assets pledged as collateral to secure the loan.

The second way out is not preferred due to the cost and negative publicity. But, one way or another, the lender has to be made whole.

THE FIVE C's OF CREDITWORTHINESS

Lenders have a formula for determining creditworthiness.

They utilize the five C's of credit:

1. Character
2. Capacity
3. Capital
4. Collateral
5. Conditions

The 5 C's form a bank's version of a black box. When it comes to using other people's money (OPM), every business owner should know the five C's of creditworthiness.

A lender will look at your **credit** history. Most SBA lenders will not lend to customers who fall under a FICO score of 660. Lenders want to know whether you pay your bills on time. They want to know how much revolving credit and other financial instruments you have outstanding. A number of factors will impact your credit score such as length of credit history, late payments, percentage of credit used and whether you have liens, filed for bankruptcy in the past five years, or public records that could adversely impact your credit.

Lending is about **character**: The ability to repay and willingness to do so reflects your character. Your job is to present the case that you can be trusted by providing the documentation required. If there was a problem in your past, where you didn't repay an obligation, own up to it and explain it. There may be mitigating circumstances, but don't make your lender play detective by not disclosing or hiding information.

Capacity is the ability of the business to generate sufficient cash to service the obligation. Your underwriter will look at the historical performance of the business. Going forward, your projections should demonstrate why the business will generate consistent or higher cash flows. Your assumptions should be anchored in logic with an explanation.

The lender will look at the overall **conditions** of the macro- and microenvironment to gauge your ability to perform. All industries have trends that affect them, which an underwriter must understand. For example, malls are going through rapid changes, as they try to compete with Amazon and online retailers.

Capital is what the business needs to sustain slow or down periods. An underwriter will assess whether or not the business has ample capital to address future shortfalls in cash. In addition, lenders want to see how much capital the business will put towards the project. They want to see that you have "skin" in the game that is at risk—not just theirs.

Real estate, equipment, stock portfolios, art collections, or receivables are forms of **collateral** to secure a loan. The value of collateral is discounted to give the lender a capital cushion, should a business default. The first way out of a loan is through the repayment of the loan as specified in the note. The second way out is through the sale of assets pledged. Without collateral, a lender will not accept the risk of approving a loan.

Don't hope for a loan. Know before you walk in the door, or click send on a credit application, what you bring to the table. The more you know, the better you will be prepared to get capital for your business. Your character means something. During the application process, the relationship you develop with your lender is important, especially if you choose a community lender. You build your case by providing the necessary documentation to show the lender you can be trusted, and you will pay the loan back.

TAKEAWAY: Your character matters.

26

INTEREST EXPLAINED:
THE COST OF CAPITAL

DO YOU REMEMBER the first time you purchased something on credit? You reached in your pocket, smiled smugly, and out came a credit card. You signed the authorization receipt, and you were off. It felt like you were doing something bad because it was so easy. Meet credit, formerly known as debt. Capital is essential to your business, but to lenders, it's a commodity seeking a return. When you borrow money, you have to pay it back with interest—unless your sweet grandmother gives you cash. Interest is rent lenders charge for the privilege to use OPM.

Let's dig into how credit works. Your credit history is the key factor in determining whether you receive credit from banks and other companies. Here's an example. The Ford Motor Company sends you a special promotion to receive zero-percent financing on a new vehicle. You received the offer because your credit score is over 700—by the way, that's a good score. Ford did a soft pull from Experian—a query which doesn't hurt your credit score—to find people, like yourself, with a specific credit score range. You were one of millions of people who received the special offer, in hopes of Ford reaching its sales goal.

After taking a Ford Explorer for a test drive—that new vehicle smell is crack for car buyers—you complete the paperwork and the dealer pulls your credit file from one of the three credit bureaus. This inquiry will be placed on your credit report. Bingo! You're approved. You drive off the lot the next day in your red Explorer.

WHEN TO GET A LOAN

Credit is a type of fuel your business uses to advance it down the road. When a business borrows capital, the most important factor is how it will be deployed to generate a satisfactory return. Every dime borrowed has to be paid back with interest. Projects that lead to sales and increase cash flow should be a priority. The key factors for a loan are the amount, the interest (fixed or variable) and the length (years or months) of the loan. Check the *Wall Street Journal* Prime Rate on Bankrate.com to see the rate. Loans are priced above the Prime rate, to generate a return for the lender. Make sure you know the fees associated with closing the loan. Is there an application, underwriting, closing or document fee? Fees add up: a one percent loan origination fee on a $50,000 loan is $500.

Suzanne Kearns, a freelance writer, wrote an article, "Is Your Business Profitable, 3 Reasons a Loan May Make Sense".

The reasons are:

1. To avoid giving up equity in your business.
2. When the ROI on the opportunity is higher than the cost of the debt.
3. To prevent a future loss of sales.[1]

Interest matters. A business receives a commitment letter: $50,000, 5-year term loan at 7.75 percent (simple interest). The monthly payment is $1,007.85 and the total amount paid will be $60,471. Total interest paid is $10,471. A nonbank lender offers a commitment letter: $50,000, 5-year term loan at 11.75 percent (simple interest). The monthly payment is $1,105.92 and total paid will be $66,335.20. Total interest paid is $16,335.20. In this example, the bank interest rate is better than the nonbank lender, with $5,864.20 in savings. With no prepayment penalties, either loan could be repaid sooner, saving on interest.

Return on investment (ROI) is a profitability ratio that measures return on capital invested in a business or on a specific project. Suppose you own a restaurant and you want to add a new hood & fire suppression system. Because the ventilation system has to go up three stories to the roof of the building, it will cost $50,000. With the addition of this hood, fire suppression system and new deep fryer, the restaurant adds new fried food items on the menu. Assuming a $50,000, 60-month term loan, at 7.75 percent, the monthly payment would be $1007.85. Assume the restaurant can increase food sales by $3,000 a month or $36,000 a year. Food costs are 30 percent or $10,800, leaving $25,200 (70%) as net profit. The restaurant could justify the expense of $12,094.20 in debt payments. ROI is equal to net profit ($25,200) divided by the cost of the equipment ($12,094.20) x 100. The ROI would be 208 percent on the investment, the first year.

ANNUAL PERCENTAGE RATE

Since the Great Recession, new alternative lenders have emerged to provide capital to small businesses. Although the terminology the lenders use to show the cost of their financial innovation sounds nefarious, it is not—and it adds

CREDIT IS A TYPE OF FUEL YOUR BUSINESS USES **TO ADVANCE IT DOWN THE ROAD.**

up to big dollars in profits for these lenders. Transparency is a disinfectant. To understand, you have to put the financial products under an annual percentage rate (APR) microscope. As an owner, you need to know the true costs of capital.

The APR is the standard for comparing financial products. Once you know the APR, you can compare the true cost across a variety of financial products: credit cards, payday loans, merchant cash advances and other offerings. A federal law requires financial products to disclose the APR to consumers, as part of the Truth in Lending Act (TILA).

Let's look at an example. A payday (a small, short-term loan) lender may charge a $15 fee to borrow a small amount, let's say $100. The casual observer may think that's a 15 percent interest rate. That's wrong because the loan must be paid back within two weeks. Calculating the numbers reveals the APR is close to 400 percent—that's not a typo. If there are additional fees, the APR would be higher.

Here's the math. The daily cost of interest is $1.07 ($15 divided by 14 days). Take that number and multiply by 365 to get a full year, which equals $390.55. Your hundred dollar loan would cost $390, if extended out for a full year— 390 percent of what you borrowed. People get hurt by these high-interest rate personal loans and the government has caught on. Kansas City businessman Scott Tucker was sentenced to nearly 17 years in prison.[2] His payday loan companies took in $3.5 billion in loan payments from over 4.5 million customers, including $1.3 billion in "improper interest rates."

The terminology they use is meant to confuse. Given that the average American doesn't love math, you can understand why this is a big problem for the public. Accion, the national micro lender, wrote "The Truth About Interest Rates for Term Loans."[3]

It suggests answering the following questions:

1. How long is the term of the loan?

2. How is the interest calculated?

3. How often are payments due?

4. Will you receive the entire loan amount?

5. What other fees are involved?

READ FINE PRINT

Always read the fine print in contracts because the devil is in the details. While it may not be pleasurable reading, you need to know the truth. Hire an attorney to go over the loan documents before signing. Monthly payments and small fees add up. An extra $50 a month on a loan, over 5 years, adds up to $3,000 dollars. In the end, don't be afraid to walk away.

TAKEAWAY: Know the real cost of money.

27

YOU WIN:
COMPETE FOR MONEY

AMERICANS LOVE COMPETITION, especially sports. In 2018, CBS news reported that 103 million people watched the Philadelphia Eagles upset the New England Patriots in the Super Bowl. You don't have to be a 320-pound offensive lineman or a gold medalist snowboarder like Chloe Kim, to know that sports push people to be their best. If you need cash for your business, you must be on the winning podium to claim your prize.

Business competitions are everywhere and even promoted on college campuses, by governments, corporations, chambers of commerce and nonprofit organizations. Competitions are not only for college students eating Ramen noodles and wearing hoodies. When too few people are lining up to give your business money, a competition with prize money is an option. At any given time, serious dollars are at stake for the winners. BusinessPlanCompetitions.com bills itself as "The world's most complete listing of entrepreneurship contests, elevator pitch events, and business plan competitions." When reviewed in November 2017, there were 122 events and over $24.5 million in prize money—that's nothing to sneeze at.

COMPETITION: THE STAKES ARE HIGH

Entrepreneurship promotes economic development and opportunity. And nothing says business, like a business plan. Business plan competitions have been around for a long time. Rice University's website calls its business plan competition "the world's richest and largest student startup competition." What started out 17 years ago with nine teams in 2001 competing for $10,000 in prize money, grew to 42 teams from around the world in competition for $1.5 million in cash and prizes. In 2016, the competition received over 750 applications. These businesses are not just for show: the businesses in the competition have raised over $1.2 billion. Rice University's competition has won numerous awards over the years. From 2009 to 2015, Princeton Review and *Entrepreneur* magazine awarded the competition a place in the Top Ten Best U.S. Graduate Entrepreneurship Programs.

Not to be outdone, the federal government launched the Strong Cities, Strong Communities Economic Visioning Challenge in 2011 to fund economic development. Hartford, Greensboro, North Carolina and Las Vegas were selected to participate because of the economic decline all have experienced. In Hartford, the contest was designed to create an economic development plan for the city. The government's rationale for supporting such a completion was to crowdsource innovative ideas to develop long-term economic development and job growth.

The Hartford competition had over one million dollars in prize money up for grabs, with the top prize of $500,000 for the winning team. With that much money available, a number of teams were formed to develop an economic development strategy for Hartford. The competition had two rounds. Hartford.Health.Works won the $60,000 prize in the semifinal round. All teams were invited to participate in the second round, which was where the big money was waiting.

Hartford.Health.Works won the top prize of $500,000 in the final round. The team's plan is to create and attract biomedical companies to the city, which is an area that the State of Connecticut has promoted as a sweet spot for growth. *The Hartford Courant* asked Mark Burton, one of three founding members of the group, "What comes next?" Mark said, "Jobs, thousands of jobs over the next decade."[1] The answer was the perfect response, because in the end, it's about jobs, jobs, jobs. Senator Richard Blumenthal concurred, "Jobs are what this program is all about."[2] That's the same reason 238 municipalities submitted applications to get the 50,000 jobs Amazon is promising for its second headquarters.

Note: My team participated in the SC2 competition. We didn't win. Within a few months of the contest ending, I started my business. I didn't want to spend the rest of my life building someone's dream. I haven't looked back.

Here are the lessons I learned:

1. If you have a dream, put in the work to make it a reality.

2. Working for someone else pays the bills, but often, it doesn't leave you as fulfilled as working for yourself.

3. You can't do it alone. Build a team and get them committed to your vision.

4. Hard work never goes unnoticed.

5. Start something, anything—just start.

My moonshot is to disrupt small-business failure by creating must-have products, which will lead to 100,000 jobs with an economic impact of $1 billion. What's yours?

PLAY TO WIN

There are many different ways to get a business off the ground and a contest is one. Competitions do have a cost; besides a modest entry fee, there's the time trap. Contests take you away from customers and the business. If you choose to get involved in a contest, make sure the upside is worth the investment in your time. People on your team will be taken away from key areas of the business to work on the contest. When all is said and done, be prepared for the emotions of winning or losing. You'll reflect on all the time you spent on the project. Of course, you want to win, but realistically, only one person or team can win. Be prepared for a release of emotions.

Prize money attracts the masses, so bring your "A" game; anything less is a waste of your time. The intangibles of a competition are numerous: feeling of accomplishment, team building, chance to push beyond limits. Only you know whether a competition is the right approach to raising capital. Should you decide to participate, play to win. And if you don't win, take the lessons learned from the competition and put them to work as a building block of your business foundation.

TAKEAWAY: Time is money.

28

BIG CORPORATIONS HAVE LOTS OF MONEY: GET SOME

STARTUPS AND BIG CORPORATIONS have become an "item." You could say they were dating. Corporations are betting that their altruistic ways can lead to a warm and fuzzy connection to their brands. It's win-win: entrepreneurs receive cash, business assistance, and corporations gain customers and positive attention. But if the assistance is not authentic, beware of the saying, "No good deed goes unpunished" because blowback on social media is fast.

Many corporations trace their roots back to small businesses, but it's hard for large, established companies to come across as hipsters. Apple and Starbucks are two companies bucking conventional pigeonholing. Entrepreneurs have street cred, which is part of their appeal to large companies. But there's nothing wrong with a deep-pocketed company bankrolling your business. Here are a few companies who have built a connection from small to big.

The Boston Beer Company, maker of Samuel Adams beer is one of the largest craft beer makers in the country—some credit the company with starting the craft beer movement in the United States. Tory Burch is a top fashion company in America producing clothes for women. Her ballerina flats are a must-have for stylish women. If you like breakfast cereals, you know Kellogg's, the food manufacturer that makes everything from Rice Krispies and Kashi, to Eggos and Cheez-Its, in over 180 countries. This trio of companies is helping emerging businesses.

Corporate programs can assist entrepreneurs to grow their businesses and source capital. When it comes to sourcing precious capital for your business, leave no cornflake (I couldn't resist) uncovered. You never know where the capital will come from. If you believe you will have a difficult time sourcing capital, now is the time to learn how corporate programs can help.

MAKE FASHION PAY

Tory Burch is a juggler: mother of three children, successful businesswoman in the world of fashion, fashion designer and philanthropist. In 2004, Tory Burch launched her namesake business in the Nolita (North of Little Italy) neighborhood of Manhattan, a boutique store with her then-husband Chris Burch.

Prior to opening her first store, Tory had worked with top designers such as Ralph Lauren, Vera Wang and Narciso Rodriguez at Loewe. She was asked to be the President of the LVMH Group, the luxury brand behind Louis Vuitton, Christian Dior and Fendi, but she turned it down because at the time she had three children under the age of four. Today, Tory Burch is an American lifestyle brand with over 200 Tory Burch boutiques around the world. Her clothing and accessories are sold in over 3,000 specialty and department stores worldwide. In 2016, sales topped the $1 billion mark.[1]

The Tory Burch Foundation was established in 2009. On the foundation website, Tory states, "As our company has grown, I've learned about the obstacles that women in business face, from balancing work and family (my greatest challenge) to securing financing. Many also lack the confidence, business networks and training they need to see their ideas through." The foundation provides access to capital, entrepreneurial education, mentoring and networking opportunities.

In terms of capital, the Tory Burch Foundation Capital Program works with Bank of America and community development financial institutions (CDFIs) throughout the country. CDFIs are community-based lenders committed to helping make capital available to underserved communities and entrepreneurs. To access the program, complete the Pre-Screening form on ToryBurchFoundation.org and a representative will contact you. If you are approved for a loan, you will receive a two percent discount as part of the program, access to a financial mentor through Bank of America, and you will become part of the Tory Burch entrepreneurial community.

CHAMPAGNE DREAMS AND BEER MONEY

James "Jim" Koch and Rhonda Kallman founded the Boston Beer Company in 1994. The company's first beer was Samuel Adams Boston Lager, named after American patriot Samuel Adams. Sam Adams is synonymous with Jim Koch—part of a long list of famous pitch men who are owners, including the late Dave Thomas from Wendy's and Frank Perdue of Perdue Chicken. Jim brewed the first batch of beer in his kitchen after finding a family recipe in his parents' attic.

Prior to starting the company, Jim Koch was working with the famous consulting firm, the Boston Consulting Group. Jim is no dummy. He earned a BA, MBA and JD degree from Harvard University. Since founding Boston Beer, the company has won numerous awards and generated considerable media attention. In 2016, Boston Beer sold roughly 4 million barrels of its products.[2] Over sixty products used the Sam Adams brand name during 2016. The company is a smaller player in the beer industry compared to Anheuser-Busch InBev and MillerCoors, which control more than 80 percent of domestic beer production in the United States.

Help for the small guys (and gals) is here. There are over 5,234 companies brewing beer in the United States, which is a dramatic increase from 1,596 in 2009.[3] To help small businesses grow, Boston Beer created Sam Adams Brewing the American Dream to provide support in the form of speed coaching, pitch room competition and loans as well as the Brewing and Experienceship (a one-year program to help craft brewers grow their businesses). Since 2008, along with its lending partner Accion, the program has loaned over $14.5 million to 1500 plus small businesses in 35 states. Visit the company's website for programs information. btad.samueladams.com

FOOD FIGHT

Kellogg's, the world's largest breakfast cereal maker, is in a food fight to stay relevant. The breakfast and snack food aisles are a competitive turf war. Hungry Americans don't like the menu and are changing their eating habits, moving away from prepackaged foods to healthy options with lower sugar, salt, fat and additives. Kellogg's has heard the message and will eliminate artificial colors and flavors from its products by 2018 and will use only cage-free eggs in the United States starting in 2025.

Founded in 1908, the Kellogg Company manufactures and markets ready-to-eat cereal and other packaged foods. Its brands include Rice Krispies, Special K, Apple Jacks, Fruit Loops, Pop Tarts, Eggos, Cheez-It, Pringles, and

Famous Amos. Despite the challenges, the company generated over $13 billion in sales during 2016, which is down from $14.5 billion in 2014. But investors are hungry for greater returns and expect more from the company. In response, the company continues to change and seek new opportunities to serve consumers.

To reserve a place at the table, Kellogg's launched a venture capital company to seed food companies of the future. The fund is named "eighteen94 capital" and will invest $100 million into startups, paving the way for new ingredients, foods and packaging. In a *Fortune* piece, Gary Pilnick, vice chairman of Kellogg's, stated, "As consumer preferences move toward more diverse tastes and trends, the pace of innovation in the packaged food industry continues to intensify."[4] By taking an equity stake in startups, Kellogg's can be close to companies that will create foods people all over the world will want to eat. General Mills, a Kellogg's rival, has made investments in a number of companies through its own venture capital arm, General Mills' 301 INC.

General Mills' 301 INC has made a handful of startup investments in recent months, including backing cottage cheese maker Good Culture, plant-based food maker Beyond Meat, and kale chips brand Rhythm Superfoods. Expect competition to heat up as food companies fight it out to see who will serve the food of the future.

TAKEAWAY: Innovation starts small.

29

PATIENT CAPITAL:
FRIENDS, FAMILY – AND FOOLS

IT TAKES CAPITAL to get a business off the ground. And in the beginning, the best person to start raising capital from is Y-O-U, which is affectionately known as bootstrapping. You may be surprised how much money you can find from unexpected sources—without even looking in your couch cushions.

The advantage of working for a paycheck over the years is that you may have a 401(k). Yes, you can use your retirement funds to seed your business. There are firms that specialize in this process, such as Benetrends Financial, Guidant Financial and FranFund. Make sure you are comfortable and prepared to put your money at risk. Talk to your financial advisor to understand the ramifications, including tax issues.

Don't overlook selling your prized possessions as a source of seed capital. We collect stuff that has value, from chicken-shaped salt & pepper shakers, art, and vintage clothing, to stamps and coins. Your possessions may be accumulating dust, and now may be the time to liquidate your collections. If you have lots of stuff, a tag sale could yield a few thousand dollars or more, all in one shot. Craiglists.org may be an alternative to a physical tag sale. Don't forget about the old car that's been sitting in your garage for years. It too has value.

Your home may be a source of untapped capital. If the property is worth more than you owe the bank, you can tap the excess equity through a home equity line of credit (HELOC). Contact your local bank branch representative or go online to complete an application. Make sure you are comfortable putting additional debt on your home.

FAMILY AND FRIENDS

After exhausting your personal resources, it may be time to tap family, friends—and fools. Dave Berkus, the author of the book, *Raising Money*, uses the word "fools" in his book to describe unsophisticated investors.[1] Often overlooked, family and friends are natural allies to tap to do heavy lifting in the early stages. Your mother, father, aunts and uncles may be willing to let you borrow money on reasonable terms, or they may purchase stock in your company. Either way what you offer to even friends and family may be considered to be a securities offering, so you have to be careful. The Securities Act of 1933 or your state may regulate the sales of debt (notes/loans) and equity in private companies, which may require you to provide a filing, register the security, or meet an exemption (for example, under Regulation D.)

If you're sure you want to offer some type of investment, get in touch with an attorney as soon as possible. A reputable attorney will offer an initial consultation at no cost. Use this time to get comfortable with the firm, their expertise, success stories, and the price structure. Get the scope of services in writing, with an estimate. When looking at multiple firms, your comfort level should be a top priority.

SURVEY YOUR WAY TO CAPITAL

Finding early boosters for your business is hard. But there is an early test you can use to evaluate the market for your product and capital. For example, if you plan on opening a restaurant, cook your family and friends a meal, and after the meal is over, ask them to complete an online and anonymous survey using Survey Monkey or another option.

An anonymous survey tool will generate unfiltered and authentic feedback. Your survey should include questions about whether they would buy your product and at what price. Add opened-ended questions about what people liked, disliked, or would change. These types of questions give your potential customers a way to tell you exactly how they feel. The feedback you receive is critical to understanding whether you have a product that people are willing to support.

Thank your friends (guinea pigs) for their participation. You have much riding on the launch of your business. Make sure your assumptions about the marketplace are valid—and not just based on family and friends making you feel good. After the results have been tabulated, be objective with the data. If all is good, it's time to consider getting your family and friends involved.

DOCUMENT, DOCUMENT, DOCUMENT

Tell your friends that you're opening a business and how their financial support, in the form of a term loan, would help you move forward quicker. Explain how the funds would be used. The rules regarding selling investments in private businesses is complex. There are platforms where you can sell investments, but only through the platforms. Contact an attorney.

The key to any financial transaction is to craft documents that meet your situation and terms that will give you the longest runway possible to get your business off the ground. Hire an attorney to draw up the legal agreement, which will specify the parameters of the deal: amount, interest rate, collateral offered, along with which state will have jurisdiction, should a dispute arise. You may also want to have a term sheet with a summary of the offering (even if debt), and risk disclosures, so that your potential investors know exactly what they are buying into.

Make sure you can work with the family members or friends, in both good and bad times. Raising capital takes time and at the end of the day, it's a financial transaction. Make sure you're not sourcing capital from someone who has a history of filing lawsuits. The value of the relationship is most important. Make it a win-win situation for all parties.

The *Wall Street Journal* Prime Rate is a good way to find out what the prevailing interest rate environment is like. In general, seek a fixed interest rate—it's too hard to figure where the economy is going in a few years. While there is a possibility for rates to fall, in general, rates tend to rise, not fall.

COMMUNICATE THE NEWS

New ventures rarely go as planned. Keep your investors updated on your progress. They may be able to help you more than you anticipate. When things go wrong, communicate. It is never easy to deliver bad news, but don't make it worse by going silent. You may have to negotiate a deferment or forbearance to get the loan back on track to performing status. Of course, it's up to your lenders. Always document any agreement and keep your attorney involved.

TAKEAWAY: Trust but put it in writing.

30

ANGELS:
CAPITAL FROM HEAVEN–
OR HELL

BRAD FELD AND JASON MENDELSON are the authors of the book, *Venture Deals*. In the book, the authors state, "Not all investors realize it, but the entrepreneur is the center of the entrepreneurial universe. Without entrepreneurs there would be no term sheet and no startup ecosystem."[1] Entrepreneurs, you may now take a bow.

Back to reality. Entrepreneurs seeking risky seed capital to jumpstart their ventures need a miracle in the form of an angel. Angel investors don't ride on clouds, but if you're lucky to get funding, you may think otherwise. David S. Rose, the author of *Angel Investing*, mentions in his book, "Angel investors are individuals who invest their own money, typically in small amounts, and typically very early in the life cycle of a company."[2] Angels provide much-needed seed capital in exchange for an equity stake in the fledgling venture.

Investors are the gatekeepers to the promised land of material riches and the good life. When it comes to seeking investors to grow your business, think of high voltage electricity with a sign reading "Warning!" While angel investors are a significant part of the entrepreneurial ecosystem, not all businesses are suited for this type of investor. Before you go down this road, articulate why this is the best option for your business. Your best investors are customers—and they will not ask for equity. Produce a superior product at a price customers are willing to pay, and your business will not have to spend time searching for investors.

DNA OF AN ANGEL

Angel investors are "accredited investors", as defined by the SEC, who have an income of $200,000 ($300,000 for a couple) in the past two years, or $1 million in assets, excluding the value of their primary residence. If you are not an accredited investor, you can invest in companies, but it must be through one of the Direct Public Offering vehicles, described in chapter 56, or via one of the approved online funding portals, which fall under Title III of the Jumpstart Our Business Startups Act (JOBS Act) of 2012. Wefunder, SeedInvest, NextSeed, and Indiegogo are such platforms, where anyone can invest.

Angel investors are often former CEOs, C-suite executives or entrepreneurs. Most angel investors are not lone wolves. They are more likely to be part of angel investor groups scattered throughout the country. These groups have become the primary gatekeepers to sourcing new opportunities. The groups bring together like-minded people, skills, and knowledge of a wide array of businesses and industries. The Angel Capital Association, a trade association for angel investors, has over 13,000 members, who are affiliated with over 260 angel groups. Visit angelcapitalassociation.org for more information.

ENTREPRENEURS SEEKING RISKY SEED CAPITAL TO JUMPSTART THEIR VENTURES **NEED A MIRACLE** IN THE FORM OF AN ANGEL.

"The American Angel," a report about angel investors and their investment activities, was published in November 2017.[3] This report is unique because it provides a profile of angel investors. The authors surveyed 1,659 people who qualify as accredited angel investors. Below are some quick facts from the report.

- 55 percent of angel investors were previously a founder or CEO of their own startup.
- Angels with entrepreneurial backgrounds write average checks of $39,000.
- Angels with no entrepreneurial background write checks for $28,000.
- 63 percent of angels in the study were located outside of San Francisco, New York and Boston.
- 89 percent of angels find prospective investments from angel groups.

In the book *Venture Deals*, the authors note, "[s]ome angel investors make a lot of small investments. Recently, these very active, or promiscuous, angels have started to be called super angels or Micro-VCs (venture capitalists)."[4] Micro-VCs raise money and invest in seed-stage companies, similar to the venture capital model.

Rose's book, *Angel Investing*, quotes Reid Hoffman, the founder of LinkedIn, as saying "If you want to be a successful angel, you have to have an appetite for risk and the ability to accept failure."[5] Investing in early-stage businesses is more grit than glamour, because most businesses won't make it to a big payout.

The dismal returns for most angels hasn't stopped the "lottery" mentality of investors ready to quickly part with their money for a ticket to the dream: a big payout. There are roughly 300,000 active angel investors, but, based on individuals with a net worth of over $1 million, the potential exists for four million people to be angel investors.[6] Angels invested $24 billion in 2016. In 2015, 71,000 businesses received angel investments—a small fraction compared to the nearly 30 million businesses in the United States.[7] Dave Berkus, the author of *Raising Money,* says that in order to raise capital, the business needs three things:

1. Address a large market
2. "Must have and be able to tell an easy to understand story,"
3. The business must have a "secret sauce" that makes the business stand out.[8]

LONG ODDS

Angels keep a low profile, so a warm introduction is the way to get past the gatekeepers. Despite angel investors' anonymity, people find their way to them. Never send an unsolicited pitch deck or business plan to any investor because it most likely won't get read. Be patient because angel investors operate on their own schedule—people with money are not in a hurry to give it away.

Your management team can make a difference with angels. It has been said many times, but it's worth saying again: invest in the jockey, not the horse. With the right management team, staff and product, you can build a moneymaker. Keep in mind that angels have various reasons for getting involved with startups. They may have specific expertise, connections, or interest in helping startups. At the end of the day, investors want to make money.

Angel groups are listed online. Gust is a platform some groups use. Make sure you review all of the angel's criteria. Follow the instructions for contacting the group, if you meet their criteria; don't expect to get an answer right away—think of the Tortoise and the Hare story. Only a tiny fraction of entrepreneurial ventures will receive angel funding. As mentioned earlier, the business must address a large market, have an easy to understand story, and possess a "secret sauce" to stand out. Are you building a business to last for twenty years? Will you change an industry or the world? If so, proceed past Go and collect $200.

TAKEAWAY: Capital miracles can happen.

31

INVESTORS: SECURITIES & THE SILICON VALLEY WAY

INVESTORS MAKE MONEY by attempting to predict the future—whether using a crystal ball, tea leaves, demographics or trends. To get to the future, bets must be placed now on virtual reality, self-driving cars and artificial intelligence (AI). Yet, one doesn't know exactly what's coming next from an entrepreneur in a garage or incubator.

Investors have the money to keep a dream alive. They provide capital, connections, and advice to startup founders, who do the day-to-day work. Financial backing from an investor has the potential to change the trajectory of a startup company. Investors are sometimes like general managers of NBA teams: they select players for their team. Each startup that dreams of doing big things needs capital. Dave Berkus refers to investors as "smart money" because of the knowledge and expertise they bring to the table. The value an investor can bring to a startup business can't be understated.

SECURITIES

Entrepreneurs seeking capital for their risky ventures is not a new phenomenon. In the sixteenth-century, when merchants ships transported goods across the world, the typical entrepreneur at that time didn't have the resources to build a ship, pay for supplies, and crew. Someone had to bear the risk that the ship wouldn't make it. The ships had to be financed until they came back from their mission. Drew Field, the author of the book. *Direct Public Offerings*, says, "Entrepreneurs began selling shares in the ships and voyages."[1] Field says that was the precursor of what "became the model for corporate IPOs."[2]

Each security is unique and can reveal a hidden vault of capital for companies. James E. Burk and Richard P. Lehmann, in their book, *Financing Your Small Business*, state a security exists "in any case in which a person provides money to someone with the expectation that they will derive a profit through the efforts of that person."[3] A security generally applies when someone buys stock in a company or makes a noncommercial loan, and it may apply when a company sells a token or coin as well.

Purchasing securities in private companies is not something anyone can do. The rules are simple. If you are not an accredited investor, as defined by the SEC, you should not be buying or selling securities, unless the company offering the securities utilizes an exemption. "The sale of equity in private companies is regulated by the Securities Act of 1933, which requires that the company either register with the SEC or meet one of the several exemptions (Regulation D)", states Bill Payne, an angel investor, in the book, *Raising Money*.[4] There may be exemptions available in each state as well.

Whenever you sell equity, whether it be common stock, preferred stock, limited partnership interests or LLC membership units, the business must be in compliance with federal and state laws governing the sale of securities.

There are two types of offerings: public and private. A private placement offering is less expensive than a public offering and is not subject to SEC and state regulatory review. An offering document is called a private placement memorandum (PPM), and is typically prepared by an attorney who specializes in securities law. A PPM is a business plan wrapped in legal disclaimers for accredited investors.

A PPM can raise alarming issues for a venture capitalist, particularly if non-accredited investors are on the capitalization (cap) table (a document that outlines what percentage of the company's shares are owned by investors). There could be legal challenges by a "disaffected" investor who lost money in the venture, which could result in a rescission of the investment and return of the money. Berkus calls the "dirty cap table" a warning sign to investors because non-accredited investors are involved in the company. Brad Feld goes one step further by saying, "When we see an email from a banker sending us a PPM for an early-stage company, we automatically know that investment opportunity isn't for us and almost always toss it in the circular file."[5] **Note:** Opinions vary about this subject. Read chapter 60 for more information about private placements.

SILICON VALLEY IS YOUR BUSINESS MODEL

The idea that an investor-backed company can make it only in Silicon Valley, Boston, or New York is ludicrous. No one holds the exclusive patent on innovation. Americans are problem solvers, and capital is like water: it can't be contained. Great ideas will always rise to the top, regardless of where the business is located. Solve a big problem and investors will find you.

Why should an investor give you money? To get the attention of an investor, your business must have the potential to gain a foothold in a large market, have an interesting story to separate your venture from that of the next entrepreneur, and have a "secret sauce," which will be your differentiator. If you meet the criteria, and want investors' funds, prepare to play by Silicon Valley's rules.

Only you can determine whether a security is right for your business. Don't fall into the trap of complaining when another business attracts capital and you didn't. The odds are long for everyone, with many factors out of your control. The experienced entrepreneur knows it is not about smoke and mirrors; customers determine success.

Making money is a byproduct of delighting customers. There's been a big rush to raise as much capital as possible— long before a cogent business idea has been articulated. Entrepreneurs, and their PR teams, send out press releases about how much money has been raised from investors. Stick to your reality where customers are real, and not something you will have in the future. When you solve a problem, customers will be delighted to pay.

TAKEAWAY: Pay attention to securities law.

"Pushin' On," The Quantic Soul Orchestra
featuring *Alice Russell, Pushin' On*

32

ASK THE CROWD:
MY KICKSTARTER EXPERIENCE

HAVE YOU EVER WONDERED what it feels like to wear a jetpack attached to your back and fly, like Ironman? Richard Browning, a British citizen and the world record holder for fastest speed in a body-controlled, jet engine-powered suit, can tell you. For everyone else, there's Kickstarter. This is my story of how I raised funds on Kickstarter to write this book.

Kickstarter is a platform of 13 million people who use crowdfunding to raise capital for their projects. It's mission is to help bring creative projects to life. Since its inception, more than $3.4 billion has been raised and over 134,000 projects (and counting) have been funded.[1] But success is not guaranteed. In fact, the success rate for funded projects is 36 percent—put another way, you have a 64 percent chance of failure. "Most successfully funded projects raise less than $10,000", states Kickstarter, "but a growing number have reached six, seven, and even eight figures."[2]

Deciding to launch a crowdfunding campaign is not easy. Whether you use Kickstarter, Indiegogo or other platforms, you must make a commitment to the process—and the emotional ups and downs along the way. Your campaign will be about 30 days, and you get the money only if you reach your goal on Kickstarter—the pressure of watching the clock is real.

Kickstarter's software doesn't require special skills, but the more expertise you bring to the table, the better your campaign will look. Rope your friends and colleagues into your project early. A team of creatives will help with writing, designing and marketing your campaign.

TELL A GOOD STORY

In the book, *Raising Capital*, David Steakley, former president of the Houston Angel Network, says, "Stories are the most important repository of wisdom, experience, knowledge, and learning."[3] People will remember a story much longer than a bunch of numbers or statistics. Before you create your Kickstarter campaign, think about the story you want to tell. Are you solving a problem? What are you doing that's different and worthy of funding? Make it about a larger cause to help others.

My campaign expanded on the challenges small-business owners face in raising capital. I created a simple video of me sitting in a chair, speaking directly to the camera, with the help of a friend, who owns a video production company—you don't have to be Steven Spielberg with a big budget to create an appealing video. The shoot took place in my friend's office break room. I explained I would take time away from my startup to write and publish this book, which is why I needed the funds. It took a few takes, varying my words, tone, enunciation and enthusiasm. I spoke from the heart, not a script. The shoot took about 30 minutes. Voila! I had a video ready to appeal to the masses—at least that's what I hoped.

A graphic designer is a visual problem solver. Your video is the first thing people will notice on your page; the friendly interactions of hierarchy, fonts, text, colors, graphics and pictures are designed to create a mood to support your story. The font and graphics must be consistent. Remember KISS: Keep It Simple, Stupid. In the end, no one has to watch your video or read your text. Make them want to watch, read and support your project. The old saying, "Luck is when preparation meets opportunity" is so true. Make your own luck by taking the time to put together a compelling project. In the end, your mission is simple: Get people to enthusiastically part with their money.

HIT LAUNCH

Once Kickstarter approves your project, you are free to launch it at any time. It can be nerve-racking preparing to launch. Up to now, only a few friends and family may know about your project, but once you launch, the world will be a click away. The prospect of that can be intimidating, especially when public failure is looming. My advice is straightforward: Set a realistic fundraising goal. Check similar projects to see what they raised. Keep your project to 30 days, to create urgency for potential funders and you.

Prior to launching, I told family and friends to make a contribution within 24 hours of going live. Kickstarter's research states that projects that reach 20 percent within the first two days tend to get funded. Develop a schedule of activities you will do to light a spark of interest. Do whatever you can to generate attention out of the gate. Make sure you have a good story because the media is inundated with requests to cover events. Any coverage from TV, radio, podcasters, bloggers and social media helps. Your job is to stoke the fire so it burns bright.

The time had come to launch my campaign. I hit the button! My project was off and flying into the universe, but I had no time to admire my work. It was time to get busy grinding.

KEEP GRINDING

I reached out to people daily, even those I hadn't communicated with in a while—now was not the time to hold onto my pride. People who are afraid to sell and put themselves out there will have difficulty reaching out to friends, family, the media and total strangers. Don't be shy! I personalized as many communications as possible. I frantically sent texts and called people when I didn't receive replies from my emails—we are all inundated with our own lives and a follow-up call helped. What's the worst thing that can happen?

I celebrated every time someone contributed to my project. I jumped up and down and screamed with excitement—your celebration rituals may vary. Even a five-dollar contribution helped me psychologically. I kept reminding people about the importance of my project to save the world on Kickstarter and the urgency of their contribution now. In the end, I did take it personally when a family member or close friend didn't contribute—it hurt. For whatever reason, they made their decision. I moved on and learned from the experience.

I didn't get a good night's sleep during the campaign. I felt butterflies in my stomach and anxiety. Not one day was easy during the campaign. I'm happy I experienced what other people have gone through—I feel part of a special community of doers. Drum roll, please. I reached my target of $5,000, but it took everything I could muster to get there. I thank my supporters who contributed. I lived a year in 30 days. Now it's your turn to carry the Kickstarter flame out into the world. Make something great. You can do it.

TAKEAWAY: Tell a good story.

PART IV
Side A:
Mostly Debt

33

START HERE:
YOUR CAPITAL SEARCH

CONGRATULATIONS! YOU MADE IT to the capital section. If you've arrived here after reading all the previous chapters, you're ready to go. Here's a quick refresher. The biggest decision you will make is whether you choose to think like an entrepreneur or a small-business owner (Chapter 1: What Are You: Entrepreneur or Small-Business Owner?). This decision is analogous to baking a cake from a Betty Crocker box or making a three-layer cake from scratch.

The next challenge is figuring out what is the appropriate business model (Chapter 3: Rev Your Engine: The Business Model) to maximize market opportunities. To succeed, focus on solving a problem or pain point for customers. Markets are people with needs, not dollar signs. Connect and serve. Delight customers (Chapter 6: Delight Customers: Happy Customers Spend) by serving each one with a smile.

In the book, *How Money Works*, it estimates that $80.9 trillion dollars exist in the world.[1] Regardless of the economy, capital is available to the business that delights customers. The chapters that follow provide an overview of the various types of capital available.

The investor class is awash in capital searching for a safe haven to generate reasonable returns. Whether you're a startup or existing business, capital is waiting for you. But no one is entitled to capital. Your job is to show why your business deserves other people's money (OPM), and how you will use the money in a safe way to generate a return by delighting customers.

KNOW YOUR CAPITAL

Meeting a friendly loan broker at Starbucks over a cup of coffee doesn't change the seriousness of the confab. As a business owner, you have to be an investigative reporter to get the facts about capital products. A healthy dose of skepticism is required when it comes to your money. Make sure the capital product will meet your needs at a price you can afford. For a refresher on the subject, review Chapter 22: Capital: Good, Cheap or Fast.

Buying capital is not like buying a box of cereal. Reread Chapter 26: Interest Explained: The Cost of Capital. Make sure you know the product you're buying, the financial terms and conditions. Compare financial products; the annual percentage rates (APR) will reveal the true cost across different products. Once you sign the loan documents, you are on the hook for whatever is in the fine print. Don't take the person's word because the devil is in the fine print. Get an attorney to review the document.

HOW YOU SEE YOURSELF, WHETHER AS AN ENTREPRENEUR OR SMALL-BUSINESS OWNER WILL DETERMINE THE TYPE OF CAPITAL SUITABLE FOR YOUR BUSINESS.

HOW TO EVALUATE THE OPTIONS

How you see yourself, whether as an entrepreneur or a small-business owner, will determine the type of capital suitable for your business. Most small-business owners are looking to make things incrementally better than the competition. On the other hand, Google dreams big. On its YouTube channel, which has over 6 million subscribers, it says, "Moonshots live in the gray area between audacious technology and pure science fiction. Instead of a mere 10% gain, a moonshot aims for a 10x improvement over what currently exists. The combination of a huge problem, a radical solution to that problem, and the breakthrough technology that just might make that solution possible, is the essence of a moonshot."[2]

All capital decisions inevitably come to a fork in the road. Review Chapter 23: Debt or Equity: The Fork in the Road for an expanded discussion on the topic. At this fork, a wrong turn can be ruinous. Putting equity into your small-business engine is like putting rocket fuel into your Toyota Prius. There's no shame in being a small business, as are 99 percent of all businesses in the U.S. Keeping your feet on the ground while serving customers every day is a prerequisite.

Raising capital is a full-time job early on and can be a distraction from building the business.

The decision to raise equity should be based on three things:

1. Serve a large market.

2. Communicate an easy-to-understand story to customers.

3. Have a "secret sauce" that gives your business a competitive advantage.

Your competitors who are raising capital will claim they also have the three things all investors look for.

Offering any type of security requires a certain level of sophistication that only an attorney can provide. Angel investors, known as accredited investors, can provide your business with the capital, connections and experts to help accelerate growth from one store to a hundred stores. Once you know the capital that suits you, it's time to find the best deal, price, conditions and terms. Your future is in your hands. It doesn't matter what the competition is doing. Focus on your value proposition, and the competition will be irrelevant. The capital that follows will give your business the options it needs to succeed, on your terms. You are now armed with powerful information to build the best business you can.

TAKEAWAY: There's plenty of money.

34

TRADE CREDIT:
FUNDED BY YOUR SUPPLIERS

OVERVIEW

Trade credit, also known as vendor financing, allows a business to buy now and pay later—like a credit card. If you have accounts payable (money owed to suppliers), you have trade credit. This type of credit benefits both the supplier and the business. The supplier gains a customer and the business receives goods on credit. Suppliers require a new business to demonstrate a pattern of paying on time before extending credit or will validate creditworthiness by reviewing your credit report. Each supplier has its own requirements, which may include a formal application process. Smaller companies tend to be less formal and grant credit quicker than larger corporations.

When suppliers extend credit, it will appear in their accounts receivable (A/R) report and on their balance sheet, and the products (goods or services) the businesses receive will appear on their accounts payables (A/P) report. To encourage prompt payment, the supplier will offer a modest discount when paid early. A typical supplier term for payment is 2/10, net 30. The business receives a two percent discount when paid by 10 days. If not paid, the full balance is due in 30 days. Many companies will charge interest on payments beyond 30 days of 1.5 percent a month or higher.

Some companies will eliminate credit terms when bills are consistently paid past the 45-day mark. If a business is cut off from credit, the transaction then becomes a cash on delivery/arrival (COD/COA), which can negatively impact cash flow. Stay on good terms with your suppliers, they provide credit when others won't, on flexible terms.

Description
Trade credit (vendor credit) is credit extended by a supplier to a business to purchase goods.

Purpose of Funds
Trade credit facilitates a supplier generating sales from its business customers.

Requirements
Suppliers will evaluate the business' creditworthiness through an application process, which may include pulling your personal and business credit report.

Technical Assistance
N/A (not applicable)

Credit Score
As part of the credit evaluation process, the supplier may pull both personal and business credit reports of the owner, along with the D&B report. The credit application may require two or more credit references.

Term

Each supplier will have its own credit process and terms. A common credit term is 2/10, net 30, which is equal to a 2 percent discount on the invoice, when paid within ten days, or the full balance becomes due in 30 days. It is common for suppliers to charge a 1.5 percent interest rate each month on the outstanding balance, which could make purchases more costly on top of the supplier's margins.

Interest

The interest charged on outstanding balances can be as low as 1 percent and up to 3 percent each month.

Fees

Some suppliers may charge an application fee to pull the credit report.

Payments

Payments are due within 30 days.

Prepayment

The terms of 2/10, net 30 encourages prompt payment.

Personal Guarantee

Suppliers may require a personal guarantee.

Collateral

While not uncommon, the supplier of credit could file a UCC-1 (Uniform Commercial Code lien) with the Secretary of State. This depends on the company's internal credit policies, including the amount of credit extended to each customer.

Rating
This is one of the rare situations where a business can get the holy trinity of credit: Good, Cheap & Fast. If bills are not paid within 30 days, the interest rate can reach up to 3 percent a month on outstanding balances.

Additional Cost
The supplier's credit agreement is one-size-fits all, similar to a credit card. It is your call whether your attorney should review the agreement. Most documents have standard boilerplate language and are not altered from customer to customer.

Where to Look
The majority of suppliers offer trade credit; just ask. Sysco, a global food distributor, has a three-page application, see it here: metrony.sysco.com/Files/Credit%20Application.pdf. Here's a good piece about calculating the cost of trade credit: thebalance.com/the-cost-of-trade-credit-accounts-payable-392835.

TAKEAWAY: Credit is hiding under your nose.

35

CREATIVE SOLUTIONS:
NOT THE USUAL SUSPECTS

OVERVIEW

You have to be creative to outlast the marathon that is business. When capital from a bank is not forthcoming, it is time to get creative. Creative solutions are unconventional ways to fund your business. Focus on solutions that do not require you to sell securities. How about providing a discount for prepaid services? A bookkeeping business could contact prospective customers in June and offer a discount on services for the next year. The same bookkeeper could contact existing customers and ask for a referral. Each referral contacted could lead to a new customer. Each referral that leads to a new customer will receive a $20 gift card. That's win-win.

For a consulting business, the company could contact clients to prepay for a new level of platinum services. Providing more services is always beneficial to a client. The platinum level can be marketed exclusively to growth businesses. Exclusivity has a way of working magic on a prospect's psyche. People often want what other people have, especially when it puts them in a favorable light. To close the sale, disclose the names of prominent clients who are part of the platinum level. A website with a newsletter subscription could add more value for prepaid orders. Discounts or prepayment for services are surefire ways to get capital in your bank account. Create a call to action with a limited-time offer to get results. You may be surprised how your creativity can lead to real cash—it's almost like winning the lottery.

The Hartford is a Fortune 500 investment and insurance company headquartered in Hartford, Connecticut. A group of employees, friends, family and business partners call themselves the HartMob. This group selects small businesses to support with their dollars and shows up on a specific date and time to spend. The website states, "It is a cash mob." How about getting your customers to start a cash mob at your business? Select a specific date and time once a quarter or month. Mention that a certain percentage of the proceeds will benefit a charity or nonprofit community group, which is a great way to connect the event to the community.

Description
Creative solutions are unconventional ways to source capital for your business.

Purpose of Funds
Raise capital now for your business.

Requirements
The owner develops the requirements and specials.

Technical Assistance
N/A

Credit Score
N/A

Term
Owner must set the terms.

Interest
N/A

Fees
N/A

Payments
The goal is to generate cash up front and awareness for the business.

Prepayment
N/A

Personal Guarantee
N/A

Collateral
N/A

Rating
This type of capital meets all three criteria: Good, Cheap & Fast.

Additional Cost
Depending on how creative you are, there may be some marketing costs to promote your offering.

Where to Look

Start brainstorming ideas. Remember, don't do anything that may be deemed a security. If you're not sure, contact an attorney. Visit the HartMob atthehartford.com/about-us/hartmob.

TAKEAWAY: The sky's the limit.

36

BARTER:
NO MONEY REQUIRED

OVERVIEW

To barter is to exchange a product from one business for goods from another business. Based on the International Reciprocal Trade Association (IRTA) website, bartering is estimated to be a $12 to $15 billion-a-year industry. The great thing about bartering is that no cash exchanges hands—a creative solution when cash is scarce. It has been said that the Mesopotamia tribes started what is known as bartering, which dates back 6000 BC. The value of money comes from its use as a medium to exchange value, not from the paper it's printed on. Since cash is accepted by everyone without question, there is an inherent trust in paper money. Bartering differs from money because it requires time to complete a transaction; the parties have to determine the value of the goods they are exchanging. Everyone knows the value of

$100 dollars, but what's the value of three hours of bookkeeping services?

The key advantage of bartering is that two or more parties can get what they want without exchanging cash. Here's how. Let's use the example of Steve, a carpenter, and Wendy, an accountant. Both businesses are going into a slow season and want to preserve cash. Steve needs someone to untangle his financial records before he applies for a loan to grow the business. On the other hand, Wendy wants to spend her precious time off in her backyard with family. To increase the quality of her family time, Wendy wants a deck to barbecue and entertain guests.

Steve agrees to build the deck for $3,000. Wendy provides an estimate of $3,000 to prepare an income statement (P & L), balance sheet and cash flow statement to go with the loan application. Both parties put their estimates in writing and agree to barter. Fast forward six months, Wendy is throwing a football around with her son and daughter, while smoke from her Weber grill permeates the air with the smell of summer barbecue. Steve has implemented a new marketing plan to increase business, as he was approved for a $50,000 loan. Another happy ending through the power of bartering.

Description
Bartering is exchanging goods between two or more parties, without money changing hands.

Purpose of Funds
The business gets the product it needs without impacting cash flow.

Requirements
Parties must agree on the value of the goods to be bartered.

Technical Assistance
Assistance may be available from a bartering platform.

Credit Score
Your credit score doesn't matter.

Term
Each owner must develop a value for their services and agree to terms of when the products will be produced, the quality and when the exchange will take place.

Interest
N/A

Fees
No cash is exchanged. However, the work performed does have a real value.

Payments
No cash is exchanged. Treat bartering like you would treat any customer who is paying. Bartering is considered taxable by the IRS Make sure you keep records of your transactions throughout the year. Many bartering platforms will do the administrative work of keeping track of all transactions.

Prepayment
A bartering platform will charge a membership fee and a fee per transaction.

Personal Guarantee
Your reputation is on the line, each time you barter. Make sure you honor the agreement.

Collateral
N/A

Rating
Bartering meets all three criteria of Good, Cheap & Fast.

Additional Cost
Bartering websites charge a fee to be on the website and for each transaction. You may have to spend money to promote your offering to the public.

Where to Look
There are a number of bartering exchanges, some of which will require you to be a member. Here's an example of a bartering website: barternetworkinc.com//index.cfm.

TAKEAWAY: You don't need cash.

37

SELLER FINANCING:
YOUR PRIVATE BANKER

OVERVIEW

Buying a competitor may be the way to turbocharge your business. Closing this type of transaction can be facilitated by the seller. Selling financing (also known as owner financing) is when the seller holds a note to help finance the deal. An acquisition can be attractive because purchasing an existing business with customers means the business will generate sales from day one. A business may seek an acquisition when the cost to generate growth through organic means is too expensive and time-consuming. With increased competition, it may be to your advantage to find companies that are smaller than yours to acquire. Rollups (acquiring many small competitors to create one large company) has become a popular strategy in large, fragmented industries.

The most important decision you may make is to acquire another company. Businesses are always for sale for a number of reasons, whether the owner is retiring, the business is struggling, or the owner's interest is waning. Your job is to perform due diligence to find out what potential problems could be lurking around the corner for the targeted acquisition. Prior to embarking on this journey, make sure you have your acquisition team assembled: accountant, attorney, business broker and other advisors necessary to provide feedback regarding the transaction.

Seller financing takes place when the owner agrees to sell the business and enters into an agreement where the buyer will make an upfront down payment and the seller will finance a portion or all of the remaining balance. Most sellers want all-cash deals, but the reality is that the majority of buyers seek owner financing. A large percentage of deals are closed with seller financing. Seller financing is the incentive to close the deal. On a typical sale, the buyer will make a down payment followed by bank financing. The gap between bank financing and the down payment is what the seller can provide to seal the deal. The seller will hold a promissory note for the portion of the financing. The note can have a five-year term with an interest rate above market, which will compensate the owner for the additional risk. With the proper vetting, seller financing can be the key to unlocking a sale.

Description
Seller financing is when the seller holds a note (loan) to help facilitate the sale.

Purpose of Funds
Seller financing is a means for a business to acquire another.

Requirements

A business broker will require the prospective buyer to sign a nondisclosure agreement (NDA) and complete a document to ascertain the buyer's financial wherewithal. Once the NDA has been signed, the buyer will receive the broker's financial writeup and the business financials. If the buyer is seeking bank funding, she will need to provide a personal financial statement, business plan, personal and business tax returns for the past three years, accounts receivable/payable aging report, interim Profit & Loss Statement, balance sheet and cash flow. Bank financing can take up to 90 days. Plan for it.

Technical Assistance

The business broker will help with putting together the sale. Your acquisition team will assist with due diligence.

Credit Score

If seeking bank financing, the buyer should have a minimum credit score of 660.

Term

The seller will give no more than 5 years of financing. Often deals can be structured as a 10-year loan with a balloon payment due in no more than five years.

Interest

The seller's financing will be a few hundred basis points (100 basis points is equal to 1 percent) above prime, higher than traditional financing due to the perceived risk the seller is assuming.

Fees

N/A

Payments
Negotiate flexible terms with the seller. Monthly principal and interest payments will be required.

Prepayment
Banks usually charge a prepayment fee, which declines over time.

Personal Guarantee
The business owner will be required to provide a personal guarantee. Seller financing will be subordinate to bank financing.

Collateral
Lenders will seek collateral to secure the loan.

Rating
Good. For most buyers, seller financing is key to making the deal work. In addition, seller financing helps the buyer get a better price for the business. This is a "win-win" situation for both the buyer and seller. Should the buyer need additional bank financing, the seller's financing will be subordinate to the bank's note. It may take a few months to negotiate seller financing. If the business for sale has many offers, seller financing will be off the table. Be patient because the first or second offer to the seller doesn't always materialize.

Additional Cost
Expect attorney's fees, which can climb depending on the complexity of the deal. If bank financing is involved, you will pay the bank's legal fees.

Where to Look

Talk to the broker to see if owner financing will be possible. A broker may not want to reveal any details about the owner financing until she knows the buyer has the wherewithal to purchase the business. Plus, as stated earlier, the owner will try to complete a deal without owner financing. However, the longer the business is on the market, the more leverage you will have.

BizBuySell is one of the top national sites for buying and selling a business. Check with local brokers in your state to find out what businesses are for sale in your area. Many have relationships with national brokers, similar to how real estate agents work.

TAKEAWAY: It may be time to buy.

38

CREDIT CARDS:
PLASTIC RULES

OVERVIEW

On December 4, 2014, *Bloomberg Businessweek* published "The 85 Most Disruptive Ideas in Our History." The magazine ranked credit number 19. Credit has come a long way. In 1950, Frank McNamara, the founder of the Diners Club Card, was the first person to complete a transaction with a credit card. From that moment on, credit changed our lives. At one time, debt was something to avoid because unpaid bills led to debtor prisons. Much later, debt was rebranded as credit and everything changed. John Lanchester, the author of the credit piece in *Bloomberg Businessweek*, writes, "The gigantic expansion of debt is possibly the single most striking feature of modern economies over the last few decades."[1]

Credit cards are usually the first credit a business receives. Credit cards are a form of revolving credit, which means that as long as the balance is paid down, the card can be used to the maximum amount repeatedly. Business credit cards have higher spending limits than consumer credit cards. To increase their utility, business credit cards may come with financial tools to manage expenses and reports to track the categories of spending. Card issuers develop programs focused on where businesses spend: office supplies, airline travel, FedEx, UPS, software, computers and hardware. Credit cards can be issued for employees to use, but the owner is responsible for making monthly payments. Prior to approval, the owner is required to provide a personal guarantee, and the card company will check personal credit scores. Over time, a business credit card can help build your business credit.

Business credit cards don't have the same rights as consumer cards. The Credit Card Act of 2009 and the Truth in Lending Act of 1968 don't apply to business credit cards, which means your annual percentage rate (APR) can change without notice. In actuality, business credit cards often extend the same courtesies as they must under the Credit Card Act, but are not required to do so. Business credit cards can apply payments above the monthly payment to the lowest rates first. A business should have at least one credit card. Caveat emptor.

Description
Credit cards are revolving credit that can be paid in full or paid over time.

Purpose of Funds
Business credit cards should be used for business purposes. Co-mingling business and personal credit cards is not recommended. You want as much separation between the two as possible.

Requirements
Your credit score and personal guarantee are necessary to receive a business credit card.

Technical Assistance
Many CDFIs and nonprofits provide workshops on using credit responsibly.

Credit Score
Your three-digit credit score is the primary criteria that determines if you will be offered a credit card. The higher the number, the better. A score of 700 and above is excellent. FICO is the primary score the three credit bureaus use: Experian, Equifax, TransUnion. Business credit card issuers may ask for personal income and business information to verify the card is for business use, which may include providing your Employer Identification Number (EIN).

Term
Credit cards have a grace period; after the grace period expires each month, the business is charged interest.

Interest
Interest rates on credit cards can escalate to APRs of 30 percent or higher. Many credit cards have variable interest rates—priced according to the Federal Funds rate—which means your interest rate can go up or down.

Fees
Some credit card issuers may charge an application fee or an annual fee. Shop around to get the best deal.

Payments
Payments are due within 30 days.

Prepayment
N/A

Personal Guarantee
A personal guarantee is required.

Collateral
N/A

Rating
For an individual with a high credit score above 700, it's possible to get a lower interest rate that is not a teaser rate. In general, credit cards can be Good, Cheap & Fast, if used properly. When the balance is paid every month, credit cards can be a cost-effective way of making purchases and keeping track of where you spend money. However, carrying a monthly balance can make credit cards expensive financing.

Additional Cost
The late fees can add up, if a bill is not paid on time. The monthly interest can increase dramatically when the credit card agreement is not followed. Read your agreement to know what the rules are.

Where to Look
Bankrate (Bankrate.com) NerdWallet (Nerdwallet.com) and CreditCards.com (Creditcards.com) are three websites you can compare the best rates for credit cards.

TAKEAWAY: You need at least one credit card.

39

MICROLOANS:
SMALL DOLLARS ADD UP

OVERVIEW

Microloans are loans up to $50,000. This type of loan product is ideal for startups and businesses that lack a reasonable credit score, operating history, and collateral necessary for traditional financing. The business must demonstrate it can make scheduled monthly loan payments on time. Lenders in this space tend to be nonprofit organizations committed to serving their mission and reaching underserved populations in low- to moderate-income communities. The Small Business Administration (SBA) has a program that provides funding to micro lenders. Micro lenders receive support from local and state governments, foundations, banks, economic development programs and private sources.

Large banks with over $50 billion in assets prefer to complete loan transactions of $1 million and up. For loan requests under $50,000, many of the larger banks will offer a business credit card. Some banks will periodically steer businesses to lines of credit that are credit scored with only the minimum requirement of two years in business. Credit cards and lines of credit based on credit scores are a bank's attempt to serve smaller clients promptly and efficiently without the cost of human underwriting. However, some large banks have partnered with alternative lenders to make referrals for deals they choose not to fund.

Community lenders harken back to the days when bankers knew their communities better and didn't rely on algorithms. Nonprofit lenders specialize in microloans. They have the expertise to assess the creditworthiness of the owner and they know the community. Small lenders require a considerable amount of time to get familiar with the owner's business and character. Some owners may have a less than optimal credit score, which must be explained in detail to the underwriter. As long as the applicant is honest, many circumstances can be overcome. The business must demonstrate it will have the cash flow to support the proposed loan.

Description
Microloans are business loans of up to $50,000.

Purpose of Funds
To help finance startups or businesses that would have a difficult time receiving traditional bank financing. Funds can be used for equipment, inventory, improvements and working capital.

Requirements
The business should have a business plan, personal tax returns, business tax returns, personal financial statement, Income Statement, Balance Sheet, Cash Flow Statement or Projections, Accounts Receivable/Accounts Payable Aging Report.

Technical Assistance

As part of their mission, nonprofits will provide technical assistance. Some lenders will require the business to meet periodically with the lender. Free or low-cost training is available in a host of areas, including QuickBooks, accounting, marketing, strategy development and management.

Credit Score

Most lenders don't have a specific cutoff score. However, a score lower than 600 would be a concern. If you have a low credit score, be prepared to explain. Mitigating circumstances, such as medical bills or a job loss, could be the difference between being declined or approved. Be candid about your situation and most nonprofit lenders will find a way to work with you.

Term

Most microloans have a maximum term of seven years.

Interest

The interest rate is usually the WSJ prime, plus two to six hundred basis points. Microloan lenders usually have fixed rates, which means the loan will not change over the duration of the loan, unless there is a default.

Fees

Fees vary from program to lender. Most lenders may charge a one or two percent loan origination fee. If the funds are used for a line of credit, the loan may have an annual renewal fee of up to two points (2 percent).

Payments

Principal and interest payments are made monthly.

Prepayment

Payments are typically made monthly to the lender. Nonprofits with the latest technology will offer online bill payments and access to account information. Some nonprofit lenders will accept payments onsite.

Personal Guarantee

Due to the nature of the loan, a personal guarantee is required.

Collateral

Lenders will look for collateral to secure the loan. The lender will file a Uniform Commercial Code (UCC-1) statement with the Secretary of the State, which uses all the business assets as collateral.

Rating

Good & Cheap. Most lenders will take up to 4 to 9 weeks to conduct their due diligence and to fund the loan.

Additional Cost

The lender will require the client to pay both the lender's and the client's closing costs. Given the size of the loan, find an attorney who will provide adequate representation and keep fees to a reasonable amount. The lender may have a list of attorneys for review.

Where to Look

The SBA maintains a list of microloan lenders. Visit their website. Accion and Uplift are two nonprofit organizations that offer this loan product throughout the U.S. See the appendix for a list of micro lenders. Visit mywaytocredit.com for a loan referral.

TAKEAWAY: Small loans can help.

40

COMMUNITY DEVELOPMENT FINANCIAL INSTITUTIONS: COMMITTED TO THE MISSION

OVERVIEW

Community Development Financial Institutions (CDFIs) are community lenders. CDFIs may be credit unions, economic development entities, nonprofit lenders, small banks, microfinance lenders, venture capital firms, or community development corporations focused on low- to moderate-income housing. They are usually nonprofit organizations committed to the mission of making capital accessible to the communities they serve. Often when a bank says "No" to a small business, a community lender will find a way to say "Yes", because their focus is on the community—not return on investment to shareholders.

The U.S. Department of the Treasury oversees the CDFI program, which was established in 1994 to make capital accessible to struggling communities. CDFIs fix the problems that are not addressed in a responsible manner by the private sector, such as access to affordable credit, financial products geared to the unbanked population (not served by a bank or similar financial institution), financial literacy training, affordable housing, and community development. The Treasury website states, "Mission-driven CDFIs fill these gaps by offering affordable financial products and services that meet the unique needs of economically underserved communities."[1]

Make sure you do your research about CDFIs because they are not all the same, or even all lenders. For example, some CDFIs are involved in affordable housing. Most CDFI venture capital firms have specific criteria for what types of businesses they are looking to invest in. Their criteria will be posted on their website.

Description
CDFIs are mission-driven organizations. Those organizations that lend to small businesses specialize in loans under $1 million, with a sweet spot of $50,000 to $200,000.

Purpose of Funds
Funds can be used to finance business expansion for equipment, inventory, commercial real estate, construction/build-out, and working capital.

Requirements
CDFIs want to see a business plan, personal tax returns, business tax returns, personal financial statement, Income Statement, Balance Sheet, Cash Flow Statement or Projections, Accounts Receivable and Accounts Payable Aging Report.

Technical Assistance
Most CDFIs will provide technical assistance (TA) to complete the application process. If approved for a loan, some lenders will require you to meet with them periodically, as part of

their TA programs. The lender many provide free or low-cost training in a host of areas, including QuickBooks, accounting, marketing, strategy development and management.

Credit Score

CDFIs don't have a hard and fast rule for a credit score, but the higher the score, the better your chance for financing. A credit score of 660 is a good place to start. However, a lower score for approval is possible. CDFIs understand that most businesses don't have a perfect credit score. The lender will review the totality of the application to decide whether to extend credit. As mission-driven lenders, projects that create or retain jobs and improve the community, are looked upon favorably.

Term

For loans to be used on equipment, inventory and working capital, the term could be up to seven years. On commercial real estate transactions, the term is typically 20 years. On building improvements, the term could be up to 10 years. Each lender's terms vary.

Interest

Interest rates are usually a few hundred points (one hundred basis points equal one percent) or more above prime.

Fees

Some lenders may charge up to a two percent origination fee. If the funds are used for a line of credit, the loan may have an annual renewal fee of up to two percentage points. These numbers are a guideline. Check with the lender for specific rates.

Payments

Payments are made monthly, directly to the lender. Some

financial institutions may require, or suggest, you open a bank account at their institution. Not all CDFIs will have the latest digital technology, such as paying online line and electronic statements. Each CDFI's level of service varies.

Prepayment
Many nonprofit lenders do not charge a prepayment fee.

Personal Guarantee
The lender will require a personal guarantee.

Collateral
CDFIs will look for collateral to secure the loan, just like a bank does. CDFIs will file a UCC-1 on any equipment purchased with the proceeds of the loan. The lender will hold the deed to a commercial property acquired until the note has been paid in full. Many CDFIs will accept a junior position on collateral behind senior lenders. Find a CDFI at ofn.org/cdfi-locator

Rating
Good & Cheap. Most lenders will take up to 4 to 9 weeks to conduct their due diligence and to fund the loan. For commercial real estate, the transaction, from application to funding, may take longer.

Additional Cost
The lender will often require the client to pay both the lender's and the client's closing costs. Legal fees on a loan of this size vary. Contact your attorney to get an estimate of legal costs.

Where to Look
CDFIs are located throughout the country.

TAKEAWAY: These lenders are committed to their missions and communities.

41

ECONOMIC DEVELOPMENT FUNDS AND GRANTS: CHEAP MONEY

OVERVIEW

Every state in America is competing to attract and retain businesses. Economic development entities on the local, regional and state level provide incentives to businesses in the form of loans, grants and tax abatement programs. Billions of dollars in incentives are doled out each year to attract and retain businesses. Some states will stop at nothing to lure businesses to move. Florida Governor Rick Scott came to Connecticut to recruit businesses in June 2017.[1] Scott's main carrot was an $85 million job growth fund, which was approved by the Florida Legislature—along with the promise of warm winters. He dangled the cash to businesses, like red meat to starving lions.

Regardless of what state you live in, there are programs for both small and large companies. The state of Connecticut has a program to help small businesses called the Express Program. The purpose of the program is to help growing small businesses that would have a difficult time receiving funding from a bank. The program offers loans up to $300,000 at an interest rate of 3.25 percent and forgivable loans and grants up to $100,000. Through the Department of Economic and Community Development (DECD), resources are available to large businesses as well: The First Five Plus Program. Funds have been disbursed to UTC, ESPN, NBC Sports, Cigna and more. Furthermore, Connecticut has a venture capital fund for fast-growing businesses managed by Connecticut Innovations (CI). CI also runs an annual contest, VentureClash, that doles out $5 million in prizes to businesses.

The best place to start your search is with your state economic development department. Most programs are designed to help existing businesses grow in the state by providing access to grants and low-cost capital. To access the funds, read the materials online. In general, larger companies have more leverage than small businesses. However, there may be a specific program for small companies at the state, regional or local level. Businesses that have a solid operating history tend to do well. The process to access the funds may take up to six months, so start early. The process is similar to what a bank wants and more. Tell your story about retaining and creating jobs, which is what economic development professionals want to hear.

Description
Economic development is a public-policy program to retain and attract companies, while promoting growth.

Purpose of Funds
Funds can be used to attract, retain or help grow the business.

Requirements
Each state's economic development program varies. Most states will want to see the same documents a bank will request: application, personal financial statement, business plan, personal and business tax returns for the past three years, Accounts Receivable/Payable Aging report, interim Profit & Loss Statement, Balance sheet and Cash Flow. Add on top of that, the state will have its own unique documents to complete.

Technical Assistance
Some states will provide assistance through a local nonprofit, SCORE, Small Business Development Centers (SBDC) or college assistance programs.

Credit Score
Many states will not pull a credit report, but will look for job retention, new hires and business growth.

Term
Some loans have terms up to 10 years. However, each program differs.

Interest
Economic development programs serve a public-policy goal and the interest rates tend to be lower than a bank's. Stimulating the state's economy is the top priority.

Fees
Most states don't charge an application fee.

Payments
Loans will have monthly payments, unless a portion or all of the loan is forgivable. Grace periods can be negotiated.

Prepayment
Economic development programs usually don't have prepayment penalties. Check your documents.

Personal Guarantee
Increasingly, states are requiring a personal guarantee.

Collateral
Lenders will seek collateral to secure the loan, but economic development programs tend to be more flexible than a bank, and will accept a second or third lien position on collateral.

Rating
Good. Cheap, but not Fast. State funding could be great for your business, especially if you are fortunate enough to receive a grant. The main disadvantage is that the programs are slow and can be bureaucratic and immersed in politics from year to year.

Additional Cost
Most grant programs have a clawback provision that will make the grant a loan if job targets are not met or if funds are not used as stated in the loan documents. Remember, you are using public dollars. It is advisable to hire an attorney to represent you at the closing. You may be required to pay the state's legal fees to close the transaction, along with your legal cost.

Where to Look
Contact your state's economic development website directly or visit eda.gov/resources/.

TAKEAWAY: These programs have a public policy goal.

42

COMMUNITY BANKS:
EMBEDDED IN THE COMMUNITY

OVERVIEW

Community banks are banks with assets under $10 billion, which defines 99.5% of all banks in the United States.[1] Many community banks are merging or being acquired to compete with much larger banks. Small banks pride themselves on relationship lending that comes down to knowing their customers and the communities. Decision-making is done within the local branch or within the footprint of where the bank does business. The sweet spot for most small-business loans is under $250,000. Large banks tend to focus on loans of $1 million and up, but small banks also can, and do, lend higher amounts.

Startups will find it hard to get bank financing. A startup with a good credit score, collateral, experience and a long relationship with the bank may be considered for an SBA loan, which is a loan guaranteed by the government. A business must demonstrate that it has the cash flow to service the proposed debt it seeks. Provided it has collateral and a personal credit score of 660 or above, with no derogatory information within the last two years, the bank will consider the request.

Small community banks are different from larger banks. The Independent Community Bankers of America (ICBA), the trade group for community banks, states the community bank difference:

1. Local focus: Deposits used to make loans in the local communities.

2. Focus on main street: Serve the local community and report to a local board of directors.

3. Relationship Banking: Know the people they serve and the community; whereas, large banks focus on algorithms, credit scores and data points.

4. Lending leadership to small business: A Federal Reserve Bank survey reported community banks are the small-business lender of choice.

5. Provide innovative solutions: Work to provide the best secure, reliable and convenient products.

6. Timely decision-making: Strive to make nimble decisions.

7. Community engagement & accessibility: Bank leadership is involved in the community.

Description
Community banks are lenders with assets under $10 billion that have a community focus. Their sweet spot is loans under $1 million. Some community lenders have the capacity to loan millions of dollars to one client, if the need is presented.

Purpose of Funds
Community lenders finance business expansion, equipment, inventory, construction/build-out, real estate, inventory and working capital, the same as much larger banks do.

Requirements
The lender requires a business plan, personal tax returns, business tax returns, personal financial statement, Income Statement, Balance Sheet, Cash Flow Statement or Projections, Accounts Receivable and Accounts Payable Aging Report.

Technical Assistance
Banks don't provide technical assistance. If the bank feels the client is not ready to go through the process, they may refer the client to a local SCORE Chapter, Small Business Development Center, Women's Business Center or nonprofit organization.

Credit Score
For some banks, the cutoff score will be 660. Commercial lenders are concerned with the ability of the business to repay the loan. If a client does have a low score, most banks will not spend time listening to mitigating circumstances.

Term
The term varies from five years all the way up to twenty-five years for commercial real estate.

Interest
Bank interest rates are usually a few hundred or more basis points above prime.

Fees

Most lenders may charge a one or two percent loan origination fee. If the funds are used for a line of credit, the loan may have an annual renewal fee of up to two percentage points. Check your commitment letter or loan closing documents. Consult with your attorney.

Payments

Payments are made monthly directly to the lender. Most banks will require the business to move its operating account to the bank or open an account at the bank. Banks will withdraw the monthly payment directly using an ACH.

Prepayment

Banks may charge a prepayment penalty. However, the prepayment declines over time. Many nonprofit lenders do not charge a prepayment fee.

Personal Guarantee

A personal guarantee is required.

Collateral

Lenders will look for collateral to secure the loan. The lender will file a UCC-1 on any equipment purchased with the proceeds of the loan. The lender will hold the deed to any commercial property acquired with bank funds until the note has been paid in full.

Rating

Good & Cheap, most lenders will take up to 4 to 9 weeks to conduct their due diligence and to fund the loan. For commercial real estate, the bank may take up to 90 days or more to close the transaction.

Additional Cost

The lender will often require the client to pay both the lender's and the client's closing costs. Legal fees on a loan of this size vary. Contact your attorney to get an estimate of the legal costs. You don't want to face sticker shock the day of the closing.

Where to Look

Start with a community bank. Search for a community bank near you at icba.org.

TAKEAWAY: Small banks are committed to community.

43

CREDIT UNION: CAPITAL FROM MEMBER-OWNED FINANCIAL COOPERATIVES

OVERVIEW

The United States banking system has three types of depository entities: Commercial banks, thrifts (savings and loans) and credit unions. A credit union is a financial institution organized as a financial cooperative for the benefit of its members owners. Investopedia states that such "Credit institutions are created, owned and operated by their participants."[1] Credit unions are operated as not-for-profits for the benefit of their members, who are its de facto owners. Most credit unions restrict membership to people who live, work, or worship within a specific region, or to employees of a participating company or organization.

Over 100 million Americans belong to a credit union. Credit unions have over $1 trillion assets combined. Credit unions have a common bond or "field of membership," which allows a person to become a member of a credit union. The size of credit unions varies from small all-volunteer organizations to the Navy Federal Credit Union, based in Vienna, VA, with 4.79 million members, $83.7 billion of managed assets, and 282 branch locations.[2] Credit unions are smaller than banks. While Navy Federal Credit Union seems big, compare it to JP Morgan Chase & Co. with its $2.55 trillion in assets under management. The ten largest U.S. banks have $11.8 trillion in assets.[3]

A member of a credit union buys shares in the cooperative through deposits. These funds are pooled together to provide financial products in the form of demand deposits, mortgages, car loans and business loans. Credit unions are not small banks; their mission is much different. They operate under the "Seven Cooperative Principles for Credit Unions," according to the Cornerstone Credit Union League website.

These are:
- Voluntary membership
- Democratic member control
- Economic participation of members
- Autonomy
- Education and training
- Cooperation among cooperatives
- Community Involvement

Since credit unions are nonprofits, they are exempt from paying corporate income tax on earnings. They only have to generate funds to cover daily operations. Thus, credit unions are able to offer loan rates that are superior to those of banks. In addition, credit unions can lend up to only 12.25 percent of their net worth, with loans under $50,000 exempt.[4] Visit NAFCU's site to find a credit union near you: CULookup.com.

Description
Credit unions are cooperatives owned and operated by their members. The average loan for a small business from a credit union is $212,000.

Purpose of Funds
Credit unions can lend to small businesses for equipment, commercial real estate, inventory or working capital.

Requirements
A credit union will seek a business plan, personal tax returns, business tax returns, personal financial statement, Income Statement, Balance Sheet, Cash Flow Statement or Projections, Accounts Receivable and Accounts Payable Aging Report.

Technical Assistance
Credit unions that are community development financial institutions (CDFI) may provide programs to educate their members about using credit responsibly and may offer their own training programs for small businesses or through partnerships with nonprofit organizations. A CDFI may apply for grant funds from the U.S. Treasury to support its mission.

Credit Score
Your three-digit credit score is a key factor in determining your credit worthiness.

Term
Terms vary all the way up to 20 years for a commercial mortgage.

Interest
Interest rates can be from up to 1 to 3 basis points lower than a similar commercial bank loan.

Fees
The lender may charge a loan origination fee.

Payments
Monthly payments are due. Many financial institutions will require the funds to be withdrawn from an account at the credit union.

Prepayment
Some lenders may charge a prepayment fee. Contact your lender to find out.

Personal Guarantee
It's standard operating procedure for lenders to seek a personal guarantee.

Collateral
The business must have collateral to secure the loan.

Rating
Good & Cheap. Credit unions are relationship-based lenders that usually have various products and lower interest on their loan products, compared to large banks. Think of a commercial bank as a department store. Commercial banks tend to offer more financial products, services and larger loans, but may lack the personalized service of a credit union.

Additional Cost
The lender may require the borrower to pay its closing cost.

Where to Look
Credit unions operate in every state. Check to find out membership requirements. Search for a credit union near you atCULookup.com or smarterchoice.org.

TAKEAWAY: Committed to serve its owners.

"Titanium," David Guetta featuring Sia,
Nothing but the Beat 2.0

44

U.S. SMALL BUSINESS ADMINISTRATION: BACKED BY UNCLE SAM

OVERVIEW

The United States Small Business Administration (SBA) is an agency whose head serves a Cabinet-level position in the President's administration. The SBA website states, "The SBA helps Americans start, build and grow businesses. The SBA was created in 1953 as an independent agency of the federal government to aid, counsel, assist and protect the interests of small business concerns, to preserve free competitive enterprise and to maintain and strengthen the overall economy of our nation."

The SBA is not a direct lender. It works with banks and other intermediaries to serve as a guarantor of loans made by others through its lending programs. In essence, the SBA is a public-policy program to make capital accessible to businesses in the U.S. by proving a guarantee to the participating lenders. Private banks and nonbank lenders are encouraged to lend to businesses when they might not otherwise do so, without a guarantee. The 7(a) Loan Program is the SBA's most popular product. In 2015, the average SBA loan was around $374,000. The SBA guarantees 85% of a loan of $150,000 or less and 75% of loans greater than $150,000, up to a maximum guarantee of $3.75 million. With the SBA's guarantee, the bank's risk is reduced dramatically. **Note:** In legal documents, the word is "guaranty." In the book, we use the familiar word "guarantee" to simplify.

The SBA approves lenders to work with its lending programs. The approval process evaluates the length of time the entity has worked with the SBA and the history of the relationship regarding the quality of deals, default rate and other factors. The Preferred Lender Program (PLP) is the highest level of approval a lender can have from the SBA. Under PLP, the lender directly approves the loan, not the SBA. The PLP is like an all-star team of SBA lenders; only the best make it to this level. Lenders are periodically reviewed to maintain their PLP status. The Certified Lender Program (CLP) gives lenders the authority to operate under streamlined rules. CLP lenders can use their own forms. The information that must be submitted to the SBA is reduced. They have a partial delegation of authority and receive a 36-hour window for the turnaround of applications. The lender must first approve the loan, followed by the SBA's approval, which adds time to the approval process.

Description
The SBA is a guarantee program to incentivize participating lenders to lend to small businesses, which might not otherwise do so without the guarantee.

Purpose of Funds
Funds can be used for any business use under the SBA guidelines.

Requirements

SBA loans are paper intensive. The bank will require the standard documents: business plan, personal financial statement, interim Profit & Loss Statement, Balance Sheet, Cash Flow, Accounts Receivable and Payable Aging Report, personal and business tax returns from the past three years. Look for a PLP or CLP, to speed up the process.

Technical Assistance

SCORE, Small Business Development Centers (SBDCs), Women's Business Centers and nonprofits may provide assistance to complete the loan process.

Credit Score

The bank will want to see a minimum credit score of 660.

Term

Each SBA loan product has different terms.

Interest

Rates vary. Contact a participating SBA lenders.

Fees

The SBA program does have a number of fees. See SBA document at sba.gov/sites/default/files/files/SBA%20 Lending%20Chart.pdf for more information.

Payments

Monthly principal and interest payments will be required.

Prepayment

There are prepayment penalties.

Personal Guarantee
Business owner will be required to provide a personal guarantee.

Collateral
Lenders will seek collateral to secure the loan.

Rating
Good. The SBA process is document-intensive and takes time. However, if you do get approved, your cost of capital will be higher than a traditional bank loan, but still very competitive.

Additional Cost
You will pay the lender's and your closing costs.

Where to Look
Review the most active SBA lenders by state for the 7(a) program at https://www.sba.gov/article/2017/oct/01/100-most-active-sba-7a-lenders. Work with lenders that are PLP or CLP lenders, which means they are experts at the process and can approve loans quickly.

TAKEAWAY: The SBA is not a lender; it guarantees loans in the program.

45

ALTERNATIVE LENDERS: ONLINE & FAST

OVERVIEW

When banks reduced lending to small businesses during the Great Recession, alternative lenders filled the void and became a viable option. Alternative lenders are nonbank lenders serving the small-business market. Lenders in this market underwrite, approve, and disburse capital in days, not months. They are lightly regulated. Banks have partnered with alternative lenders to provide solutions to businesses seeking small capital loans. In the future, banks also may offer alternative loan products.

Competition in this space continues to grow each year and there is no shortage of product offerings from peer-to-peer lenders such as Funding Circle, Prosper, Lending Club and Upstart; online lenders such as OnDeck Capital and Kabbage; and microloans from nonprofit lenders Accion and Kiva.

BlueVine, Fluid, and Fundbox provide accounts receivable financing. American Receivable is a well-established player in accounts receivable financing. There are many merchant cash advance (MCA) companies.

Each product has a specific niche. While having many different products on the market is good for businesses, the onus falls on the owner to know the product and read the fine print. The trick is to make sure you are working with a lender you trust. Check online reviews about the lender. Most owners who explore these types of products may have traditional bank financing relationships but hit a lending ceiling. Another group of owners may not be able to get bank financing. Alternative lenders are an option. The products in this category tend to be more expensive than traditional bank financing. What you get in this category is a streamlined online application process and products that are geared to your situation. Lenders evaluate cash flow, not your credit score.

The key is to understand each product and compare its cost based on the annual percentage rate (APR), which is the standard when it comes to comparing financial products. You must be confident that you can use the capital to generate a return higher than your cost for the capital. If you can't, you may be headed for long-term survival challenges. Check a CDFI to see if you qualify. Their products tend to be lower in price and high on serving the long-term interest of businesses.

Description
Alternative lenders serve the capital needs of small businesses when traditional financing is not available.

Purpose of Funds
Funds can be used for just about any business need. Many lenders specialize in loans under $100,000.

Requirements

The companies in this category underwrite credit differently than banks. Some will underwrite strictly on the cash flow of the business, requesting credit card sales and bank account data. Some product offerings are not loans per se, they are cash advances on future sales. Know the difference. For-profit nonbank lenders have the strictest lending terms and highest interest rates.

Technical Assistance

N/A

Credit Score

For peer-to-peer lenders, your credit score matters. The higher your score, the better interest rate you will receive. Most alternative lenders have found other ways to evaluate creditworthiness beyond a simple credit score. Some will look at your social media profiles to gauge business and personal support, along with product reviews and feedback.

Term

Each funder has different terms, with some terms as short as 90 days to one year.

Interest

Many of these lenders don't provide the Annual Percentage Rate (APR), which is the standard in consumer loans. Don't get taken in by the terminology they use, like "factor rate." Go to this website to convert to APR: https://www.nerd-wallet.com/blog/small-business/merchant-cash-advance-small-business/.

Decide whether this type of funding is right for your business. Ask yourself, will the funding help my business in the long-term and can I afford this.

Fees
There are a number of different fees. Read each one because you will be paying them.

Payments
Some lenders may withdraw fees directly from your account daily, using an ACH.

Prepayment
N/A

Personal Guarantee
Many lenders will want a personal guarantee.

Collateral
Some lenders will put a blanket lien on all business assets, known as a UCC-1 on the business.

Rating
Good. Fast. As mentioned earlier, this is the most expensive capital available to your business, since it is outside of the traditional banking system. Business borrowers don't have the same protections that consumers have.

Additional Cost
If you are late on any payments, there will be fees. Read the fine print in your agreement.

Where to Look
Do a quick online search of the top lenders in each category. Opportunity Fund is a nonprofit based in California that has a merchant capital advance-type product: https://opportunityfundloan.org/loans/easy/ Search for a CDFI near you at https://ofn.org/cdfi-locator.

TAKEAWAY: There is no shortage of capital products.

46

COMMERCIAL REAL ESTATE:
OWN YOUR SPACE

OVERVIEW

Commercial real estate, building improvements, rebuilding equipment or purchasing new equipment are all considered long-term fixed assets. These are assets that cannot be easily converted into cash. Commercial real estate is the focus here. Financing fixed assets requires an experienced lender to assist the owner in completing the transaction. A lender's emphasis is on the strength of the business to generate sufficient cash flow to service the debt.

One of the key metrics a commercial real estate lender will examine is the debt-service-coverage ratio (DSCR). This metric demonstrates the property has sufficient cash flow to service the proposed loan. Your DSCR will determine how large a loan the property can support. DSCR is the relationship between the net operating income (NOI) of a property divided by the annual loan payments. In the example below, the proposed loan is $720,000, amortized over 20 years at an interest rate of 4.94%. The owner will put down $180,000. Annual loan payments are $56,734.20.

Net Operating Income is cash flow available to service debt. Divide the net operating income by annual debt service for the loan. Lenders want to see a DSCR of 1.20x or greater, which means that the business will have 1.20x of cash for every dollar of debt service. The loan-to-value (LTV) metric is the percentage of the value of the property a lender will finance. Commercial lenders are conservative and will finance LTV anywhere from 75 to 90 percent. The LTV is calculated by taking the loan amount and dividing it by the property value. Lenders will finance based on the lesser of the purchase price or market value. The SBA's 504 program is designed specifically for acquiring fixed assets and will finance up to 90 percent of the project. The example below is not a 504 program loan. See page 344 to learn about the SBA's 504 program.

Purchase Price	$900,000
Gross Potential Rent (GPI)	200,000
LESS: Vacancy 10%	($20,000)
Effective Gross Income (EGI)	$180,000

Operating Expenses

Real Estate Taxes	$30,000
Insurance	$10,000
Repairs & Maintenance	$5,000
Lawn Care	$5,000
Cleaning	$20,000
Utilities	$7,000
Management Fee	$10,000
G&A	$7,000
Replacement Reserves	$9,000
Total Expenses	$103,000

Net Operating Income (NOI)	$77,000
Less:	
Annual Debt Service or Annual P&I Payment*	$56,734.20
Debt Service Coverage Ratio (DSCR)	1.36
Cash Flow Available After Debt Service	$20,265,80

$720,000 loan, amortized over 20 years at an interest rate of 4.94%

Description

A commercial mortgage is a loan for a commercial property, which is a long-term fixed asset. The commercial property may be an apartment complex, mixed-use building, office building, warehouse or shopping center. The property is the collateral. For more information about commercial real estate lending, see appendix for Underserved Markets: Community Lenders Extend a Helping Hand.

Purpose of Funds

Purchase commercial property. Lenders may want to see the business occupy 51 percent of the building—anything below that percent threshold is considered speculation. A property with tenants is viewed favorably. If there is a construction component to the project, the lender may assist with bridge financing (temporary financing), until permanent financing can be put into place, after work has been completed.

Requirements

Banks will want to see the standard documents: Business plan, personal tax returns, business tax returns, personal financial statement, Income Statement, Balance Sheet, Cash Flow Statement or Projections, proforma for the building, Accounts Receivable and Accounts Payable Aging Report.

Technical Assistance

Under the SBA's 504 program, a local community development organization will be part of the deal along with a bank.

Credit Score

Commercial lenders are concerned with the ability of the business to repay the loan, not as much with the credit score because the collateral will be the property, reducing risk.

Term

Commercial real estate transactions will have a term of up to 25 years. The SBA 504 program will finance up to 90 percent of the project costs. Banks typically will finance 80% LTV, the lesser of the appraised value or purchase price.

Interest
Check Bankrate.com or a participating SBA lender, to gauge mortgage rates.

Fees
Some lenders may charge a loan origination fee.

Payments
Payments are made monthly directly to the lender. On a bridge loan, only interest payments will be made, until the final payment is due.

Prepayment
Banks will charge a prepayment penalty. However, the prepayment declines over time. Many nonprofit lenders do not charge a prepayment fee.

Personal Guarantee
A personal guarantee is required.

Collateral
For commercial real estate, loan-to-value (LTV) is important. The property is the collateral to secure the loan, and the lender will hold the deed to any commercial property acquired until the note has been paid in full. The lender will file a UCC-1 on any equipment purchased with the proceeds of the loan.

Rating
Good & Cheap. For commercial real estate, the bank may take up to 90 plus days to conduct their due diligence and to close the transaction. It's not fast, but you will get the best rates available through conventional lenders or one that participates in the SBA 504 program.

Additional Cost

The lender will often require the client to pay both the lender's and the client's closing costs. Legal fees on a loan of this size vary. Contact your attorney for an estimate.

Where to Look

Contact your local bank or participating SBA lender.

TAKEAWAY: Why rent, when you can own?

47

ACCOUNTS RECEIVABLE FACTORING: SELL YOUR ASSETS

OVERVIEW

Cash is king. Accounts receivable factoring (also known as invoice financing) is selling your receivables to another party who will provide cash in exchange for the receivables. A receivable is money owed to a business in the form of an invoice. Factoring is designed to help a business improve its cash flow by getting paid quicker.

Here's a simple explanation: ABC Metal Supplier provides West Machine Shop with credit terms to purchase materials, which creates an I.O.U. or receivable for ABC Metal Supplier. ABC benefits because the credit terms attract a new customer. But ABC will not get paid for 30 days or more, creating a cash flow problem. Receivables are assets on the balance sheet. Factoring is selling that asset. The factoring company now owns the receivables and is responsible for collecting the debt. In exchange for selling the receivables, the business will receive an upfront payment of 80 percent (could be more or less) of the value of the receivables. A certain percentage of the receivable is paid in cash, minus a discount rate (invoices that may not be collected) and a reserve (funds held back until the receivables are paid). When paid, the company receives the final payment, minus fees.

There's no limit to how often a company can sell accounts receivables. The quicker a business gets paid, the better. Selling on credit, which is what accounts receivables are, does have a cost. That cost is the possibility the business extending credit will not receive some, or all of the funds owed. A factor assumes risk by buying the accounts receivables. The factor provides other services such as weekly or monthly reports on the status of accounts receivables sold. Selling receivables to a factoring company transfers the ownership of the receivable to the factoring company. Once this happens, the receivables come off the balance sheet as a short-term asset. Factoring is not the same as asset-based lending (ABL), which can be called commercial finance. An ABL will lend strictly against collateral to secure a loan, when cash flow is insufficient. The credit facility (loan or line of credit) is secured by all business assets such as inventory, equipment, and accounts receivables. A lender will develop a borrowing base that the business can borrow against. The LTV may be as much as 80 percent of the assets.

Description

Accounts receivable factoring is selling accounts receivables to a company (factor) and receiving cash up front, minus a fee and certain amount held back (reserves) until the receivable is paid. The factor owns the accounts receivable, manages the assets, and collects on the debt.

Purpose of Funds

Funds to be used at the owner's discretion. Companies sell their accounts receivables to generate cash quicker, versus waiting 30 days or longer from a customer.

Requirements

The factor will evaluate the strength of the receivables. For example, the receivables must be less than 30 days old. The factor will look at the credit worthiness of the invoices outstanding. The owner has the option to choose which invoices they want to factor.

Technical Assistance

N/A

Credit Score

The factor weighs the strength of the accounts receivables under consideration for sale, not the credit of the business selling the accounts receivables. Therefore, the credit score is not relevant.

Term

Funds are repaid in weeks or months. Terms vary by factor.

Interest

The interest (or discount rate) on this product is two to six percent of the invoice total. Rates can be weekly or monthly. Fees can be on the full invoice amount or the advance.

Fees

The factor will provide a list of fees: application, credit check, due diligence, ACH or wire, service, lockbox and early termination. These fees can add up.

Payments
The business selling the receivables gets cash, usually 80 percent of the receivables being sold, less a percentage held back until the customer pays the bill. A business may sell receivables as frequently as they desire.

Prepayment
Some companies charge an early termination fee.

Personal Guarantee
N/A

Collateral
The factor doesn't advance 100 percent of the receivables. In essence, the factor is using the accounts receivables as collateral.

Rating
Good. Fast. This type of financing is good from the standpoint in that it helps the business collect cash quickly. However, the business receives less than the full value of the receivables. If the business can use the cash to generate additional sales, the cost may be worth it. It is recommended a business do a cost-benefit analysis to weigh the pros and cons.

Additional Cost
There may be legal costs for an attorney to evaluate and explain the factoring agreement.

Where to Look
Factors are all over the country. Do your homework and look for factors that have the best reputation. Search online reviews for positive and negative reviews from customers. BlueVine, Fundbox, Fluid and American Receivable are some of the companies in this industry.

TAKEAWAY: Getting paid quicker is the game.

48

PRIVATE LENDERS:
A HARD BARGAIN

OVERVIEW

When the Great Recession hit, and investment yields declined, investors plowed money into lending to small businesses. They viewed this market as an asset-class with above-market return potential and lower risk than comparable investment opportunities. Private lenders are investors or companies that are willing to lend to you when a bank will not. They are sometimes referred to as "hard money" lenders, because residential or commercial real estate is the hard asset that secures the loan. A short-term loan secured by real estate may be a better way to describe a hard money lender.

Investopedia refers to hard money lenders as, "A loan of 'last resort' or a short-term bridge loan. The borrower can use a single-family home, commercial, mixed-use, multifamily, industrial properties or land as collateral. Private lenders

244

work best for construction loans, fix and flip, land loans and when the borrower has less than stellar credit. This type of loan is usually for one to five years. If a business owner needs money fast to capitalize on an opportunity, this may be the right fit.

Securing a bank loan can take 90 days or more; whereas, a private lender can approve a deal on paper in a day or so. A hard money lender will require the borrower to complete a loan application, which will include personal information, and may pull your credit report. If the borrower has judgements, liens or other derogatory information in his file, the lender may choose not to proceed. For many hard money lenders, the value of the property is the key factor in the decision-making process of whether to lend. The lender will offer a loan-to-value (LTV) of between 50 to 70 percent of the value of the property—lower than a traditional bank. The advantage of a hard money lender is speed. A primary drawback of this type of financing is the cost. Hard money lenders want to generate a twenty percent return on investment, given the inherent risks. See appendix for When Banks Say "No": Private Lenders Step Up.

Description
Private lenders, which are nonbank entities or investors, lend against hard assets, primarily real estate.

Purpose of Funds
Funds are used for any business need, at the discretion of the business owner.

Requirements
Lenders will request documentation: personal financial statement and personal/business tax returns for the past two years. Some private lenders may require additional information. However, the value of the property will drive the

decision process for the lender and will serve as the collateral securing their investment.

Technical Assistance
A bookkeeper or accountant can be of assistance in putting together the necessary documents.

Credit Score
The lender may review your credit score, but the value of the collateral securing the loan is the driving force in the underwriting process. However, a negative credit report with recent derogatory information could persuade a lender to pass on the deal.

Term
Loan terms are usually one to five years, often referred to as a bridge loan, which gives the business time to search for permanent financing. Each deal varies based on the lender's criteria.

Interest
This type of funding is expensive. Investors are looking to make a 20 percent return on investment. The interest rate on the loan can be up to 15 percent. Most private lenders charge an application fee as well.

Fees
Lenders usually charge an application, appraisal, underwriting, late, legal and collections fee.

Payments
Payments are monthly.

Prepayment
There is no advantage to pay the deal off quicker because the return to the investor is locked in.

Personal Guarantee

The real estate is the collateral securing the loan. Some lenders may also request a personal guarantee.

Collateral

Real estate is the primary collateral.

Rating

Good. Fast. Businesses that seek this type of funding cannot get traditional funding, or if they can, the business can't afford to wait months for the funding. Businesses are paying for speed and the risk to the lender.

Additional Cost

If payments are late, there could be additional fees and legal costs of collections. Review the commitment letter for the details.

Where to Look

Talk to your banker, accountant or attorney. Most private lenders don't advertise and are accessible only through referrals. Worth Avenue Capital and the Raymond C. Green Companies are two examples of private lenders.

TAKEAWAY: Private lenders can be expensive.

49

EQUIPMENT FINANCING:
TO LEASE OR BUY?

OVERVIEW

Equipment can make a business more productive and efficient when utilized to maximum capacity. A number of financing products exist to acquire equipment. Some businesses choose to purchase used equipment because they can get like-new assets with a long useful life, at competitive prices. The big challenge is figuring out if it makes sense to purchase or lease equipment. Both purchasing and leasing have advantages that will impact your cash flow and bottom line. In a purchase scenario, the equipment can serve as collateral to secure the loan. Banks finance equipment. The useful life of the equipment will dictate how long the term of the financing will be. The advantages of purchasing are that you own it and get the best price by paying up front. Some of the disadvantages of purchasing are the large down payment, the asset depreciates, the cost of repairs and maintenance. Plus, a bank loan could take up to 60 days or more to complete the closing.

A lease requires no money down, no upfront payment or collateral. When the end of the term of the lease approaches, the owner can renew the lease, terminate it or purchase the equipment for the fair market value. Equipment that tends to breakdown or require expensive repairs after a certain period could push you toward a lease. The advantages of leasing are, no collateral, no large out-of-pocket down payment, and no liens or personal guarantee required. It is often easier to qualify for a lease than a loan to purchase equipment. With a lease, you're not locked into a long-term commitment. You get the latest equipment along with the tax incentives of leasing. (Talk to your accountant for tax implications.) Your credit score will not be a factor in the lease. The biggest disadvantage of a lease is that is usually more expensive than purchasing.

There are two types of leases worth exploring: capital lease and operating lease. A capital lease is a type of ownership where the asset is on the company's balance sheet. This type of lease is for equipment that has a long useful life with few technological changes. Capital leases may be eligible for depreciation. For example, a pizza oven may be a capital lease. An operating lease (known as a service lease) is for equipment that is updated frequently due to wear and tear or technological obsolescence. A copier is a piece of equipment that meets that criteria. The business gets to use the equipment without taking on ownership. The cost of the operating lease is an operating expense. The more your lender understands about your business, industry, and cycles, the better she can help you get approved for the financing that fits your needs.

Description
Equipment can be purchased or leased. From a leasing prospective, there are two options: capital or operating lease. Consult with your accountant regarding the tax benefits. Tax laws may push you in one direction over the other.

Purpose of Funds
Capital to purchase or lease equipment for your business.

Requirements
If you purchase the equipment, the lender will want to know about the business, but the equipment will serve as the collateral for the financing. Most banks will want to see personal tax returns, business tax returns, personal financial statement, Income Statement, Balance Sheet, Cash Flow Statement or Projections, Accounts Receivable/Accounts Payable Aging Report. On the other hand, a lease will not require as much documentation because the equipment will serve as the collateral.

Technical Assistance
Talk to your local banker or an equipment leasing company. Make sure you get your accountant involved in the decision-making process.

Credit Score
Commercial lenders will pull your credit report. Leasing companies will not use your credit score as a factor to lease the equipment to you.

Term
The term will vary depending on whether you purchase or lease the equipment.

Interest
Leasing is usually more expensive financing than buying. Run the numbers. Calculate the true cost of the equipment.

Fees
A lease does not require money up front. Banks will charge a fee to provide the capital.

Payments
Monthly payments will be required.

Prepayment
A bank may charge a prepayment penalty.

Personal Guarantee
For a bank loan, a personal guarantee is required.

Collateral
The equipment is the collateral, which is sufficient to secure the loan or lease.

Rating
Good & Fast applies to equipment leasing. On the loan side, Good & Cheap is the standard.

Additional Cost
The lender will often require the client to pay both the lender's and the client's closing costs on a loan. Review your lease. The lease will require the business to have general liability insurance coverage, or there could be a return fee and late fees.

Where to Look
Contact your local bank or leasing company.

TAKEAWAY: Leasing has upside.

PART V
Side B:
Mostly Equity

50

CROWDFUNDING:
SMALL DOLLARS FROM MANY

OVERVIEW

One vehicle to raise capital for your business is crowdfunding. Crowdfunding is soliciting small contributions from the public using the internet.

Before we jump into crowdfunding, let's get familiar with the three types:

1. Donation
2. Reward
3. Investment

Donation-based crowdfunding is receiving money for nothing specific in return. People who contribute want to be part of helping someone and supporting a cause. GoFundMe is one of the more popular websites where anyone can solicit or receive funds. Its website states, "Launched in 2010,

GoFundMe is the world's largest social fundraising platform, with over $5 billion raised so far. With a community of more than 50 million donors, GoFundMe is changing the way the world gives."[1]

Reward crowdfunding is contributing to a project and receiving merchandise, a discount on the product, or other type of thank-you gift. Kickstarter is the largest platform for reward-based crowdfunding. On Kickstarter, projects have received over $3.5 billion pledged to date. Over 139,000 projects have successfully reached their funding goals. The success rate is approaching 36 percent on Kickstarter. Indiegogo is similar to Kickstarter. The primary difference is that a Kickstarter campaign is not successful unless it meets its goal by the deadline. If the project doesn't meet its goal, it doesn't receive any of the pledged funds. In contrast, all funds pledged on Indiegogo go to the campaign, regardless if the goal is reached.

With the passage of the JOBS Act in 2012, and SEC regulations on May 16th 2016, the general public can participate in a new form of investment crowdfunding (also known as regulation crowdfunding). Some people refer to this category as equity crowdfunding, which is a misnomer because all investments don't have to be equity. Loans and royalty streams can be offered. However, non-accredited investors must go through the SEC/FINRA approved platforms, or registered broker-dealer platforms, to invest. The two main challenges with this type of investment is that i) this is an indirect form of fundraising, since a company is prohibited from directly soliciting investments from the public (instead they must send them to a platform to learn more and ask questions); and ii) there is no liquid secondary marketplace to sell shares, such as the New York Stock Exchange. Wefunder, an investment crowdfunding platform, says, "It's safest to assume you cannot resell your investment to another investor."[2] "Regulation Crowdfunding specifically prohibits resale of securities for one year, except to the issuer, an accredited investor, a family member or to one's trust."[3] See appendix for *Wefunder x Hopster.*

Description
Crowdfunding is soliciting small contributions from the public over the internet. There are three different categories of crowdfunding, with DPOs included with investment crowdfunding.

Purpose of Funds
To secure capital to grow the business.

Requirements
While investment crowdfunding has been opened up to the masses, non-accredited investors must use approved platforms. As always, talk to an attorney about securities investment issues.

Technical Assistance
Resources are plentiful on crowdfunding. The best thing to do is to observe successful crowdfunding campaigns. Look for projects that are similar to your business or industry. Check out their websites, story, product names, logo and products.

Credit Score
N/A

Term
Varies based on the type of crowdfunding the owner embarks on.

Interest

Investment crowdfunding may be equity, a loan or royalty stream. Check Bankrate for the prime interest rate, to see what the commercial interest rate environment looks like.

Fees

Kickstarter and Indiegogo charge almost ten percent, which includes merchant processing fees. Check each platform for a breakdown of the fees.

Payments

N/A

Prepayment

N/A

Personal Guarantee

N/A

Collateral

N/A

Rating

Good & Cheap. Crowdfunding takes a considerable amount of effort and time. Certain skills will have to be hired to assist with your campaign, whether it be a graphic designer or copy editor. Some campaigns have hired social media and public relations teams.

Additional Cost

Don't cut corners when it comes to hiring an attorney regarding investment crowdfunding. Offering securities can be very risky if not done right. This type of legal work can be expensive but will save you money in the long run.

Where to Look

GoFundMe, Kickstarter, Indiegogo, and Wefunder are examples of donation, reward and investment crowdfunding. Here are platforms for accredited investors looking for opportunities: CircleUp, AngelList, SeedInvest and EarlyShares.

TAKEAWAY: Go direct to your supporters.

"Beautiful," Snoop Dogg featuring Pharrell,
Uncle Charlie Wilson, *The Best of Snoop Dogg*

51

ACCREDITED INVESTORS: PROS WITH MONEY SEEKING A RETURN

OVERVIEW

Whether you call them angels, micro-VCs, venture capitalists or family offices, they have one thing in common: money. They have it, and you want it for your business. On the investor trail, angel investors will be the first ones encountered. Angel investors are high-net worth individuals who are accredited investors. The SEC defines an accredited investor as someone who has made over $200,000 ($300,000 as a couple) the past two years, or has over $1 million in assets, not including their primary residence. A business with over $5 million can also qualify as an accredited investor. When soliciting capital, make sure you talk to an accredited investor, or things could go sideways. Angels usually invest about $35,000 per deal or $300,000 as a group.

Micro-VCs are seed-stage investors who invest from $25,000 to $500,000 in promising start-up businesses. Their funds are usually less than $50 million. They deploy a business model similar to venture capital (VC) firms. The purpose of such funds is to invest in early-stage companies. Today, many VC funds put aside capital to invest in seed-stage companies, because the competition for the next big thing is fierce. VCs want to mark their territory by investing in young, innovative companies. At stake is the next Uber-like valuation.

The U.S. venture capital (VC) industry invested $84 billion in 8,035 companies over 8,076 deals in 2017, which was a record amount distributed since the early 2000s.[1] VC firms raise money from insurance companies, hedge funds, institutions and wealthy individuals to invest in early-stage companies with high-growth potential. The investors are called limited partners (LPs) and the fund is run by a general partner (GP). The business model is to invest in growing companies and cash out when they are acquired or go public. Apple, Google, Amazon, Facebook and Microsoft were all companies that received investments. VCs seek to find the next "It" company and make a fortune. They tend to invest millions of dollars in the early stages and will invest in follow-on rounds.

Family Offices are private wealth advisory firms who serve ultra-high-net-worth individuals (ultra-HNWI). They manage both the financial and investment needs of their clients, providing a complete solution for wealth management. Family offices touch all aspects of wealth: business, taxes, wealth transfer, charitable giving, insurance and budgeting. Nothing has to be outscored. A single family office (SFO) serves one family; whereas, a multi-family office (MFO) serves more than one wealthy family. MFOs can serve hundreds of clients, with billions under investment. *Bloomberg Market's* "Annual Ranking of the Richest Family Offices" ranked Northern Trust number two in the world with $112 billion under management for

3,457 families.[2] Family offices have the resources to invest in early-stage businesses. If you can get to a gatekeeper—and find the hidden door—with a warm welcome, family offices are an option for startup capital.

Private equity (PE) investors seek to buy 100 percent of underperforming companies. PwC predicts that the entire private equity, hedge fund and alternatives industry is expected to double to $21 trillion under management globally by 2025, a more than double increase, according to the *Wall Street Journal.*[3] At the heart of what they do is turning around an underperforming business and selling it within five years: a fix-and-flip strategy. PE firms leverage funds from investors or banks and use little of their own funds. Their skill set is turning around the company and seeking a liquidity event to cash in on their investment. They see value where no one else does—like the person who sees treasure in a blighted building where others see junk. If your business has had success in the past, but is struggling, PE may be interested in kicking the tires.

See appendix for Raising Capital, And A Business: An Interview with Michael Duncan.

Description
Angel investors are high-net worth individuals who are accredited investors, who provide seed or early-stage funds to grow private businesses, in exchange for equity.

Purpose of Funds
Capital used to start or grow a business.

Requirements
High-growth startups or businesses that have the potential to dominate their industry.

Technical Assistance
Investors will provide access to their network and mentoring to their portfolio companies.

Credit Score
Investors bet on entrepreneurs and the management team, not their credit scores.

Term
Most investors want to be out of a company within five to seven years of making the initial investment.

Interest
Investors want a 10X return or higher. It's not unheard of for an investor to make a 20 or 30X return. Investors get their return when the business is sold, not from interest payments.

Fees
Securities are complex. Most deals require attorneys, accountants and consultants.

Payments
The return happens when the business goes public or is acquired.

Prepayment
N/A

Personal Guarantee
N/A

Collateral
No collateral is required to receive an equity investment.

Rating

Good. If you are working on a startup business, accredited investors may be your solution to funding.

Additional Cost

An accountant, attorney and advisor are mandatory.

Where to Look

If you believe you have an idea that will revolutionize your field, you may want to consider accredited investors. Read about the top angel groups and VC firms. Learn about their investment strategies. Look for compatibility with companies that are in their portfolios. Search for a local angel group in your area or state. Visit the Angel Capital Association to find angels at angelcapitalassociation.org/directory/. Search Gust.com, a website linking companies looking for capital and accredited investors.

TAKEAWAY: Accredited investors are the standard.

52

ACCELERATORS & INCUBATORS:
JUMPSTART YOUR IDEA
OR BUSINESS

OVERVIEW

Accelerators and incubators are like brother and sister. Accelerators are focused on scaling a business and incubators on innovation of ideas. The purpose of an accelerator is to stimulate and expedite the growth of a business. Startup accelerators work with businesses in the early stage; whereas, an incubator helps create ideas that will become a business in the future. Accelerator programs will work with a business for a few weeks to three or four months. During this time, the accelerator provides technical assistance to the business. The top accelerators are like prestigious colleges—they are very selective and will connect you to their powerful network of successful people, if you are accepted.

Y Combinator (YC), 500 Startups, Techstars, MassChallenge, Plug and Play, Coplex and Dreamit have been mentioned as the best accelerators in the country. These programs often have an application process that seeks to find the best startups or ideas. Once accepted into an accelerator program, the founders of the business must relocate to where the accelerator is located for a period of up to three months. The accelerators hand out capital to a startup business and receive up to 10 percent of the business in equity. At the end of the formal program, the companies attend a pitch session to entice investors to invest.

On the other hand, incubators charge a fee for access to discounted services, training and mentors, a much different business model from accelerators. Universities sponsor incubators to help commercialize research into useful products and viable businesses.

An article on the TechRepublic website, "Accelerators vs. Incubators: What startups need to know," states, "If an accelerator is a greenhouse for young plants to get the optimal conditions to grow, an incubator matches quality seeds with the best soil for sprouting and growth."[1] Incubators can be affiliated with a college, government entity or corporation. Businesses in the incubator share a location with other startups and can stay indefinitely until the business achieves certain milestones. There is usually an application process for acceptance into the incubator. Idealab has been a successful incubator, with over 45 IPOs from 150 companies created since 1996.[2] A co-working space is not an accelerator or incubator. Know the difference.

Description
Accelerators are focused on scaling a business and incubators on innovation of ideas.

Purpose of Funds
Capital comes in the form of dollars, resources (physical space or equipment) and human talent. Accelerators help grow an existing business and incubators serve as places to grow a nascent idea.

Requirements
Accelerators and incubators have an application process to gain admission. A business must have a scalable idea in a large market with growth potential. If your business is not in a growing industry or lacks an innovative idea, it may not be worth your time to apply for an accelerator program.

Technical Assistance
You will have access to some of the brightest entrepreneurial minds and mentors. Going through an accelerator program is like getting a college degree from a selective university. Incubators provide assistance to grow your idea and put you on track by connecting you to the entrepreneurial ecosystem in your area.

Credit Score
N/A

Term
Investors are seeking to exit their investment within a five to seven-year period.

Interest
Equity often comes in the form of convertible notes—another way of saying it's a loan that will convert to equity at some point in the future. A Simple Agreement for Future Equity (SAFE) is common for some accelerators, including Y Combinator (YC): ycombinator.com/documents/

Fees
Before accepting equity, hire an attorney to review the documents

Payments
Investors seek to cash out of the investment. Prior to that time, no payment is required. Incubator participants will be charged a fee.

Prepayment
N/A

Personal Guarantee
N/A

Collateral
N/A

Rating
Good. Raising capital is a job in and of itself. It can take up to a year to raise funds for a business. Equity is often a good option for a business that is in the early stage. At this point in development, most startup businesses don't have the cash flow or a proven track record to get traditional financing.

Additional Cost
This varies depending on the expertise required.

Where to Look
Review the top accelerator programs and their criteria. Many cities outside of Silicon Valley, New York City and Boston, have developed accelerator programs to attract the best new startup businesses. Incubators are available in cities throughout the U.S.

TAKEAWAY: Money and mentors to help you grow.

53

SMALL BUSINESS INVESTMENT COMPANIES: GOVERNMENT-FUNDED VCs

OVERVIEW

Created by Congress, and launched in 1958, the Small Business Investment Company (SBIC) Program is run by the SBA, which issues debt to venture capitalists, private equity funds and other types of investments that match the funds to invest in fast-growing, small businesses. "The SBIC Program leverages the full faith and credit of the U.S. government to increase the pool of investment capital available to small businesses," according to the SBA website.[1] Since its inception, the program has invested over $67 billion in 166,000 businesses. In 2015, the program invested $6.2 billion in 1,200 companies. As an investment program, the goal is to increase access to capital for growth-stage businesses.

For every dollar private investors (pensions, foundations, banks and high-net worth individuals) invest in an SBIC,

269

the SBA invests $2 of government-guaranteed debt, up to a maximum of $150 million. SBICs invest the funds in businesses. The private investors are "Limited Partners" (LP) in the SBIC and assemble the matching funds required to access SBA-guaranteed leverage. SBIC fund managers are responsible for compliance with SBA regulations and limited partner relations. Fund managers create their investment strategy and monitor companies with the ultimate goal of a liquidity event (exit from the investment).

The SBIC Program defines a small business as a business with a tangible net worth of less than $19.5 million AND an average of $6.5 million in net income over the previous two years at the time of investment. A business may also be deemed "small" using SBA's North American Industry Classification System (NAICS) code standards. A small business is defined as having a tangible net worth of less than $6 million AND an average of $2 million in net income over the previous two years at the time of investment. Apple, Intel, FedEx, Tesla, Costco Wholesale, Pandora, Whole Foods, Staples and Amgen have received SBIC Program funds.

Description

The SBIC Program invests in fast-growing, small businesses through issuing debt to venture capitalists, CDFIs, private equity funds and others who invest in America's small, high-growth businesses.

Purpose of Funds

The goal is to increase access to capital for growth-stage businesses, to be used at the business owner's discretion.

Requirements

SBICs have their own due diligence process, which usually includes reviewing a company's business plan, business tax returns, Income Statement, Balance Sheet, Cash Flow

Statement or Projections, Accounts Receivable and Accounts Payable Aging Report. Ultimately, investors are investing in the management team's ability to grow the business.

Technical Assistance
SBICs are encouraged to help their portfolio companies grow. They provide connections to new customers and other sources of assistance helpful to the business.

Credit Score
Long-term growth is the key criteria, not credit score, when it comes to an investment.

Term
Funds have a life span of ten years. Investors are seeking a liquidity event within five to seven years of making the initial investment. SBICs are constantly raising new funds, after their initial capital has been deployed. New monies in a fund are usually deployed within two to three years. During this time, a fund may make follow-on investments in the company as other investors come in.

Interest
N/A

Fees
There are legal fees involved with closing an equity investment. Contact your attorney to learn more.

Payments
With a typical equity investment, there are no monthly, quarterly or annual payments. In theory, your investors are aligned with your interests and seek to make their return at a later time when they sell their investment in the business.

Prepayment
N/A

Personal Guarantee
Equity investments do not require a personal guarantee.

Collateral
No collateral is required to receive an equity investment.

Rating
Good. This type of investment is suited for the entrepreneurial company that is growing fast, and for which debt is not a viable option. In the end, equity is not cheap because the owner is giving up a stake in the company.

Additional Cost
There may be additional costs in the form of hiring experts to value the business and close the transaction.

Where to Look
Search the SBIC database: sba.gov/funding-programs/investment-capital#paragraph-11.

The Small Business Investors Alliance (sbia.org) is a trade group for venture capital, or visit the National Venture Capital Association (NVCA) at nvca.org.

TAKEAWAY: SBICs grow businesses.

54

BUSINESS DEVELOPMENT COMPANIES: DEBT, EQUITY AND A HELPING HAND

OVERVIEW

Congress created Business Development Companies (BDCs) in 1980 in an amendment to the Investment Company Act of 1940. During the late 1990s and early 2000s, the number of business development companies grew. The purpose of a BDC, which can be a publicly-traded company, is to finance small businesses. BDCs can support startups, growth companies and mature businesses. They are unique in that they can lend, invest or offer a combination of the two for their portfolio companies. BDCs provide growing companies with capital and guidance. A key requirement is that 70 percent of their assets must be loaned or invested in small- and mid-sized companies.

A BDC is a combination of a venture capital firm, lender and public holding company. Investors in a BDC don't own shares in the individual companies, they own shares in the BDC, a type of closed-end fund that raises a fixed amount of capital through an IPO. A closed-end fund is defined as "a publicly traded investment company by the SEC," according to Investopedia. It raises a fixed amount of capital through an IPO and a manager oversees the portfolio of investments. BDCs invest in small- to midsize-businesses, with an emphasis on middle-market companies. Investopedia defines middle-market companies as firms with revenue from $10 million to $1 billion dollars.

Unlike venture capital or private equity, BDCs give the general public an opportunity to invest in small- to mid-sized businesses through the sale of their stocks. The BDCs invest in businesses, whether via debt, equity or a combination of the two. Prior to the JOBS Act legislation, BDCs were one of the few ways the general public could invest in private small- to mid-sized businesses.

Description
BDCs invest in small- to mid-sized companies. BDC funds are used to help businesses grow, whether that be for working capital, inventory, a strategic acquisition or to purchase equipment.

Purpose of Funds
The goal is to increase access to capital for growth-stage businesses, to be used at the business owner's discretion.

Requirements
Each investment company has its own due diligence process, which usually includes reviewing a company's business plan, business tax returns, Income Statement, Balance Sheet, Cash Flow Statement or Projections, Accounts Receivable

and Accounts Payable Aging Report. Investors are investing in the management team's ability to grow the business.

Technical Assistance

The BDC is encouraged to help their portfolio companies grow. They provide connections to new customers and other sources of assistance helpful to the business.

Credit Score

Long-term growth prospect is the key criteria, not credit score, when it comes to the BDC making an investment.

Term

Debt terms can be similar in length to a bank loan of 5 to 10 years, depending on the use of the proceeds. Equity investments vary.

Interest

Interest rates are higher than bank financing, due to the perceived risk.

Fees

Contact your attorney to learn more.

Payments

For debt products, there will be monthly, quarterly or annual payments on the debt.

Prepayment

Depends on how the deal is structured.

Personal Guarantee

Equity investments do not require a personal guarantee.

Collateral

No collateral is required to receive an equity investment.

Rating

Good. This type of investment is suited for the entrepreneurial company that is growing fast, and for which bank debt is not a viable option. In the end, equity is not cheap because the owner is giving up a stake in the company.

Additional Cost

There may be additional cost in the form of hiring experts to value the business.

Where to Look

BDCInvestor tracks publicly traded BDCs. Review some BDCs at bdcinvestor.com/business-development-company-list/.

TAKEAWAY: Closed-end fund invests in businesses.

55

MEZZANINE FINANCING:
THE CAPITAL MIX

OVERVIEW

Mezzanine financing is a hybrid instrument of debt and equity. This type of financing is subordinate to venture capital and senior lenders. Picture a triangle. At the top of the triangle is equity, which is an ownership stake in the company. See image below. At the bottom of the triangle is senior debt secured by a claim on the business' assets. Mezzanine sits in the middle of the triangle, like an escalator connecting one floor to the next.

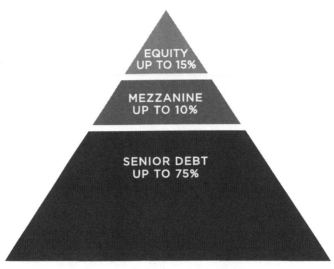

MEZZANINE FINANCING % OF DEAL

Mezzanine financing appears as equity on the balance sheet, which can make the company more attractive for future debt financing. Interest on the debt can be paid in monthly, quarterly or yearly installments, based on the agreement with the lender. Should the business face difficulty, interest can be deferred to a future date by rolling it into the outstanding balance. Mezzanine lenders take on greater risk than debt lenders and have no claim on assets like senior lenders, should something go wrong. No collateral is required for mezzanine financing. However, the company must demonstrate long-term growth potential. Borrowers like that interest is tax-deductible. The debt portion of the financing converts to equity in the event of default, and can be sold at any time.

Lenders who provide mezzanine financing receive warrants or options as part of the deal, to compensate for risk and to generate a fair return on their capital. The Motley Fool states, "A mezzanine debt investment will include a free "kicker," usually in the form of a small slice of ownership, or an option (warrants), which entitle the debt investor to buy equity in the company at a future date."[1] The equity, warrants and options compensate the lender for the perceived risk. Mezzanine financing is high risk with the potential for high reward for the lender. A typical mezzanine interest rate is 12 to 20 percent, according to Investopedia.

Description

Mezzanine financing is a hybrid financial instrument that bridges both debt and equity capital structures. Private equity firms use mezzanine financing to acquire businesses. Some businesses will seek mezzanine financing when debt from a bank is not available.

Purpose of Funds

The goal is to increase access to capital for growth-stage businesses, to be used at the business owner's discretion.

Requirements

To attract mezzanine financing, a business must have a stable operating history and a track record of success. The mezzanine funder will review previous financing and write-ups about the company and perform due diligence. The reputation and strength of the lenders and investors can influence a deal. The firm will review the business plan, business tax returns and interim Profit & Loss Statement, Balance Sheet and cash flow. Mezzanine lenders are looking at the future prospects of the business and the industry.

Technical Assistance

N/A

Credit Score

N/A

Term

The terms vary for each deal.

Interest
The interest rate for mezzanine financing can be up to 20 percent.

Fees
Some of the fees will be rolled into the loan.

Payments
Interest payments on the loan can be monthly, quarterly or yearly.

Prepayment
N/A

Personal Guarantee
N/A

Collateral
N/A

Rating
Good. Mezzanine deals are more expensive than bank financing, but in the long run, much cheaper than all equity deals.

Additional Cost
Expect accounting and legal fees.

Where to Look
One mezzanine finance company is Escalate Capital: escalatecapital.com.

TAKEAWAY: Capital structured as debt and equity.

56

DIRECT PUBLIC OFFERING: THE BEN AND JERRY'S WAY

OVERVIEW

A direct public offering (DPO) is a term used to describe the process of selling securities through public solicitation to unaccredited investors. It is also known as investment crowdfunding, but it differs from the new JOBS Act crowdfunding rules that allow for an indirect offering via a registered platform.

A DPO is a tool for a for-profit or nonprofit revenue-producing business to raise capital directly from the public by offering securities, without hiring a broker-dealer, underwriter, or registering the offering with the SEC. DPOs must still be filed with one or more states where the offerings will take place.

In the past, it was believed that only accredited investors could partake in securities of private companies. However, long before the JOBS Act was signed into law in 2012, DPOs opened up investing in private companies to the masses. Ben & Jerry's and Annie's Homegrown (now owned by General Mills, the parent company of Pillsbury and Cheerios) are two companies that used a DPO to raise capital over 30 years ago. The DPO remains one of the most cost-effective securities vehicles to solicit funds from the public.

The cost of going public is not feasible for a small business for many reasons, including the complexity, cost, and lack of access to underwriters who only service very large companies. Smaller companies find themselves cut off from the typical sources of capital. However, exemptions exist within securities laws to allow companies to raise capital without having to follow the typical registrations with the SEC.

DPOs are legal based on existing laws that provide for one of the following exemptions: Regulation A+, Regulation D - Rule 504, and Rule 147 (the "intrastate exemption").

- Rule 147. A DPO that raises funds from residents in only one state is exempt from federal registration, but the offering must receive state approval. Generally, there is no limit to how much can be raised for an intrastate DPO.

- Regulation D – Rule 504. Companies that wish to raise funds from residents of several states can do so under Rule 504. The maximum amount that can be raised is $5 million in a 12-month period. The offering must be approved by securities regulators in each state where general solicitation takes place, and one of those states is the principal reviewer of the offering.

- Regulation A+ (previously knowns as Regulation A) is a type of DPO, but requires filing with the SEC. An offering under Regulation A is allowed in two different tiers, and can raise up to $50 million in Tier 2. Moreover, it allows investors to "test the waters" to gauge the interest in offering securities prior to filing with the SEC.

The pros of a DPO are:

- Cost is lower than other options.
- Public solicitation allows companies to talk to potential investors directly, including advertising.
- Companies can raise more with a DPO than on the JOBS Act platforms or through intrastate crowdfunding.
- By going direct to customers, the DPO can strengthen the connection between the company, organization and its supporters.
- Companies can use the same marketing strategies normally used to reach their customers.

The cons of a DPO are:

- The owner does some of the work to get the DPO ready, including business plan development, financials and projections.
- The company principals must devote significant time with a larger pool of potential investors, many of whom may need education about investing.
- The offer has to be registered in every state where the offering will take place, including one primary state filing that will be reviewed.
- Since the DPO will not be listed on a major stock exchange, investors may have a liquidity problem when it comes to selling because there is no secondary market for DPOs, such as the New York Stock Exchange.

Description

A direct public offering (DPO) is a term used to describe the process of selling securities through public solicitation to unaccredited investors.

Purpose of Funds
Raise capital for a business or nonprofit. Make sure the funds spent are consistent with the offering approved by regulators.

Requirements
Businesses or nonprofits with access to a large customer or fan base tend to do well. The offering must remain in compliance with state securities regulators.

Technical Assistance
Cutting Edge Capital is a company that specializes in DPOs. Visit their website for more: cuttingedgecapital.com

Credit Score
N/A

Term
This varies based on what was presented in the offering. For example, a company could offer loans with a specific interest rate or royalty financing.

Interest
Your investors should have a connection to your business or mission, so they don't expect a dividend or interest rate higher than the business can afford.

Fees
Hire an attorney and other professionals to prepare your offering documents for approval by your state or the SEC (if a Regulation A).

Payments
This varies based on the security offered.

Prepayment
N/A

Personal Guarantee
N/A

Collateral
N/A

Rating
Good. Cheap. It will take time and skill to develop the DPO documents, which is why an experienced securities attorney is a prerequisite. Securities law is complex and regulators are stern when it comes to protecting the public from unscrupulous businesses.

Additional Cost
This varies depending on the expertise you hire. For some, marketing is difficult, so they will need to hire marketing expertise. If successful, you may have to create a system to communicate directly to many investors on a regular basis.

Where to Look
Cutting Edge Capital is an expert at DPOs. The company helps companies navigate the complex world of securities law by providing strategic consulting, a DPO marketplace and legal services. Visit cuttingedgecapital.com/ for more information.

TAKEAWAY: No SEC registration required. State filings are required.

57

INITIAL PUBLIC OFFERING: WELCOME TO WALL STREET

OVERVIEW

An initial public offering (IPO) is when a private company offers stock in its company to the public—it's going big, not home. This is the first time the company sells shares of stock to the public (see previous chapter on Direct Public Offerings), and it signals to the world the company is prepared to play on a bigger stage as part of the world capital markets. Capital is more readily available and on better terms to a public company than it is to a private company. Companies use an IPO not only to raise capital, but also as a way to gauge continuing interest, and as a public message to their competitors that they plan to fight and win.

All is not rosy in the IPO markets. In the U.S., many fast-growing companies are not rushing to be public companies for a number of reasons. The *Wall Street Journal* reported,

"Firms raised about $1.7 trillion through private offers of debt and equity in 2016, compared to about $1.5 trillion through public sales of debt and equity, according to an August report from SEC economists."[1] Some companies have soured on the process. The *New York Times* reported that, "the total number of companies listed on the United States stock market plummeted by nearly half, to 3,671 last year from 7,322 in 1996.[2] The number of IPOs in 1996 was 706 and only 105 in 2016, according to the *New York Times*. A number of reasons for the decline have been batted around, from increased regulations to a focus on short-term measures of beating Wall Street's expectations at the expense of long-term goals.

It's not cheap to go through the IPO process. The *Wall Street Journal* reported that Snap Inc. paid $100 million to go public in March 2017.[3] Spotify, the music streaming service, will use the novel approach of a direct listing (not using the typical underwriting and syndicate that purchases the stock and then sells it in the public offering), while paying roughly $35 million to go public, a significant savings over a traditional IPO. Many people are involved in launching an IPO, driving up the cost. Companies usually hire an underwriter to determine the type of security to offer, the price and the number of shares to be issued. In addition to the underwriter, a firm will put together a team consisting of certified accountants (CPAs), lawyers and people familiar with the SEC. Financial statements will be audited and the prospectus will be sent to the SEC for a date to be set for the offering. The lead underwriter will work to get the offering ready for the regulators while simultaneously testing the market for the appeal of such an offering. Regulation A+ can serve as a means to evaluate the market for the proposed offering. If feedback from investors and the economic climate are not favorable, companies may choose to wait for a better time for the IPO.

Description
An initial public offering (IPO) is when a private company offers stock in its company to the public for the first time.

Purpose of Funds
A company seeks an IPO to raise capital from the public capital markets.

Requirements
A business must be ready and assemble a team to create demand for the IPO. The company must have something the market perceives as valuable today and well into the future.

Technical Assistance
Companies must hire an underwriter and team to get through the regulatory scrutiny of launching the IPO. This is no small undertaking. The people who have experience going through the process don't come cheap. Be prepared to pay.

Credit Score
N/A

Term
N/A

Interest
N/A

Fees
The fees will be in the tens of millions of dollars to launch a successful IPO.

Payments
N/A

Prepayment
N/A

Personal Guarantee
N/A

Collateral
N/A

Rating
Good. A company may spend several years planning for an IPO.

Additional Cost
A number of experts must be hired to get the IPO approved.

Where to Look
Visit Nasdaq for more information about IPOs. Here is an article on Facebook's IPO: mergersandinquisitions.com/initial-public-offering-process-ipo/#comments.

TAKEAWAY: Most companies don't go to Wall Street—perhaps that's a good thing.

58

INITIAL COIN OFFERING: IS THIS THE FUTURE OF MONEY?

OVERVIEW

A company uses an initial coin offering (ICO) to raise capital by offering investors proprietary digital tokens known as cryptocurrency. These digital tokens are a new type of currency linked by decentralized computers all over the world that record each transaction. Cryptocurrencies are part of the blockchain, the distributed ledger system that records transactions. The computer network is not owned by any country, company or one individual. In fact, just about anyone with ultrafast computing power can be part of the system that records transactions and creates (mines) new tokens. Paul Krugman, the Op-Ed Columnist for the *New York Times* and an economist, described Bitcoin (a popular cryptocurrency) as, "an asset that has no physical existence, consisting of nothing but a digital record stored on computers."[1] Libertarians and others like this currency because people can remain anonymous and access funds with only their password. A major drawback is the currency is not universally accepted and lacks protections to deter theft and other "real world" crimes.

Companies that raise capital through an ICO accept payment in cash or a cryptocurrency, like bitcoin. The twist is that investors who partake in the ICO do not receive stock, they receive tokens that can be held as an investment, or used to buy a company's current or future products. Investors are excited, and the value of cryptocurrencies has been on a wild rollercoaster ride—some fear a bubble is growing. *Reuters* reported, "Over $3.7 billion was raised through ICOs last year, up from less than 82 million euros in 2016."[2] Companies create demand by issuing a fixed amount of tokens and hyping the currency up as the future next big thing. They hire celebrities to pitch the currencies, adding fuel to the fire and driving up the value.

The jury is still out on what will happen with the plethora of cryptocurrencies. As reported on *Fortune.com*, China banned ICOs and called on exchanges to stop trading the currency. One certainty is regulation. Gibraltar will issue the first regulations for cryptocurrencies. The planned regulations will create disclosure rules for "adequate, accurate, and balanced information to anyone buying tokens," *Reuters* reported.[3] Countries around the world will be watching. Government officials in the U.S. have sent mixed messages about the currency. On one hand, they praise the innovation of the technology. On the other hand, the SEC Chairman Jay Clayton said that ICOs are securities and should be regulated as such.

Description
A company uses an initial coin offering (ICO) to raise capital by offering investors proprietary digital tokens known as cryptocurrency.

Purpose of Funds
Businesses raise capital from the public to launch or create new products.

Requirements
The SEC believes that most cryptocurrencies are securities and should be registered as such. Regulations of some kind is expected in the future.

Technical Assistance
If you plan to create a cryptocurrency and sell it to the public, contact a securities attorney.

Credit Score
N/A

Term
N/A

Interest
N/A

Fees
Hiring a securities lawyer can run in the tens of thousands of dollars.

Payments
N/A

Prepayment
N/A

Personal Guarantee
N/A

Collateral
N/A

Rating
Stay away from cryptocurrencies until more is known.

Additional Cost
Launching a cryptocurrency without registering the offering with the SEC could lead to legal action in the future.

Where to Look
Here are two articles about cryptocurrencies:

- "An Explanation of Initial Coin Offerings": nytimes. com/2017/10/27/technology/what-is-an-initial-coin-offering.html.
- "Bubble, Bubble, Fraud and Trouble": nytimes. com/2018/01/29/opinion/bitcoin-bubble-fraud.html.

TAKEAWAY: A security is a security.

59

REVERSE MERGER:
IT'S COMPLICATED

OVERVIEW

A reverse merger or reverse takeover is when a private company acquires the majority of shares of a public shell company. In 2015, 79 companies used the reverse merger to go public and 214 used it in 2014, according to PrivateRaise, a data service of The Deal.[1] There are a number of reasons to be a public company:

- Access to capital markets and a broader pool of investors and other capital, such as loans..

- Public companies trade at higher multiples than private companies.

- Public markets provide liquidity to investors.

- Company stock serves as an incentive to attract and retain top talent.

- Stock can be used to pursue mergers and acquisitions.
- Public companies that have an attractive story and solid business fundamentals may attract analysts to cover the company. With more coverage, the possibility exists to attract more demand for the stock, moving up the price of the stock, which benefits the company, employees and investors. Attention has become the new currency.

Companies that want the benefits of being publicly-traded without going through the arduous and expensive process of a typical IPO, often explore a reverse merger. An SEC report states, "The legal and accounting fees associated with a reverse merger tend to be lower than for an IPO."[2] The way a reverse merger works is that a private company acquires a shell company. Investopedia defines a shell company as, "a corporation without active business operations or significant assets."[3] A private company will acquire the outstanding shares of the shell company and exchange its shares for public company shares, which consummates the deal. Since the company doesn't have to spend time raising capital, the business can now focus on its core business without distractions.

The main challenge of the reverse merger is that the shell company must be vetted for any negative issues that could harm the newly merged company. The shell must be "clean" and not "tainted" from issues in the past— that could haunt the company like a ghost. You don't want outstanding liabilities to take the company down. The acquiring company's management must be prepared to deal with both regulatory and compliance issues of a public company, which is often difficult for most small businesses. A management team that is competent on the operational and financial side will have to add compliance and regulatory skills. A reverse merger works when the company has considerable upside from the economics of its business model and the market opportunity.

Description
A company seeks to go public to get access to capital and the other benefits of being a public company without going through the traditional IPO process. A reverse merger or reverse takeover is when a private company acquires the majority of shares of a public shell company.

Purpose of Funds
Access to public capital markets on a public exchange to grow the business.

Requirements
Must be in compliance with public company regulations.

Technical Assistance
Hire an attorney and accountant familiar with reverse mergers, and make sure you have the right team to develop a plan going forward.

Credit Score
N/A

Term
N/A

Interest
N/A

Fees
While less expensive than an IPO, costs can add up to a few hundred thousand dollars.

Payments
N/A

Prepayment
N/A

Personal Guarantee
N/A

Collateral
N/A

Rating
Good. Fast. The company must have strong market opportunities and financial health to take on the uncertainty of purchasing a shell company. A reverse merger can take three to four months, which is less time than a typical IPO requires of at least one year plus preparing.

Additional Cost
Uncertainty goes along with purchasing a shell company. A reverse merger may require more due diligence than a typical IPO. Considerable time must be spent making sure the shell company is "clean." In the long run, this path to becoming a publicly-traded company is rife with issues for the company. Invest in an experienced securities attorney and advisors. The price range of a reverse merger varies from $150,000 to $600,000, including the cost to purchase the public shell. A public shell is a commodity and can increase in price substantially.

Where to Look
Here's a blog post about reverse merger: blog.vcexperts. com/2017/06/15/going-public-transactions-for-smaller-companies-direct-public-offering-and-reverse-merger/.

TAKEAWAY: This is a creative way to become a public company.

60

PRIVATE PLACEMENT OFFERING: WEALTHY INVESTORS WANTED

OVERVIEW

A private placement offering is the method of raising capital through issuing an unregistered security to a limited number of investors, typically accredited. "Private placements include offering types ranging from friends and family investments in a new retail establishment, to angel investments in a social enterprise, to institutional and venture capital investment in a growth company," states CuttingEdgeCapital.com.[1]

Under a private placement offering, a company may sell shares of its stock, warrants, bonds or some other interest in the company for cash. This approach to a security has minimal regulation and does not have to be registered with the SEC, based on the Regulation D (also known as Reg. D) exemption of the Securities Act of 1933, but a Form D is required to be filed once funds are accepted. Investopedia says, "A private placement is different from a public issue in which securities are made available for sale on the open market to any type of investor."[2]

Private placements can be done in two ways: one is completely private (Reg D 506(b), where the company brings in investments from investors that they typically know or have gotten to know first, and who self-identify as accredited. The other is a private placement done via general solicitation (Reg D 506(c), where the company may solicit investors in any way they want, as long as the accredited investor has been verified via an approved process set up by the SEC.

An investment into a private placement does not require a formal prospectus and detailed financial information may not need to be disclosed (though most investors want to see this). FINRA.org states on its website, "Issuers selling securities in a private placement generally have fewer disclosure requirements than issuers that sell securities in a public offering."[3] However, many companies will use a prospectus, typically known as the private placement memorandum (or PPM). A PPM typically describes the background, terms of investment, financial information, projections, uses of funds, management and risks when investing in a private placement. The purpose of the PPM is to disclose material information about the company and the securities, so that an investor has been provided all information that would be reasonably expected before making an investment. A PPM gives investors key information, and protects the company by having been transparent. The actual offering documents are separate from the PPM. The supporting documents are subscription agreement, investor suitability questionnaire, the company's organizational documents such as business operating agreement, limited partnership agreement and shareholders agreement or a promissory note (for debt offerings), to name some, not all the documents.

A PPM is like a business plan with the proper disclosures, and it has typically been reviewed by a securities lawyer. The issuance of a private placement memorandum does not result in the company going public like an IPO would. A private placement is not a listing on a public exchange; it's private. If the securities being offered in a private placement are bonds, they do not have to be rated by a credit rating company. Since a bond is not rated, the interest rate on the bond will typically be higher commensurate with the perceived risk.

Private placements can take much less time to prepare and complete, and when done, the company can move forward with growing the business. As they say, time is money.

Description
A private placement offering is the method of raising capital through issuing an unregistered security to a limited number of investors, typically accredited.

Purpose of Funds
Capital to be used at the owner's discretion to grow a business. The PPM will define how the funds raised will be used.

Requirements
Must be in compliance with SEC regulations regarding an unregistered security.

Technical Assistance
Hire an attorney familiar with private placements, drafting PPMs and securities laws that are relevant.

Credit Score
N/A

Term
N/A

Interest
N/A

Fees
Contact an attorney to get an estimate.

Payments
N/A

Prepayment
N/A

Personal Guarantee
N/A

Collateral
N/A

Rating
Some venture capitalists don't want to deal with companies that have raised capital using a PPM. Their rationale is that if the company couldn't raise funds from venture capitalists, it probably will have a hard time growing the business. But that is just one opinion. Private placements are used to raise a tremendous amount of investment capital every year.

Additional Cost
Unknown compliance costs may not be stated in the estimate from an attorney, but they are relatively low.

Where to Look

See sample private placement memorandum: sec.gov/
Archives/edgar/data/1456857/000135028410000016/
exhibit101ppmfinal.htm and https://www.manhattan
streetcapital.com/sites/default/files/Parklands%20
PPM%20.pdf.

TAKEAWAY: Issue securities to wealthy investors.

61

⟹BONUS CHAPTER

CAN'T STOP, WON'T STOP: MORE CAPITAL OPTIONS

This book was written to solve hair-on-fire problems about capital for YOU. Value is what drives the success of a business—like paying for coach airfare and being upgraded to first-class; that's value. When value exceeds price, people buy. Give your customers more than what they expect, and they will keep coming to your door—or website.

Companies are innovating in the capital-raising space, with new products. Your business and circumstances are unique, so capital products should be tailored to your needs. Make capital fit. It's the difference between purchasing a sweater off the rack at Target or going to a couture designer. This chapter provides a summary of the capital sources that may be overlooked, along with our rating system: Good, Cheap or Fast.

The summaries are a quick overview, not an in-depth analysis. Use this section as a reference. Do your due diligence to make sure the capital product will meet both your short- and long-term needs. Don't believe the hype; instead, read the fine print to discover what's really going on. In the end, the buck stops with you—and your pockets. Here are capital sources you should consider on your journey to building the best business. Good luck!

HOME EQUITY LINES OF CREDIT: USE YOUR HOME

Overview

Americans are using their homes as their banks again, drawing down $156 billion in 2015, which was the largest amount since the Great Recession, according to Investopedia.[1]

A home equity line of credit (also known as HELOC, pronounced "hee lock") is a line of credit granted to homeowners to use in any way they choose. It's like a credit card that uses your home as collateral. HELOCs are usually secondary loans because a first loan (mortgage) is on the home.

Marketers send homeowners pre-approved offers for HELOCs based on preselected credit scores and income. Your home must have equity in it to access capital: Market value of your home minus mortgage balance is equal to equity. Lenders will provide up to 85 percent of the value of the home as a HELOC. Banks use loan-to-value (LTV) to determine how much they will lend, which is calculated by dividing the balance of the mortgages on the property by the present market value. The interest rate is variable (floating, based on the prime rate). When the prime rate increases or decreases, your rate will do the same.

A line of credit is a revolving product, meaning that once you pay down the line, you can continue to access credit. You pay interest only on the amount outstanding. The payment on the line of credit is usually interest only, up to a certain time frame (for example, 1 or 5 years), at which time, the HELOC will be due in full. A HELOC is not the same as a home equity loan. The latter is a loan against your home paid in fixed, equal monthly payments.

Rating: Good, Cheap & Fast
Be careful because you can drain all your equity in your home by using it as your bank. If the market value of your home drops, you could be left owing more on the home than it is worth—this is called being underwater or upside down.

Where to Look
Contact your local bank branch to inquire about a HELOC. When you access your online bank account, there may be an option to apply for a HELOC online. Visit Bankrate.com for mortgage rates.

INSURANCE: CASHING OUT

Overview
Life insurance is what protects your loved ones when something happens to the policy holder. But not all insurance is created equal. Term life insurance is cheaper than other types of insurance, and pays a specific death benefit during the covered period. Permanent or whole life insurance not only provides a death benefit, but you can also borrow against the money the policy accumulates above what is required for the death benefit. Your savings component is invested to generate a return on the funds. The earnings that accrue are called the "cash value." Borrowed funds from a life insurance policy have a specific interest rate that will be charged per the agreement. In essence, you are borrowing against yourself. The cash value can be used as collateral for certain types of obligations.

Permanent insurance varies and some types are better positioned for growth and structured to borrow against. Make sure the insurance funding and loans are structured properly to take advantage of tax-free benefits. One should consider the length of time an insurance policy has been funded before considering it as a funding source for your business. Drawing from newer policies (less than 10 years old) may inhibit or erode the growth potential because the interest rates can be higher than the growth rate. The higher overall costs may cancel out tax benefits and potential future growth. Life insurance shouldn't be your first option when it comes to funding your business. But if you have done your homework, it is an option to consider.

A participating life insurance policy receives dividend payments from the life insurance company. It is named participating because the policy holder gets to share in the surplus earnings in the life insurance. A nonparticipating policy doesn't have the right to share in the surplus earnings of the company, thus it does not receive dividend payments. The IRS considers the dividend a return on premium. In essence, the IRS says the policy holders paid too much. The website Life Ant states, "instead of being classified as a dividend by the IRS, a life insurance dividend is actually considered to be a return of premiums paid for tax purposes." These funds are returned to the policy holders.

Rating: Fast
This brief section is not meant to be the unabridged version of insurance and investments. For more information, contact an insurance professional or financial advisor.

Where to Look
Review your life insurance policy. Contact your insurance agent to go over your policy.

BORROW AGAINST PRIVATE EQUITY STOCK: YOUR FUTURE NEST EGG

Overview

Private market holdings are shares of private companies that can be pledged to secure a loan. The stock must be vested in order to leverage it. Companies may have "cliff" or "step" vesting rights.[2] Cliff vesting means you get access to all benefits and stock on a specific date. Step vesting is acquiring access over a number of years. For example, a company may vest 25 percent of the stock each year over four years. Some equity plans can vest in a year or much longer; each company is different. Senior management and employees of private companies receive shares and options to purchase additional shares of stock in the company as an incentive. The promise of equity is a tasty carrot to dangle in front of recruits and employees.

Private stock is illiquid and hard to value. But the stock may have tremendous value, if the company goes public one day. Since the market for shares of private companies is not as robust as the New York Stock Exchange or Nasdaq, the value of the shares cannot be fully realized until sold. But senior executives and other employees may want to buy a house or pay college tuition for a son or daughter. A number of companies have sprouted up to provide an option to employees who own shares in private companies. A "secondary offering" is the vehicle to sell shares. In a secondary offering, "money from outside investors goes directly to existing shareholders—employees or early investors—unlike a primary funding round, where the capital raised goes to the company to fund its operations and growth", according to Carolyn Said, a reporter at the *San Francisco Chronicle*.[3] Companies will partner with a firm to provide a secondary offering to help employees turn their shares into cash. Accredited investors, banks, hedge funds and institutions provide the capital.

For employees who want to cash in their private shares, SharePost has created a new solution to loan money, using the stock as collateral. The company works with 10 large banks to provide capital, using the value of the stock as collateral. Executives and employees get the benefit of access to cash and still keep the equity, which may continue to go up in value, prior to going public. Check to make sure the company doesn't have a first right of refusal to purchase your stock. For employees with options, the options can be exercised using borrowed money.

Note: If you have publicly-traded stock, you can borrow against your shares from a plethora of options: Morgan Stanley, Bank of America, and Interactive Brokers have securities-based loan programs. As of September 2017, Morgan Stanley had $40 billion and Bank of America $39.3 billion of these loans.

Rating: Good, Cheap & Fast
The market for shares of private companies is growing. Based on all the options available, the SharePrice product offers a real solution to people who own shares and options in private companies. This capital checks all the boxes.

Where to Look
Sharepost and EquityZen are platforms that enable borrowing against private market holdings. Nasdaq Private Market is a solution provider that can manage secondary offerings for companies.

MERCHANT CASH ADVANCE: BEWARE OF FAST MONEY
Overview
A merchant cash advance (MCA) is not technically a loan: It is an advance against future sales from credit or debit

cards. This loan product has been compared to payday loans or car title loans, which have a reputation of preying on low-income customers who are down on their luck.

There are two ways MCAs are structured to be paid back:

1. The business receives a lump sum injection of cash in exchange for future credit card sales.

2. A business could receive cash up front that is paid in fixed daily or weekly debits from the business owner's bank account. This method is known as automated clearing house (ACH) withdrawals. The ACH payment method is popular and the industry targets businesses that are not tied to credit card sales.

Payment is received via ACH in daily or weekly increments, which include interest and fees. A factor rate is determined based on the perceived risk of the deal. 1.2 has lower risk than 1.5. Multiply the cash advance by the factor rate to get the total amount to be paid back. An advance amount of $40,000 multiplied by a factor rate of 1.45 equals $58,000. The total fee for the example given is $18,000. Percent of sales and fixed daily withdrawals are the two payment structures. Suppose your company does $60,000 a month in credit sales and the MCA company withdraws nine percent (holdback) or $5,400 per month. It would take 11 months to repay the advance. Depending on sales, if could be quicker or longer to repay the advance. Faster repayment equals higher APR.

Under a fixed repayment structure, the daily or weekly payments withdrawn don't change. A business with $60,000 in weekly credit card sales would pay $1,350 per week. You pay the exact amount every week, regardless if your credit card sales increase or decrease, which could have a profound impact on your cash flow. Contrast your payment with a term loan of $58,000 at 9 percent amortized over 60 months. The monthly payment would be $1,203.98 a month, a significant savings from the above examples. The annual percentage rates (APR), when all fees and interest are calculated, tend to be over three digits, which is dramatically higher than in other products.

Rating: Fast
Due to the cost, it is difficult to recommend an MCA as a viable long-term solution. The fees add up quickly. Know your situation and what will work best for your business. Caveat emptor.

Where to Look
Nerd Wallet produced a special report on MCAs: "It's the 'Wild West Out There.'" View it here: nerdwallet.com/blog/small-business-special-report-mca/.

NONPROFIT: SUPPORT THE GOOD GUYS AND GIRLS

Overview
Doing good costs money, and nonprofits have capital needs, just like a business. What separates a nonprofit from a business is its mission, state nonprofit designation and IRS tax-exempt status. Nonprofits have access to capital from many of the same sources that for-profit businesses do: banks, credit unions, community development financial institutions (CDFIs), credit cards and more. Yet, the bulk of their money comes from grants. Grants are funded by foundations and federal, state and local governments. Nonprofits hire skilled people to write persuasive grant applications. Researching and applying for grants is a time-consuming process, with no guarantees. Successful nonprofits increase the odds in their favor by innovating and producing measurable results. Just like a business,

a nonprofit has to develop a business model that will distinguish it from competitors.

Nonprofits have a number of different places to find capital. Individuals, small businesses and corporations can make tax-deductible donations. This is a big advantage and many nonprofits have annual campaigns to raise funds. Nonprofits can solicit donations merely with a donation button on their websites. Any nonprofit that is not taking advantage of this is leaving cash on the table. Some nonprofits receive bequests (also known as planned giving) as part of a will. Increasingly, nonprofits are operating businesses (e.g., Goodwill and Homeboy Industries) as part of their missions. Nonprofits have partnered with retail companies. During the year, large retail chains solicit cash donations from customers at the register and may match the total up to a specific number.

The for-profit sector has begun to come up with innovative ways to find solutions to problems plaguing society, such as homelessness, domestic violence, and high unemployment in impoverished areas. Social impact bonds (known as results-based financing) are private-public partnerships on a priority subject area where capital is deployed to solve social issues. Investors provide capital to a social service provider. The provider implements its solution. If the solution addresses the problem in a measurable way, the government pays the investors a return on their money. Goldman Sachs has been instrumental in developing social impact bonds.

Rating: Good & Cheap

A line of credit is a simple solution for most nonprofits. Plan ahead because it can take up to 60 days to get the capital you need.

Where to Look

Banks, credit unions, nonprofit lenders and CDFIs provide lines of credit and other creative ways to finance a nonprofit. Bridgeway Capital, a Pittsburgh-based lender, assists community ventures, including small businesses and nonprofits. Check your local CDFI for more information: ofn.org/cdfi-locator.

PAWNSHOPS: YOUR STUFF HAS VALUE

Overview

If you need capital for your business, selling your possessions at a tag sale or on Craigslist or eBay can work. When you need more, sometimes you have to take it to the next level by going to a professional. A pawnbroker is where you go to pledge property you own as collateral. The pawnbroker will assess the item and lend cash against the asset. You get your merchandise back when you pay the money back. There are no consequences if you decide not to redeem your merchandise. The item will be sold and there are no credit consequences to you.

Pawnbrokers are nonbank financial institutions (NBFI). DK's book *How Money Works: The Facts Visually Explained*, describes an NBFI as "an organization that does not have a banking license, or is not supervised by a banking regulator."[4] Pawnbrokers are regulated, but they have a seedy image. It can't be denied that they provide a valuable service—in a world where people rent storage units for overflowing items, pawnbrokers are liquidators of sorts. But not all are created equal. If you have high-end items such as jewelry, furs, luxury watches, fine art, luxury handbags, gold, precious metals, fine wine and luxury cars—don't go to the pawnbroker on the corner, go online. Paul Aitken is the CEO of asset lending site Borro. "We're about as similar to a private bank as we are to a pawn shop," Aitken explains.[5] Luxury items not only retain their value but may go up in value over time. You might think about searching your possessions for luxury items.

Borro has three capital products: Sales Advance, Bridge Loan and Term Loan. The sales advance loan product is up to a 70 percent advance on the item they sell for you. Interest is 1 to 2 percent a month. The company charges a 15 to 20 percent fee to sell your asset. A bridge loan is a temporary loan secured by your belongings. Once the loan is repaid, you receive your belongings. This product has a six-month term and the interest rates vary from 2.99 percent to 4.99 percent per month. The term loan product starts at $250,000 with terms of 18 to 36 months. A set-up fee for asset appraisal and logistics is charged. There is an annual service fee based on the length of time they will have the asset. The interest rate is fixed and is charged each month. Borro's interest rate on this product varies based on the asset.

Rating: Good & Fast

Know the interest rate limits in your state. When other options fail, and you have valuable items, a personal loan from a pawnbroker may be a viable option.

Where to Look

Pawnshops are located across the country. Pawngo and IPawn are online options. Pawngo calls itself the premier asset-based lender. IPawn is "an affordable trusted and friendly online pawn shop."

AUCTION HOUSES: GOING ONCE, TWICE, SOLD

Overview

Consignment of antiques and collectibles is an option for some. While they don't give money upfront, these companies charge only a commission and specialty auction houses will get the best price for valuable collectible items. Kathy Worthington, the editor of this book, sold antique trains using a high-end toy auction company that uses online bidding for their live auctions. She received $19,000 for a tiny Schlitz freight car.

Christie's, Sotheby's and Bonham's are examples of world renowned auction houses at the high end. Bunte's Auction Services (Illinois) and Stanton's (Michigan) and Vickers and Hoad (Sydney, Australia) are mid-range auction houses. There are many auction houses scattered all over. Some low-range auction houses conduct garage sale type auctions, specializing in specific items. Do your homework. Here's a good read to learn how long it takes to sell, buyback policies, transportation fees, catalogues, and more: antique-hq.com/finding-the-right-auction-house-to-sell-your-antiques-248/.

Rating: Good & Cheap

The professionals will handle the details of getting the best price for your prized possessions. Be aware of all the fees and nuisances of an auction. At the end of the day, there's a market for just about everything from antique watches to collectible trains.

Where to Look

Check the websites of established auctions houses mentioned above, which will provide invaluable information to make you almost as knowledgeable as the pros. Here's a good read about questions to ask before consigning a work: artsy.net/article/artsy-editorial-5-questions-auction-house-consigning-work.

PEER-TO-PEER LENDING:
TECHNOLOGY-ENABLED LENDING

Overview

Peer-to-peer (also known as P2P) is a type of lending facilitated by the Internet. P2P lenders merge technology, data analysis and underwriting. P2P companies are intermediaries between investors that fund the loans and the business owners seeking capital—a two-sided market. Investors may be an individual, bank, hedge fund or institution. P2P platforms specialize in lending to both consumers and businesses. Here we will focus on business P2P lenders that perform the underwriting function but don't actually fund the loans. Lending Club, a P2P lender that launched in 2007, went public on the New York Stock Exchange on December 11, 2014. The company's website states, "We are America's largest online marketplace connecting borrowers and investors."[6] Since its inception, the company has facilitated over $33 billion in loans to over 2 million customers. Lending Club's market capitalization is valued at $1.34 billion.[7]

P2P lenders work with banks to fund transactions and to provide the necessary infrastructure. Lending Club works with WebBank in Salt Lake City, Utah. P2P platforms offer capital as small as $5,000 up to $500,000, and most have a minimum requirement of one year in business. Your credit score should be at least 600. Annual percentage rates on this capital range from 7.5 percent all the way to 40 percent. Given that the prime rate may increase, expect rates on this type of capital also to increase over time. Some of the P2P platforms will require the business to have a minimum amount of revenue of $20,000 per year to qualify. Loan terms vary from one to five years. A number of the lenders quote a funding time as fast as a few days, but most will fund in one to two weeks—still much quicker than a bank.

Like any other capital product, do your homework and read the fine print. To qualify for a loan, a business cannot have a recent bankruptcy or tax lien and must own at least twenty percent of a business. P2P lenders grade loans into categories, with a specific type of risk profile based on the credit score and other propriety information. These lenders will not ask for collateral for small loans or a business plan, and will not visit your business. Expect to pay an origination fee. Origination fees can vary from 1.99 to 6.99 for some platforms. Be aware: The factor rate is not the same as the APR; know the difference. Some loans will require daily payments withdrawn by an ACH.

Rating: Good & Fast
The good thing about P2P lenders is the higher your credit score, the better interest rate you will receive. Businesses with poor credit can still get funds, but at higher interest rates. P2P capital is attractive for some, considering that banks don't offer small loans, unless via a credit card.

Where to Look
FundingCircle, LendingClub and StreetShare are companies that provide small-business loans.

ROYALTY FINANCING: LEVERAGING FUTURE REVENUE

Overview
Royalty financing (also known as revenue-based financing) is when an investor provides upfront cash in exchange for a specific percentage of future revenues. Royalty Exchange generates over a $100 billion in royalty payments annually. This type of financing has been used successfully in gas, mining, film production, pharmaceuticals and music, which is where it has its roots. In royalty finance, a company borrows money and agrees to give a small percentage of

future revenue per month in return. Lighter Capital CEO, BJ Lackland, says, "The amount of capital is determined by a multiple of monthly revenue (i.e. 3-4x), allowing companies with negative cash flow or limited assets to access growth capital."[8]

Royalty financing is considered a security; therefore, you should talk to an attorney before entering into such an arrangement. What makes this attractive is that no equity or control in the business is given up. Unlike a bank loan, where the interest rate may be fixed, the business pays a percentage of revenue over time, until the loan is fully paid back. During good times, when revenue is increasing, more capital is paid back; in slower times, payments decrease with revenue. Royalty payments are usually in the range of two to six percent of revenue, with a cap on the total amount to be repaid. This type of investment is subordinate and unsecured, which makes it seem like equity, except for the income stream paid monthly to investors. No personal guarantee, collateral or financial covenants are necessary.

"It's especially applicable for companies that have lumpy, seasonal, or hard to predict revenues," says Andy Sack, the founder of Lighter Capital, on the AVC.com blog.[9] Marco Vangelisti, an impact investor who spent twenty years in finance, calls royalty financing a "self-liquidating investment."[10] The quicker the owner pays back the investors, the higher the return on investment will be. Investors must develop an acceptable return on their investment, which is a multiple of how much they want as a return. For example, let's say an investor provides $50,000 to a company and expects to receive a premium of $25,000 (1.5) factor rate and 4 percent of revenue. If the business does $1.2 million in revenue, it would take almost nineteen months to repay the loan, assuming revenue doesn't dip below $1.2 million. "We take about a month to review a deal", says Lighter Capital CEO

BJ Lackland. The due diligence process includes reviewing financial statements, bank transactions and bios. Lighter Capital also reviews LinkedIn profiles, existing debt and customer information.

Rating: Good
This type of financing can turn out to be quite expensive, when compared to a term loan. However, if few options are on the table, royalty financing could be just what the business needs to grow, without giving up equity.

Where to Look
Visit Lighter Capital to learn more: lightercapital.com.

ROLLOVER AS A BUSINESS STARTUP: BET YOUR RETIREMENT ON IT

Overview
A rollover as a business startup (ROBS) is a transaction where your retirement account, which may be a 401(k) or traditional individual retirement account, is used to start or purchase a business. Your retirement funds may be the biggest nest egg you have, so this type of transaction requires thought. You are putting your retirement at risk, should the venture fail. In addition, you will lose out on any potential gains you could have made on the money in your retirement account.

The owner will setup up a C corporation, or other structure that allows for shareholders. A new 401(k) plan will be created, and the owner's retirement funds will be rolled into the new 401(k) plan. In general, most types of retirement plans will qualify. The funds rolled over are used to buy stock in the new entity, which is now available to the business. If you don't qualify for a traditional bank loan, a ROBS is an option to access capital for your business. No debt will be incurred—a long-term benefit for any new business. By using a ROBS, there is no ten percent penalty for withdrawing funds from your retirement before you reach 59.5 years of age and no distribution tax to the government. The fee to implement a ROBS is roughly $5,000, plus monthly administration and filing fees for the retirement plan. Consult with your attorney and accountant before proceeding.

It takes money to make money. Make sure you have a long-term plan to build the business and to fund your retirement when the time comes. Some people want the option to work as long as they can. The difference between the person punching the clock and the person jumping out of bed to get to work may be linked to purpose, which fuels passion. An engaged mind is a healthy mind. Work brings out the best in some people long after others have retired to the golf course or other interests.

Rating: Good & Cheap
If other options don't work, this may be the best option without taking on debt, but your future retirement will be at risk. Weigh the pros and cons.

Where to Look
There are a number of companies that specialize in this type of transaction such as Benetrends Financial and Guidant Financial.

TAKEAWAY: Give more than they expect.

EPILOGUE

Have you missed in your aim?
Well, the mark is still shining.

Did you faint in the race?
Well, take breath for the next.

—Ella Wheeler Wilcox

Fix your business model, and capital will flow.

APPENDIX

APPENDIX

ABC Wholesale Company Profit and Loss Statement
For the Quarter Ended March 31, 200X

Net Sales		$200,000
Cost of Goods Sold:		
Beginning inventory	- 45,000	
Merchandise purchases	- 120,000	
Freight	- 15,000	
Cost of Goods Available For Sale		180,000
Less ending inventory	- 50,000	
Cost of Goods Sold		- 130,000
Gross Margin		70,000
Selling, Administrative and General Expenses:		
Salaries and wages	- 22,000	
Rent	- 6,000	
Light, heat and power	- 1,000	
Other expenses	- 4,000	
State and local taxes and licenses	- 1,000	
Depreciation and amortization on leasehold improvements	- 500	
Repairs	- 1,500	
Total Selling, Administrative and General Expenses		- 36,000
Profit From Operations		34,000
Other income	2,500	
Other expenses	- 500	
Net Profit Before Taxes		36,000
Provision for income tax	- 14,400	
Net Profit After Income Tax		**$21,600**

Courtesy of Zions Bank

DOODADS CO. BALANCE SHEET AS OF DEC 31, 20XX

Assets	$$
Current Assets	
Cash On Hand	$ 300
Cash in Bank	$ 2,200
Accounts Receivable	$ 1,600
Merchandise Inventory	$ 5,500
Prepaid Expenses	
Rent	$ 1,200
Total Current Assets	**$10,800**
Fixed Assets	
Equipment and Fixtures	
(less Depreciation)	$ 1,200
Total Assets	$12,000

Liabilities	$$
Current Liabilities	
Accounts Payable	$ 1,100
Notes Payable, Bank	$ 2,200
Accrued Payroll Expenses	$ 500
Total Current Liabilities	$ 3,800
Long-Term Liabilities	
Notes Payable, 1998	$ 5,500
Total Liabilities	$ 9,300
Net Worth*	$ 2,700
Total Liabilities and Net Worth	$12,000

*Assets = Liabilities + Net Worth

Courtesy of Zions Bank

ABC Wholesale Company Cash Flow Statement
For the Year Ended 200X (In Thousands)

Cash Flow From Operations	
Net Income*	**$200**
Additions (Sources of cash)	
Depreciation	100
Increase in Accounts Payable	30
Increases in Accrued Income Taxes	10
Subtractions (Uses of cash)	
Increase in Accounts Receivable	(150)
Increase in Inventory	(25)
Net Cash Flow From Operations	**165**
Cash Flows From Investing Activities	
Equipment	(400)
Cash Flows Associated with Financing	
Activities Notes Payable	30
Net Change in Cash	**(205)**

*Net income is taken from the income statement.

Courtesy of Zions Bank

MICHAEL DUNCAN

RAISING CAPITAL, AND A BUSINESS: AN INTERVIEW WITH MICHAEL DUNCAN

Note: I interviewed Michael Duncan, the founder and CEO of Bankjoy, a startup located in Troy, Michigan (a Detroit suburb) that provides mobile banking solutions to community-based financial institutions, including credit unions and banks. Duncan is a Y Combinator alumnus and Kettering University graduate. This interview was condensed, edited for clarity, and took place over the telephone.

Why did you start Bankjoy?

It started because I had been working at a credit union, and I realized that there was a big need to enhance the technology there, especially the customer-facing technology, such as mobile banking and online banking. We saw big banks, like Chase and Capital One, investing tons into growth and online banking offerings, and the community-based financial institutions (the credit unions, the community banks) having a hard time keeping up with them, and realized there was a big need across the board.

We started Bankjoy to help them be competitive and not only to provide better, more advanced mobile banking and online banking, but also to open up the data and products and services through modern APIs (application programming interfaces), which are what software, data and devices use to communicate on the Internet. To learn about APIs, visit https://www.youtube.com/watch?v=s7wmiS2mSXY.

What is your business model?

We provide a software product to banks and credit unions. They pay for it on a monthly basis. It's a subscription, and they sign a multiyear contract, like SaaS (software as a service). The contract is based on the size of the bank or credit union.

There are upfront fees. Fees that we charge for training, installation, customization, branding and things like that. The important metric, especially for fundraising purposes, is recurring revenue. For any business that is thinking about fundraising, upfront fees and one-time fees are awesome to get cash in the bank. But I think any kind of recurring metrics they can put together are going to be a lot more impressive to traditional kinds of investors.

You were living in Michigan when you were accepted into the Y Combinator program. What was it like leaving your home and going out to Silicon Valley to immerse yourself in the program?

It was equally exciting and scary at the same time. I've been in Michigan most of my life. I was literally leaving my family, friends, and loved ones to pursue this business. This had been a dream for a very long time, to apply the skills I had developed over time in software engineering, and I wanted to build something that was going to have an impact on the world. I saw this as a great opportunity to do that. It was in line with what I wanted to do with my life. The person I brought with me (he has since left the company) felt the same way. He was extremely excited. He was leaving everything behind. He packed up a van and drove across country. And we went on the journey together.

What was the thought process around giving up equity to Y Combinator?

It was a no-brainer! Ours was an extremely early-stage company that had no traction. The value that Y Combinator brings is a brand that they have built successfully over many years. As part of their portfolio, they have the top companies in the world.

They have a fantastic Demo Day that the program leads up to, where you get to speak to Silicon Valley's top investors. It exposes you to, and gives you access to, a network of some great companies with founders who are at all different levels of experience, from very experienced veteran founders to new guys. It's really a great network to grow with and find support when you need it.

Y Combinator pioneered the SAFE (Simple Agreement for Future Equity) agreement. Is that what you executed?

Yes, the SAFE; that's really popular, although much more popular in "the Valley" than it is anywhere else. It is what Y Combinator developed and introduced to the world. We used that, obviously with Y Combinator, but with other investors, as do many companies there that come out of the Valley.

How much equity does Y Combinator take?

Six to seven percent is what they traditionally take. It's $120,000. That's the standard amount now.

When did you receive the money?

If I recall correctly, it's in that first couple of weeks [in the program], when the money arrives.

Did you use the capital for basic living expenses?

Exactly...living expenses, keeping our salaries as low as possible. [We] used the rest for just paying the bills of the company, the different kinds of services we needed, the office space—the basic business expenses, which at that stage are not very much. A hundred and twenty thousand dollars between two people can last quite a while.

Does Y Combinator help you find an apartment?

That's part of the network. The network is supportive. If one Y Combinator company is moving out of a place, they will post it up and say that they're moving, and it's available. We saw lots of different opportunities. We ended up getting an Airbnb that was a pretty good price. It was a house full of startups. We got our own room. It was just a good place for us to sit and work without a lot of distractions.

During this time, were you staying up late at night and eating ramen noodles every day?

Yeah, ramen noodles were definitely part of the equation. A lot of DoorDash, a lot of meal delivery just because we didn't have time to go out and get food. As much as I missed all the people who were here in Michigan while I was out there, having my co-founder and me working on the scene together, we could go as late as we wanted to. No interruptions. We didn't have any events planned, nothing to do on the weekends. We just sat and worked, with the goal of getting this product out as quickly as we possibly could. That consumed our days and nights, until we passed out every single night.

What was it like fleshing out the idea and building a business model?

We knew what we were there to build, and what we wanted to take to market. We knew we had to build a minimal viable product (MVP) that we could take to market to just make sure that we were building the right thing. Y Combinator's motto is: "make something people want". The way you achieve that is by building something small, showing it to people, and getting their feedback by letting them use it, and making quick iterations.

We built a minimal viable product. We were doing about 20 demos per week with different credit unions, and we got a lot of great feedback. That drove the direction of our product, made it what it is today; and we found tremendous market product fit from talking to users and making something they wanted.

Walk us through the Demo Day experience at Y Combinator.

[The] three months are used by a lot of startups to gain the sort of traction that would be attractive to investors. Every company is at a different stage. Some are a little bit more mature. They already have revenue, raised money, [or] may have big teams. There are companies that came in with just an idea, two people—like we did.

Our goals were a little different from some of those mature companies. For us, we wanted to demonstrate that we wanted to build something. Let's make sure we talk to a lot of our prospective customers. Make sure we are building the right thing, and demonstrate that by showing that we can at least get some letters of intent to show there is a demand for what we are building.

We went up on stage on Demo Day to show our traction, with some good letters of intent from credit unions to banks that liked our software and wanted to do a deal with us. It takes time to close those sorts of deals, especially when you're new. But we had letters of intent in hand to show that we were going on the right path: They liked our pricing, they liked our product.

How much time do they give you?

I don't recall exactly, but it's like five or seven minutes or so. There are no questions allowed. The batch size is about 120 to 140 companies. They flip through them over two days. There's one startup after another getting up on stage giving their pitch, and they get down, and the next one comes up.

What happened after Demo Day was over?

We thought that the best place in the world to go raise money was probably in the Valley. And we spent a few more months in the Valley, doing that until we had raised $1.1 million. Then we came back [to Michigan] and got to work. We hired another engineer. We got to work on closing these deals we had LOIs (letters of intent) for, and eventually ended up closing a couple of those deals. We just worked hard on delivering the software.

We spent that year working on closing the deals. It was a process we had to learn. We had to learn about developing contracts and negotiations. We spent that year refining the product, officially closing our first deal. Went into the next year, working on the delivery of that process. That whole second year was really about software development, delivery, and continued refinement of the process through conversations with credit unions and banks. We got to the point that year where we were delivering software to financial institutions.

What year was this activity happening?

It was 2016 when the first client came online, and we began making money. It wasn't a lot of money, a few grand every month is what we were making, but we were proud of that three grand a month. We kind of had a watershed moment that same year as well. We closed our first major deal with a company that gave us more than 200 credit unions that we could [possibly] deploy our software to. We then began to close direct sales right after that, one after another, month after month, and our business began to really take off. We have been riding that wave ever since.

What was the company like during this period of increasing sales?

It was a time of bringing in some additional people and talent. It was learning how to build a team. We were learning how to do all kinds of things all at once. We were still doing our sales. We began building channel partnerships to strengthen our ability to sell and sell more. We were building all the software too, so we could get it delivered to these clients.

A lot of things were happening at once and then we realized we needed more capital. We went out to raise more money. So far, we have raised $1.75 million. That's got us to the point where we are right now. We currently have 11 financial institutions that are live, and we are getting ready to turn on a bunch more throughout the year. We have turned that corner.

Last year was all about getting the software ready, getting it built. Now we are at a stage where the product is completely ready. It's ready for deployment. We are queueing up these deployments one after another and we are delivering. We are shipping software, and we are earning revenue. Our growth rate is reflective of that right now.

How many employees do you have?

Right now, we are a team of six, that's mainly developers. I still do a quite a bit of software development too, at this stage. We also have a project manager and a VP of sales, who is currently our only sales person.

How are your investors helping you and what's the relationship like now?

Our investors are super supportive, in terms of helping us understand the kinds of metrics we need to have to go out and raise the next round, [Series A]. Helping us set our priorities, goals and connecting to new sales opportunities, so we can grow our pipeline. They've been very supportive in helping us understand how to deal with the growing pains as the team grows, revenue grows.

What lessons did you learn in terms of starting the business and raising capital?

It's important that if you're a startup raising capital from investors, VCs or angels, you are targeting the right kinds of investors, and you understand what they are looking for in a startup. Each investor has its typical check size, typical target, and different space it invests in, and a focus, or set of focuses they really know about. They can offer some expertise, advice and assistance.

Know who your investors are. Don't waste time talking to investors who are not targeting your stage. If you're early stage, don't go after growth-stage investors. They will talk to you. They will spend your time, but it's not going to end up in any kind of check.

Once you get the money, focus on growth. Building your business is the best thing you can do to go out and raise money. Limiting your time to talking to investors is probably a good thing. Talk to investors when you need to raise money and show them all the growth and the great things you have done with your company.

Understand there are differences in investors' [expectations] on a regional level. There are far more liberal expectations on the West coast, where they have seen many SAFE agreements, and they are not opposed to them. They are willing to help get deals done fast, if you're not raising a ton of money.

Expectations in the Midwest or East Coast may be a bit more conservative or traditional. The process may take a little bit longer in some cases. The valuation of your company will be a little bit lower, more conservative, more traditional. Going in with the proper expectations, knowing what those are, will help save a lot of time in the negotiating process, as well.

Angel investors are usually a little more easygoing if you're raising a small round. They may do something a little more liberal than you can do on the East coast. There's a lot of variance in the VCs across the regions. VCs in the Midwest or East Coast are going to take you through a lengthy process and smaller rounds. They are not going to give you as liberal of an evaluation. I think knowing and having those expectations will save a lot of time.

How do you vet investors?

I think the best way to vet investors is to look at their portfolios. They are going to check your references, depending on the investor. You can also check their references and talk to the companies they have invested in. Usually it's easy to find them, if they have got the money. Also, how supportive are they going to be. What kind of investors are they? Startups are a great source to get that sort of information.

In our experience, we follow up on our references. We do our due diligence, just as much as they do.

What's the goal for revenue in 2018?

Our goal is $1.5 million in revenue. We have all of that booked. It's realizing revenue we have already booked. We are just delivering now. We continue to sell and to get ourselves to a point where we can reach next year's milestones.

How much money do you expect to raise in your series A round?

Probably a minimum of $3 million dollars, to help us achieve the next milestone. That's going to be a fun raise because I get to learn a lot of new things. We are going to build an executive team, develop a board, and do all those things that growing companies do.

MICHAEL CIABURRI

WHEN BANKS SAY "NO": PRIVATE LENDERS STEP UP

Note: I asked Michael Ciaburri, the CEO of Worth Avenue Capital based in Connecticut, to write a piece about private lenders. Like most capital, private lenders are not right for all businesses. Do your homework before proceeding.

During the last several years, the private lending space has continued to grow both in the number of institutions that are competing in the marketplace as well as the amount and volume of loans that are being originated by these lenders.

As the banking industry continues to be over burdened with regulations from a complex and onerous regulatory environment, private lenders have gained a competitive advantage over commercial banks in terms of being able to provide capital to businesses of all types in an expedient and streamlined manner.

In the past, private lenders were known as the "lender of last resort" in which a commercial borrower would solicit a private lender for financing only after fully exhausting the commercial banking participants for their capital needs. Recently, however, various borrowers have begun to use private lenders as their "go-to" providers for their financing needs and are foregoing dealing with banks altogether. A recent transaction that my company funded late last year clearly illustrates this phenomenon.

Towards the end of November of last year, I received a call from a former bank client of mine whom I hadn't spoken with in many years. This client is the principal of a very successful family-owned commercial contracting company in Connecticut, who had several existing bank borrowing relationships already in place when he contacted me. In fact, this company had unused lines of credit (LOC) with two different banks in the seven-figure range that were available to his company for short-term working capital needs.

After meeting with his outside CPA firm earlier that week, the accounting firm advised the company that there existed a short "window" of opportunity in which the company could benefit from the pending new tax laws by taking on debt that would allow them to save approximately $200,000 in tax savings for the coming fiscal year. The "catch" was that the company needed to close on a new $2 million loan by year end.

Once the company had received this advice from their outside CPA firm, they immediately contacted their commercial loan officers at the respective banks to try and quickly arrange the necessary financing. The company did not want to access their unused lines of credit at those banks. Instead, they wanted a new and unrelated commercial loan in order to keep their LOCs separate from this particular financing need. Despite offering the banks excellent real estate collateral with sufficient existing equity, and offering to pay off the loan in 45 days or less, both banks were less than receptive to their loan request.

Subsequently, the company contacted me and I quickly gave them a same-day verbal approval for their loan request and then issued them a Letter of Intent (LOI) the next day. We ultimately closed and funded the loan just before Christmas, thus accomplishing the borrower's goal of closing the transaction by year end.

The borrower had liquidity events that they knew would come to fruition during January of 2018 and they ultimately paid off our $2 million loan in full within 38 days.

As of this writing, this same company has reached out to me again and we will be meeting to discuss another financing need that the company has in which they may have a chance to purchase a commercial property at a below-market price and they need to move quickly to take advantage of the opportunity.

This aforementioned example is just one of many in which my company has been able to fund a commercial loan to a business for opportunistic purposes.

Michael Ciaburri is the CEO of Worth Avenue Capital. He is a former bank CEO.

MARK COUSINEAU

UNDERSERVED MARKETS:
COMMUNITY LENDERS EXTEND A HELPING HAND

Note: I asked Mark Cousineau, the CEO of Community Investment Corporation based in Connecticut, to write the following observations about community-based lenders.

Throughout the United States there is a network of private, non-profit economic development lenders, each established to address unmet business capital needs within their area of operation. Community Investment Corporation (CIC) is one of the network organizations serving small businesses based in both Connecticut and Rhode Island. These organizations are as varied as the local economies they serve.

CIC has a dual focus of assisting small businesses that are not quite bankable while also assisting healthy businesses looking to grow and create jobs: 1) **Access to capital** and 2) **Incentive loan** programs. Access to capital programs (and in some cases, business counseling services as well) focus primarily on lending to underserved markets. Think of underserved markets as subsets of the overall business population where borrowing opportunities are more limited.

Underserved markets are usually identified by groups (women, minority, veteran, disabled) or locations (low- to moderate-income census tracts, Enterprise and HUB Zones). Startup businesses are also considered underserved because they lack a performance history (who bets on a horse that has yet to run a race?) CIC participates in the U.S. Small Business Administration's (SBA) Microloan and Community Advantage Programs because those programs are well suited for access to capital lending within its territory. Both programs offer enough flexibility for CIC to make loans to small business borrowers who exhibit an acceptable level of creditworthiness but are not quite bankable.

Incentive loan programs are markedly different from access to capital programs. They offer advantageous loan terms typically not available through traditional lenders. These programs target successful small businesses with the specific goal to encourage owners (incentivize them) to take the next step to expand their business, create jobs and grow the local economy. The next step may be purchasing a business location, adding machinery and equipment or both. CIC participates in the SBA's 504 Loan Program to provide incentive financing.

The SBA 504 Program is designed to finance long-term fixed assets such as owner-occupied real estate, machinery and equipment. The 504 Program is offered exclusively through SBA Certified Development Companies (CDCs) in partnership with local banks. CDCs are regulated by the SBA and must have the professional staffing and program expertise to successfully deliver the loan product.

It is likely most readers never heard of the SBA's 504 Loan Program. It is an incentive loan program used exclusively to finance the purchase of owner-occupied real estate (including ground-up construction and renovations) and the purchase and installation of machinery and equipment. No inventory. No working capital. No business acquisition. To qualify as "owner occupied," the business must occupy 51% of the rentable space of an existing building purchased with loan funds or 60% of a new constructed building with an intention to occupy 80% in the future.

Banks provide financing for buildings and equipment every day, so what makes the 504 Loan Program different? CDCs like to describe the 504 Loan Program as "Bringing Wall Street to Main Street." The program blends a modest down payment with a long-term fixed rate loan structure to create a financing package similar to those only available to larger corporations. The combination of program benefits creates an incentive for small business owners to purchase real estate and equipment to drive business growth and create jobs.

CDCs partner with local banks (SBA uses the term "Third Party Lender" or TPL) to provide a 504 Loan package. In a routine 504 Loan transaction, the TPL finances 50% of the Total Project Cost and takes a first-lien position on the project assets. (The SBA uses the term "Total Project Cost" to describe **all** items to be financed using the 504 Program.) The TPL negotiates its own rates and terms with the small-business owner. The CDC finances the next 40% of the Total Project Costs and takes a second-lien position on the project assets. The small-business borrower provides the final 10% as a down payment (equity injection).

When you evaluate whether the 504 Program is right for your small business, start by evaluating the down payment requirement. It can be as low as 10% of the Total Project Cost for a borrower who has been in business for 2 years or more. To put that in perspective, in the current market, most banks require a minimum down payment of 20% or more.

Soft costs can also be included in the Total Project Costs and are eligible for financing in a 504 Loan transaction. Soft costs are out-of-pocket expenses you are required to pay in addition to the purchase price of the real estate and/or machinery and equipment. They include items such as architectural and engineering fees, the cost of surveys, environmental and appraisal reports and certain legal fees, title searches and title insurance.

By their nature, soft costs are transaction expenses that add little or no value to the collateral (project assets) used to secure a loan. While not a soft cost, installation fees for machinery and equipment have the same characteristic. They are a necessary expense that does not add value to the collateral being installed. That is why soft costs and installation costs are generally not financed by banks. The SBA 504 Program accepts a higher collateral risk so borrowers can finance up to 90% of those costs and conserve additional cash to grow their businesses.

Here's an example of the amount of cash conserved on a $1 million owner-occupied real estate deal: With a conventional loan, you will likely be required to make a 20% down payment based on the $1 million Total Project Cost.

CONVENTIONAL LOAN – $1 MILLION PROJECT

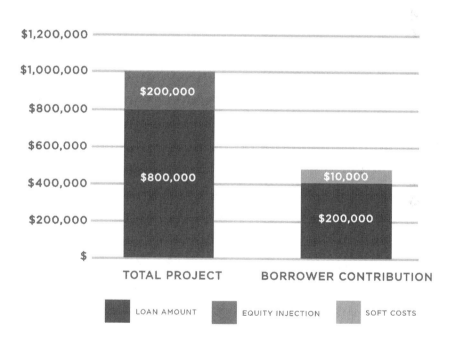

You will also be responsible for approximately $10,000 in soft costs from appraisal and environmental report fees to title searches and title insurance.

All in, you can expect to take a minimum of $210,000 out of your pocket to purchase your business location.

With a 504 Loan package, the Total Project Cost will be increased to include the $10,000 in soft costs referenced earlier, bringing the Total Project Cost to $1.010 million.

SBA 504 LOAN – $1.010 MILLION PROJECT
(INCLUDES SOFT COSTS)

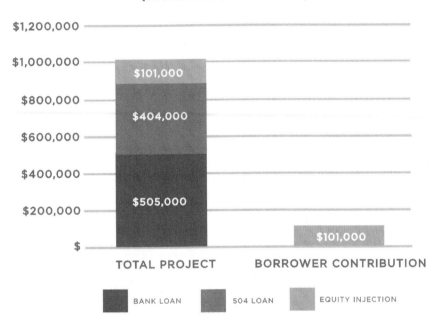

You will be responsible for a 10% down payment based on the higher Total Project Cost.

All in, you can expect to take $101,000 out of your pocket to purchase your business location using a 504 Loan.

We have all heard the truism "Cash is King". It implies that cash is your most versatile, valuable form of asset. Doesn't it make sense to apply that thinking when evaluating loan products?

The chart below shows, in dramatic fashion, your ability to conserve $109,000 in cash using an SBA 504 Loan.

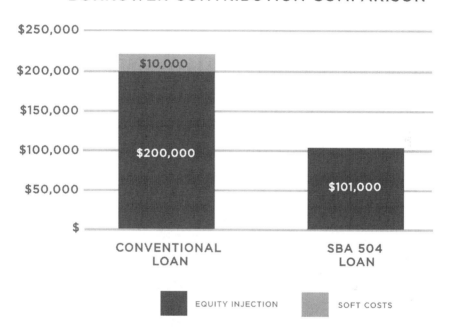

BORROWER CONTRIBUTION COMPARISON

When your cash down payment converts to an interest in real estate at closing, that cash is locked into your real estate. It is unavailable for any other purpose until you refinance the real estate or sell it. Both strategies will cost you money in fees and the refinance strategy is totally dependent on market conditions. In a down market, the cash invested in your real estate, may disappear and refinancing may be impossible because of a lower appraised value. Alternatively, selling your real estate in a down market has its own set of issues, not to mention it creates a need to find another home for your business.

Clearly, the preferred strategy for getting hard-earned money out of real estate *is to never put it in*. A 504 Loan keeps your cash on the sidelines for when you need it.

After a 504 Loan is closed and loan repayment begins, you will realize the benefits of the program's secondary incentives– a below market fixed-interest rate paired with an extended loan term (20 years for real estate, 10 years for most machinery and equipment). You will have a lower monthly payment on the 504 Loan portion of the financing package that is stable for the life of the loan thanks to the fixed rate.

To be eligible for 504 Loan financing, a small business must meet a job opportunity or economic development goal. This ensures that 504 Program loans have a positive impact on the local economy. The current job opportunity goal is 1 job for every $65,000 of 504 Loan financing. If business owner cannot reasonably project meeting the job opportunity goal within 2 years, there are any number of alternate economic and community development goals available to meet the eligibility standard.

There is no typical 504 Loan borrower or project. Medical, dental and veterinary practices and engineering, accounting and legal firms have all used the program to purchase or construct office space. 504 Loans have been used to finance manufacturing facilities, warehouses, retail facilities, grocery stores, horse farms, child care facilities, hotels, breweries, restaurants/caterers, funeral homes, sports facilities, autobody shops, auto repair shops, gas stations, mini-storage facilities and banquet halls. Those projects may or may not have included machinery and equipment.

These are the 504 Loan basics. If you think the 504 Loan Program is a good fit for your financing needs, your next step is to contact your local CDC for more details. The National Association of Development Companies (NADCO) is the CDC industry's trade association and the best resource to locate a CDC near you at nadco.org.

EVERETT COOK

WEFUNDER x HOPSTERS
How a craft brewery used regulation crowdfunding to spark a projected 7X increase in revenue

By Everett Cook

Lee Cooper knew his business had growth potential. Hopsters, a craft brewery where customers brew their own beer, had recorded $1.3 million in sales in 2015 in a 2,000 sq. ft. facility in Newton, a suburb of Boston. Business was so good, and the model so scalable, that Cooper knew building a larger facility in Boston proper could boost his profits significantly. This was a pick and shovel business within an established model. All he was missing was the capital.

He tried the bank at first, but couldn't get nearly enough to build out the new location. Cooper then hired a specialist, agreeing to 10% of the raised funds in exchange for connections to hospitality investors and VCs. The process took months and raised only $400,000, not enough for the full expansion.

Cooper hadn't heard of regulation crowdfunding, which allows customers and community members to invest in his business, until a friend in the industry sent him a tip. He then went to Wefunder. After exploring all other options, this is the model that worked.

The fee was less than half of what the specialist charged and the process took less time. By the time the deal closed, he'd raised $1.3 million through Wefunder from 720 investors. Then, he was able to go to the bank and receive a better deal on a $750,000 loan, giving him enough total capital to start his expansion plans.

"They obviously wouldn't have given me that if I didn't raise the Wefunder money," Cooper said about the bank. "The best thing about selling equity is that you're selling someone a piece of your business. The bank doesn't want your business.

They just want the money back." This winter, Hopsters is opening their second location in an up-and-coming neighborhood of Boston called Seaport. It's 3 times as large as the original brewery. Revenue is projected to increase from $1.3 to $9 million as a result, and if everything continues to scale as planned, Hopsters plans to open 16 more locations by 2022.

"Without Wefunder, without this market, I don't know how I would have got the money," Cooper said. "I would've had to go rob a bank, so it just wouldn't have happened."

HOW COOPER COMPLETED A SUCCESSFUL CAMPAIGN

From the beginning of the campaign, Cooper focused on the specific story of his brewery. This seems like a small step, but he found it to be vital to his campaign.

The story that he pitched wasn't complicated—if you invest in Hopsters, you can own your own piece of a neighborhood brewery.

This is the message he consistently sent out through the campaign. Things like investment videos, community events, and Facebook groups all heard the same idea. Cooper didn't try to sell the uniqueness of the Hopsters model, or his revenue numbers. He sold the very concept of his campaign. This proved valuable for all of his investors, but particularly for the local ones who frequently visited the bar. This audience proved to be crucial, as the majority of Hopsters investors came from Massachusetts.

UNDERSTANDING HIS KNOWLEDGE GAPS

Cooper was not a crowdfunding expert when he started his Wefunder campaign and didn't pretend to be.

"I get a lot of calls saying, 'Hey, I'm thinking about running a crowdfunding campaign, what made you successful?' " Cooper said. "I say, 'Get yourself a good lawyer. Get yourself a good accountant. Educate yourself. Find out what your story is, put the effort in to make time to sell the crap out of it, and you'll do well.' "

The reason? He knew he would get hundreds of questions from both current and potential investors. Cooper thought nobody would give money to a business led by someone who didn't know what he was talking about. So he hired the right people and then spent a lot of time figuring out the ins and outs of the process, both of which helped his investment base.

"It was definitely an emotional rollercoaster because we wouldn't just have been able to open the brewery, and crowdfunding is a great thing, but it was a lot of work," Cooper said. "I spent some money on legal fees between making sure the subscription agreement makes sense, making sure that I did the accounting piece of it. I mean, it's not easy, but you know what? People were giving me close to $2 million, bank's giving me close to a million bucks. It shouldn't be easy."

COMMUNICATION DURING THE CAMPAIGN BECAME KEY

Cooper talked with investors during his campaign, especially at the brewery, but the real conversations happened online. Every Hopsters investor was invited to a private Facebook group where they were asked three questions: Why did you invest, what can we do better, and how can we get you more involved?

"Everyone's being inundated with a million different pieces of information these days," Cooper said. "People prioritize you and give you time as long as you provide a great communication that gets them involved and gives them what they want."

Cooper had been sending out content to his 15,000 Facebook followers, but also paid to boost ads on the site during the campaign. Eventually, he noticed that a lot of his investment dollars were coming in as a result of those boosts. So he contacted Facebook's PR team, thinking they would blow him off. Instead, they set up a story with CNBC, who ran a long article on the Hopsters Wefunder campaign. Cooper estimates that national article brought in $150,000 to the campaign, and it only happened because he asked.

WHY REGULATION CROWDFUNDING PROVED SUPERIOR

Cooper prefers equity over debt for several reasons, but a big one is that his investors are also his customer base. He consistently meets patrons in the brewery who introduce themselves as investors in Hopsters, which he knows is huge for the business.

These customers are the world's best advertising. They introduce Hopsters to their friends, offices, and social channels, doing the sort of grassroots marketing you just can't pay for. This is true at the old location, but will be even more important in the new one.

"These are people that are going to speak highly about you, going to give you good feedback, and they're going to spend the time on supporting the business," Cooper said. "But they'll only be as receptive to the time that you put in building a relationship with them."

There were other advantages to having a customer base as investors, because Hopsters is Cooper's passion— its success or failures are his own. To have more than 700 people from all over the world invest their own money into his idea was something no less than extraordinary.

"When I hit that million dollars, there was so much ... not anxiety, but there was so much build up and so much tension about getting that," Cooper said. "When I hit that million dollars, I remember like it was yesterday, but I'm sitting in my office and I saw it hit a million bucks, I closed the door, and I cried. I don't cry, I never cry, but I had a five-minute moment there."

ABOUT MY KICKSTARTER SUPPORTERS

ACCESS REHAB CENTERS provides a range of physical therapy and rehabilitation services in Connecticut. I am proud to serve on the board of directors of this fine organization. If you need the best care, visit AccessRehab.com to find out more.

ANDREW WOODS is the executive director of Hartford Communities That Care (HCTC), a nonprofit organization dedicated to serving youth in Hartford, Connecticut. I had the pleasure of serving on the board of directors. Andrew is an inspiring leader who is passionate about helping youth succeed.

ERIC C. HAMPTON worked for the State of Connecticut for twenty-three years, helping businesses access capital and other assistance. Our paths crossed over the years serving small businesses. Thank you for being there for me and businesses over the years.

JOHN E. ROBINSON works for a nonprofit lender in Hartford. John is committed to helping small businesses succeed. He is an avid golfer and former athlete. John once scored five touchdowns in a high school football game and was inducted into the New Britain Sports Hall of Fame.

KENNETH "KC" WARD is the phenomenal chef, father of two, husband, and business owner of two restaurants in Connecticut: FLORA in West Hartford & Rooster Company in Newington. KC operates the restaurants with his wife, Jaime. Visit one of KC's restaurants for an amazing meal.

NORMANDO "NORM" MOQUETE JR. is the founder and CEO of Pinnacle Maintenance, a business that specializes in facilities maintenance services for commercial and residential real estate. Norman is one of the most organized business owners I have ever met. Don't stop growing your business.

SUZANNE MCKENZIE is a lover of all things art, including Andy Warhol. She is the founder of Able Made and the Ucal McKenzie Breakaway Foundation, which educates youth about healthy lifestyles through its soccer clinics. Give generously to the foundation at UcalBreakaway.com.

TONY JORGENSEN is an attorney and business owner in Hartford, Connecticut. We have worked together on many projects. Tony is my go-to attorney for legal advice. He's a die-hard Los Angeles Lakers fan. Thank you for being there for me and my businesses over the years.

WENDELL PRICE is my brother; Patricia Price is his wife. She's the best sister-in-law, whose kindness is what makes the world a better place. I couldn't write this book without my family. Thank you Wendell and Trish for the sacrifices you have made to help me.

I appreciate and thank all the people who contributed to my Kickstarter campaign: Biota Li Macdonald, Sophia Ononye, Jayuan Carter, John Lobon, Dr. John Gevinski, Angelique Boucher, Brendan Burns, Toure Diggs, Nicole Peterkin, Dontrese Brown, Ed McKeon, Tamar Draughn, Jim Zoldy, Loraine Shea, Michael Howey, Kevin McCarthy, Michael Obomalayat, Donovan Price, Beth Gardner, Jay Oboma, Julian Sawyer, Kathy Worthington, Gert and Bob McCarthy, Patricia Geronimo, Christine and Thomas Kainamura, Jonny Price and Madeleine Cannon.

FUTURE READING

If you're lucky, you will live a long, happy life and find meaningful work.

The people who achieve success don't do it on their own. Business is about people and serving others. *Fast Company* magazine asked Apple CEO Tim Cook, "So what matters?" Cook replied, "It's always products and people. The question at the end of every year, or every month, or every week, or every day is, 'Did we make progress on that front?'"[1] *Fast Company* asked, "What makes a good year for Apple? Is it the new hit products? The stock price?" Cook replied, "Stock price is a result, not an achievement by itself. For me, it's about products and people. Did we make the best product, and did we enrich people's lives?"[2]

When you make great products and treat people well, you will succeed. But what is success? Success is a dynamic learning process of understanding what you did right and wrong—but it's constantly changing. Failure is the twin of success. Both need each other, like the Persian Proverb reveals, "He who wants a rose must respect the thorn." Failure is an opportunity to say, "I can do better." The company can do better. The world must do better.

One of the best ways of learning and improving is to read books. I make an annual commitment to read books on all subjects—not just business—to keep my mind filled with thoughts that will propel me to be a better human, learner and business owner. Here's a collection of ten books that have been helpful for me. If you have books that have helped you, send me a note at info@LootScout.com. Happy reading!

The E Myth Revisited: Why Most Small Businesses Don't Work and What to Do About It, Michael E. Gerber
-for business builders

Venture Deals: Be Smarter Than Your Lawyer and Venture Capitalist, Brad Feld and Jason Mendelson
-for catching a VC

As A Man Thinketh, James Allen
-for confidence

How Money Works, DK
-for understanding money

The Law of Success: The Master Wealth-Builder's Complete and Original Lesson Plan for Achieving Your Dreams, Napoleon Hill
-for success

Everybody Writes: Your Go-To Guide to Creating Ridiculously Good Content, Ann Handley
-for creating content

The Elements of Style, William Strunk Jr & E.B. White
-for writing

The Magic of Believing, Claude M. Bristol
-for going for It

Go for No! Yes is the Destination, No is How You Get There, Richard Fenton & Andrea Waltz
-for selling

Do the Work!, Steven Pressfield
-for procrastinators & nonbelievers

SOMETHING TO THINK ABOUT

"When you feel tired, you should accelerate. That's when you start winning. So, and I've learnt that with developing new technology, that when you feel like giving up is precisely the point everybody else gives up. So, it's at that point you must put in extra effort. And you do that and then success is literally just around the corner."

–James Dyson, Founder of Dyson
Source: "How I Built This," NPR interview, February 12, 2018

"People are successful because of what they do right. And they lose because of what they do wrong. It's like sports. You win because of what you did right" [1:39].

–LL Cool J
Source: Drink Champs

"Get your revenues up, keep your costs down. That was my Harvard MBA, and I was set."

–Robert Johnson
Source: "How I Built This," NPR interview, December 14, 2017

"You have to create your own lane, otherwise you're just another piece on the table."

–Big Daddy Kane
Source: Drink Champs

Q: What is a free man?
"A free man I think is someone who is true to himself, and who makes his dreams come true. So we will always have dreams, and we will need to fulfill them because it's all possible if you put enough work into it."

–Jossi Wells
The Flying Frenchies
The Freeman Movie

NOTES

ACKNOWLEDGEMENTS

1. "George Eliot Quotes," *BrainyQuote*, accessed May 23, 2018, https://www.brainyquote.com/quotes/george_eliot_161679.

INTRODUCTION

1. "Brevity is the Soul of Wit," *Literary Devices*, accessed May 23, 2018 https://literarydevices.net/brevity-is-the-soul-of-wit/.

2. Corey "Raekwon" Woods, "C.R.E.A.M." Lyrics, *Genius*, accessed May 23, 2018 https://genius.com/1401502.

3. Napoleon Hill, *The Law of Success* (New York: Penguin Group, 2008), 560.

CHAPTER 1
WHAT ARE YOU: ENTREPRENEUR OR SMALL-BUSINESS OWNER?

1. Ben Lamm, "Stop Calling Everyone an Entrepreneur—They Aren't," *Entrepreneur*, March 22, 2017, https://www.entrepreneur.com/article/294549.

2. Lamm, "Stop."

3. Malcolm Gladwell, *David and Goliath* (New York: Hachette Book Group, 2015), 117.

4. Kurt Badenhausen, "Lebron James-Backed Blaze Pizza Is Fastest-Growing Restaurant Chain Ever," *Forbes*, July 11, 2017, https://www.forbes.com/sites/kurtbadenhausen/2017/07/11/lebron-james-backed-blaze-pizza-is-fastest-growing-restaurant-chain-ever/#36da010152b2.

5. Investor Relations, "What is Facebook's mission," *Facebook*, accessed May 23, 2018, https://investor.fb.com/resources/default.aspx.

6. Barbara Farfan, "Google Business Profile and Mission Statement," *The Balance Small Business*, March 29, 2018, https://www.thebalancesmb.com/google-business-profile-2892814.

7. Elon Musk, "The Mission of Tesla," *Tesla*, accessed May 23, 2018, https://www.tesla.com/blog/mission-tesla.

8. "Frequently Asked Questions," *U.S. Small Business Administration Office of Advocacy*, Small Business Administration, June 2016, https://www.sba.gov/sites/default/files/advocacy/SB-FAQ-2016_WEB.pdf.

9. SBA, "Frequently."

10. Michael E. Gerber, The E-Myth Revisited (New York: HarperCollins, 1995), 3.

11. Gerber, *The E-Myth*, 13.

12. Gene Marks, "The Difference Between An Entrepreneur And A Small Business Owner, " Forbes, June 6, 2012, https://www.forbes.com/sites/quickerbettertech/2012/06/06/the-difference-between-an-entrepreneur-and-a-small-business-owner/#6923aacc6635.

13. Lamm, "Stop."

CHAPTER 2
BUILT TO LAST: YOUR VISION, MISSION & CULTURE

1. "Fiscal Year 2016 Annual Financial Report," The Walt Disney Company, accessed May 23, 2018, https://ditm-twdc-us.storage.googleapis.com/2016-Annual-Report.pdf.

2. Daniel W. Rasmus, "Defining Your Company's Vision," *Fast Company*, February 28, 2012, https://www. fastcompany.com/1821021/defining- your-companys- vision.

3. Jeremy Quittner, "The One Thing Warren Buffett Says Every Business Must Do" *Fortune*, June 8, 2016, http://fortune.com/2016/06/08/warren-buffett-delight/.

4. "Ikea 2017 by Numbers," *Ikea*, https://highlights.ikea.com/2017/facts-and-figures/.

5. "Our vision and business idea," Ikea, accessed May 23, 2018, https://www.ikea.com/ms/en_SG/about_ikea/our_business_idea/index.html.

6. "Company Facts," *Walmart*, accessed May 23, 2018, https://corporate.walmart.com/newsroom/company-facts.

7. "Walmart's Vision, Mission, Generic & Intensive Strategies," *Panmore Institute*, March 25, 2017, http://panmore.com/walmart-vision-mission-statement-intensive-generic-strategies.

8. "Our Mission.", The Walt Disney Company, accessed May 23, 2018, https://www.thewaltdisneycompany.com/about/.

9. "Our Vision and Business Idea", Ikea, accessed May 23, 2018, https://www.ikea.com/ms/en_SG/about_ikea/our_business_idea/index.html.

10. Walmart, accessed May 23, 2018, https://corporate.walmart.com/_news_/photos/walmart-helps-people-around-the-world-save-money-and-live-better-anytime-and-anywhere-in-retail-stores-online-and-through-their-mobile-devices.

11. *Merriam-Webster Dictionary*, accessed May 23, 2018, https://www.merriam-webster.com/dictionary/culture.

12. Napoleon Hill, *How to Sell Your Way Through Life* (NJ; John Wiley & Sons, 2010), 114.

13. Mike Isaac, "Uber Founder Travis Kalanick Resigns as C.E.O.," *New York Times*, June 21, 2017, https://www.nytimes.com/2017/06/21/technology/uber-ceo-travis-kalanick.html?_r=0%20-.

14. James Allen, *As A Man Thinketh* (Pennslyvania: Executive Books, 2001), 12.

CHAPTER 3
REV YOUR ENGINE: THE BUSINESS MODEL

1. "Breaking Down 'Business Model'", *Investopedia*, accessed May 23, 2018, http://www.investopedia.com/terms/b/businessmodel.asp.

2. Andrea Ovans, "What is a Business Model," *Harvard Business Review*, January 23, 2015, https://hbr.org/2015/01/what-is-a-business-model.

3. Joan Magretta, "Why Business Models Matter." *Harvard Business Review*, May 2002, https://hbr.org/2002/05/why-business-models-matter

4. "Dollar Sales of Ice Cream in the United States in 2017, by Type," *Statista*, accessed May 23, 2018, https://www.statista.com/statistics/587733/dollar-sales-ice-cream-us-by-type/.

5. "Amazingly Sharable Ice Cream Facts," *eCreamery*, July 19, 2015, https://www.ecreamery.com/amazingly-sharable-ice-cream-facts.html.

6. "About Us.", *Baskin-Robbins*, accessed May 23, 2018, https://www.baskinrobbins. com/content/baskinrobbins/en/aboutus.html.

7. Baskin-Robbins, "About Us,"

8. Robert Ferris, "Tesla Passes General Motors to Become the Most Valuable US Automaker," *CNBC*, April 10, 2017, https://www.cnbc.com/2017/04/10/tesla-passes-general-motors-to-become-the-most-valuable-us-automaker.html.

9. Ferris, "Tesla Passes."

10. Jeff Desjardins, "Tesla Is the World's 4th Largest Automaker by Value," *Business Insider*, August 21, 2017, http://www.businessinsider.com/tesla-stock-price-worlds-4th-largest-automaker-by-value-2017-8.

11. Mark Johnson, *Seizing the White Space*, accessed May 23, 2018, https://www. innosight.com/wpcontent/uploads/2016/10/STWS_ Business_Model_Analogies.pdf.

12. Samantha Schmidt, "Blockbuster Has Survived in Most Curious of Places— Alaska," April 26, 2017, *Washington Post*, https://www.washingtonpost.com/ news/morning-mix/wp/2017/04/26/blockbuster-has-survived-in-the-most-surprising-of-places-alaska/.

13. Dealbook, "Blockbuster Files for Bankruptcy," *New York Times*, September 23, 2010, https://dealbook.nytimes.com/2010/09/23/blockbuster-files-for- bankruptcy/.

14. James Briggs and Holly V. Hays, "Angie's List to be Acquired by HomeAdvisor Parent Company," USA Today Network, *The Indianapolis Star*, May 2, 2017, https://www.usatoday.com/story/money/nation-now/2017/05/02/angies-list-acquired-homeadvisor-parent-company/308711001/.

CHAPTER 4
YOUR MAP: FROM BUSINESS PLAN TO PITCH DECK

1. Anita Balakrishnan, "Scandals May Have Knocked $10 Billion Off Uber's Value, A Report Says, " *CNBC*, April 25, 2017, https://www.cnbc.com/2017/04/25/uber-stock-price-drops-amid-sexism-investigation-greyballing-and-apple-run-in-the-information.html.

2. "History," Laz Parking, accessed May 23, 2018, https://www.lazparking.com/ our- company/about/history.

3. Anthony Price, "Don't Bring a Business Plan to Investors," *Hartford Business Journal*, February 29, 2016, http://www.hartfordbusiness.com/article/20160229/ PRINTEDITION/302259916.

4. Price, "Don't Bring."

5. Evan Baehr, Evan Loomis, *Get Backed* (Harvard Business Review Press: Boston: 2015)

6. Price, "Don't Bring."

7. Price, "Don't Bring."

8. Price, "Don't Bring."

9. Price, "Don't Bring."

CHAPTER 5
SATISFY NEEDS & WANTS: YOUR VALUE PROPOSITION

1. "The Few Sentences You Need to Dominate Your Market." *Kissmetrics*, accessed May 23, 2018, https://blog.kissmetrics.com/dominate-your-market/.

CHAPTER 6
DELIGHT CUSTOMERS: HAPPY CUSTOMERS SPEND

1. "Company Profile 2018," Starbucks, April 2018, https://news.starbucks.com/uploads/documents/AboutUs-Company_Profile-4.30.18.pdf.

CHAPTER 7
FOCUS: EXCEL AT ONE THING

1. Jim Croce, *Time in a Bottle, Genius*, https://genius.com/Jim-croce-time-in-a-bottle-lyrics.

2. *In Time, IMDB*, https://www.imdb.com/title/tt1637688/.

3. Susan Weinschenk, "The True Cost of Multi-Tasking," *Psychology Today*, September 18, 2012, https://www.psychologytoday.com/us/blog/brain- wise/201209/the-true-cost-multi-tasking.

4. Og Mandino, *The Greatest Salesman in the World, Part II: The End of the Story* (New York: Bantam Books, 1989), 112.

5. Cal Newport, *Deep Work*, YouTube, accessed May 23, 2018, https://www.youtube.com/watch?v=zfoCyFvADtU.

6. Cal Newport, *Deep Work*

7. Robert Safian, "Why Apple Is The World's Most Innovative Company," *Fast Company*, February 21, 2018, https://www.fastcompany.com/40525409/why-apple-is-the-worlds-most-innovative-company.

8. Safian, "Why Apple."

9. Safian, "Why Apple."

10. Safian, "Why Apple."

11. "Facts & Figures," Chicken Soup for the Soul Beta, accessed May 23, 2018, http://www.chickensoup.com/about/facts-and-figures.

12. "Visualization Techniques to Affirm Your Desired Outcomes: A Step-by-Step Guide," Jackcanfield, accessed May 23, 2018, http://jackcanfield.com/blog/visualize-and-affirm-your-desired-outcomes-a- step-by-step-guide/.

CHAPTER 8
CHANGE THE GAME: MEET LAVAR BALL

1. Kyle Boone, "LaVar Ball says Lonzon will play for the Lakers: 'I'm going to speak it into existence,'" *CBSSports*, February 26, 2017, https://www.cbssports.com/college-basketball/news/lavar-ball-says-lonzo-will-play-for-lakers-im-going-to-speak-it-into-existence/.

2. Nick DePaula, "How the Big Baller Brand is trying to disrupt the entire sneaker industry," *ESPN*, August 4, 2017, http://www.espn.com/nba/story/_/id/20225342/how-big-baller-brand-trying-disrupt-entire-sneaker-industry.

3. Movie Quote DB, accessed May 23, 2018, http://www.moviequotedb.com/movies/jerry-maguire/quote_11809.html.

4. Logan Bradley, "Facebook Reads The Comments, Lengthens 'Ball in The Family' Episodes," *SportsTechie*, March 5, 2018, https://www.sporttechie.com/facebook-reads-comment-lenghten-ball-in-the-family-episodes/.

5. Barbara Farfan, "Quotes From McDonald's Founder Ray Kroc," *The Balance Small Business*, May 12, 2018, https://www.thebalancesmb.com/mcdonalds-ray-kroc-quotes-2892155.

6. Christopher Klein, "10 Things You May Not Know About Martin Luther King Jr." April 4, 2013, https://www.history.com/news/10-things-you-may-not-know-about-martin-luther-king-jr.

7. Klein, "10 Things."

8. Yohuru Williams, "Susan B. Anthony." *Biography courtesy BIO*, accessed May 23, 2018, https://www.history.com/topics/womens-history/susan-b-anthony.

CHAPTER 9
WHEN IT DOESN'T WORK: PIVOT

1. Eminem, "Lose Yourself," *Genius*, accessed May 23, 2018, https://genius.com/Eminem-lose-yourself-lyrics.

2. "The Last Kodak Moment?" *Economist*, January 14, 2012, http://www.economist.com/node/21542796.

3. "Last Kodak?" *Economist*

4. Heraclitus, *Wikiquote*, accessed May 23, 2018, https://en.wikiquote.org/wiki/Heraclitus.

5. David Gelles, "The WeWork Manifesto: First, Office Space. Next, the World," *New York Times*, February 17, 2018, https://www.nytimes.com/2018/02/17/business/the-wework-manifesto-first-office-space-next-the-world.html.

6. David Gelles, "The WeWork,"

7. Quentin Hardy, "Young Tech Sees Itself in Microsoft's Ballmer," *New York Times*, August 25, 2013, https://www.nytimes.com/2013/08/26/technology/young-tech-sees-itself-in-microsofts-ballmer.html.

8. Hardy, "Young Tech."

9. Geoff Colvin, "Warren Buffett's Very Ordinary Management," *Fortune*, December 14, 2016, http://fortune.com/2016/12/14/warren-buffetts-very-ordinary-management/.

10. Colvin, "Warren Buffet's."

CHAPTER 10
IT TAKES A TEAM: PLAY TO WIN

1. Adam Bryant, "Marla Malcolm Beck's Three Keys to Hiring: Skill, Will and Fit," *New York Times*, January 10, 2015, https://www.nytimes.com/2015/01/11/business/corner-office-marla-malcolm-becks-three-keys-to-hiring-skill-will-and-fit.html?_r=0.

2. "Independent Contractor Defined," Internal Revenue Service, accessed May 23, 2018, https://www.irs.gov/businesses/small-businesses-self-employed/independent-contractor-defined.

3. Mark K. Smith, "Bruce W. Tuckman – forming, storming, norming and performing in groups," *Infed*, 2015, http://infed.org/mobi/bruce-w-tuckman-forming-storming-norming-and-performing-in-groups/.

4. Paul Flannery, "Explaining the World Through Kevin Garnett Quotes," *SBNation*, November 8, 2012, https://www.sbnation.com/2012/11/8/3617850/kevin-garnett-boston-celtics-quotes.

CHAPTER 11
EMPLOYEES WANT MEANING: TREAT 'EM RIGHT

1. Jim Emerman, "Working Longer For Much More Than A Paycheck," *Forbes*, August 6, 2015, https://www.forbes.com/sites/nextavenue/2015/08/06/working-longer-for-much-more-than-a-paycheck/#61333ca31924.

2. Fyodor Dostoyevsky, "Quotable Quote," accessed May 23, 2018, https://www.goodreads.com/quotes/6715871-if-one-wanted-to-crush-and-destroy-a-man-entirely.

3. Roman Krznaric, *How to Find Fulfilling Work* (New York: Picador, 2012)

4. Krznaric, *Find Fulfiling*, 57.

5. Krznaric, *Find Fulfiling*, 58.

6. Krznaric, *Find Fulfiling*, 62.

7. Napoleon Hill, *How to Sell Your Way Through Life* (New Jersey: John Wiley & Son, 2010), 97.

8. "Can Your Passion Be A Career, " *Barking Up the Wrong Tree*, https://www.bakadesuyo.com/2013/07/how-to-find-your-passion-in-life/.

9. "Quotable Quote," *Goodreads*, accessed May 23, 2018, https://www.goodreads.com/quotes/431261-where-your-talents-and-the-needs-of-the-world-cross.

10. Jim Asplund, "When Americans Use Their Strengths More, They Stress Less," *Gallup*, September 27, 2012, http://news.gallup.com/poll/157679/americans-strengths-stress-less.aspx.

11. Abraham Maslow, *The Pursuit of Happiness*, accessed May 23, 2018, http://www.pursuit-of-happiness.org/history-of-happiness/abraham-maslow/.

CHAPTER 12
THE ENTREPRENEURIAL UNIVERSE: KNOW YOUR ECOSYSTEM

1. Allen, *As A Man*, 25.

2. "The Dangerous Quest for Coffee that Inspired Dave Eggers' New Book," *CBS News*, February 24, 2018, https://www.cbsnews.com/news/dave-eggers-author-mokhtar-alkhanshali-talk-new-book/.

CHAPTER 13
MARKETING: JUST DO IT

1. Diana Kander, *All In Startup* (New Jersey: John Wiley & Sons, 2014)

2. Edmund Jerome McCarthy, Basic Marketing: A Managerial Approach. (Pennsylvania: R.D. Irwin, 1960)

CHAPTER 14
LISTENING IS SELLING: SOLVE PROBLEMS

1. Napoleon Hill, *How to Sell Your Way Through Life* (New Jersey: John Wiley & Sons: 2010), 6.

2. Frank Bettger, *How I Raised Myself from Failure to Success in Selling* (New York: Fireside: 1992), 35.

3. Bettger, *How I*, 37.

4. Bettger, *How I*, 39.

5. Geoffrey James, "6 Emotions That Make Customers Buy," *Inc.*, February 8, 2012, https://www.inc.com/geoffrey-james/6-emotions-that-make-customers- buy.html.

6. Richard Fenton and Andrea Waltz, *Go for No! Yes is the Destination, No Is How You Get There* (Self-pub.: Accelerated Performance Training, 2007)

CHAPTER 15
ACCOUNTING: THE NUMBERS ARE THE BUSINESS

1. David Kestenbaum, "The Accountant Who Changed The World, " *All Things Considered*, October 4, 2012, https://www.npr.org/sections/money/2012/10/04/162296423/the-accountant-who-changed-the-world.

2. Double-entry bookkeeping system, Wikipedia, accessed May 23, 2018, https://en.wikipedia.org/wiki/Double-entry_bookkeeping_system.

3. David Kestenbaum, "The Accountant,"

4. Business Builder 3, "How to Prepare a Profit and Loss (Income) Statement," *Zions Bank*, accessed May 23, 2018, https://www.zionsbank.com/pdfs/biz_resources_book-3.pdf.

5. Business Builder 2, "How To Prepare And Analyze A Balance Sheet," *Zions Bank*, accessed May 23, https://www.zionsbank.com/pdfs/biz_resources_book-2.pdf.

6. Business Builder 4, "How To Prepare A Cash Flow Statement," *Zions Bank*, accessed May 23, https://www.zionsbank.com/pdfs/biz_resources_book-4.pdf.

CHAPTER 16
FIND AN ATTORNEY: PROTECT YOUR BUSINESS

1. Matt Pilon, "Russian Lady Hit with Music Lawsuit," Hartford Business Journal, October 24, 2016, http://www.hartfordbusiness.com/article/20161024/PRINTEDITION/310209898/russian-lady-hit-with-music-lawsuit.

CHAPTER 17
WHERE TO FIND HELP: CONSULTANTS ARE EVERYWHERE

1. Atul Gawande, "Personal Best," *The New Yorker*, October 3, 2011, https://www.newyorker.com/magazine/2011/10/03/personal-best

2. Gawande, "Personal Best."

3. Mark Garrison, "A Startup Is Disrupting the Consulting Industry," *Marketplace*, October 9, 2015, https://www.marketplace.org/2015/12/09/business/startup-disrupting-consulting-industry.

CHAPTER 19
EXPANSION MODE: GROWTH BY ACQUISITION

1. "Small Business Transactions Reached Record Highs in 2017, up 27 Percent from 2016, According to BizBuySell.com Report," BizBuySell, January 10, 2018, https://www.bizbuysell.com/news/article130.html.

CHAPTER 20
CELEBRATE SMALL VICTORIES: TAKE A VICTORY LAP

1. Anna Robaton, "Why So Many Americans Hate Their Jobs," *CBS News*, March 31, 2017, https://www.cbsnews.com/news/why-so-many-americans-hate-their-jobs/.

2. Robaton, "Why So Many."

3. Steve Jobs, City Council Meeting, 6/7/2011, City of Cupertino, *YouTube*, accessed May 23, 2018, https://youtu.be/gtuz5OmOh_M.

4. Jobs, "City Council Meeting."

5. Jobs, "City Council Meeting."

6. Nola Taylor Redd, "How Old Is the Universe?" *Space*, June 7, 2017, https://www.space.com/24054-how-old-is-the-universe.html.

7. Kathy Gurchiek, "Millennial's Desire to Do Good Defines Workplace Culture," *SHRM*, July 7, 2014. https://www.shrm.org/ResourcesAndTools/hr-topics/behavioral-competencies/global-and-cultural-effectiveness/Pages/Millennial-Impact.aspx.

8. Gurchiek, "Millennial's Desire."

9. Quote Investigator, https://quoteinvestigator.com/2014/09/02/job-love/.

10. Nelson Mandela, *Goodreads*, accessed May 23, 2018, https://www.goodreads.com/quotes/26904-after-climbing-a-great-hill-one-only-finds-that-there.

CHAPTER 21
CREDIT: YOU NEED IT

1. Tamara E. Holmes, "Credit Card Market Share Statistics." Creditcards, June 22, 2016, https://www.creditcards.com/credit-card-news/market-share- statistics.php.

2. Holmes, "Credit Card."

3. The Notorious B.I.G., "Ten Crack Commandments," Genuis, accessed May 23, 2018, https://genius.com/The-notorious-big-ten-crack-commandments-lyrics.

4. The Notorious B.I.G.,"Ten Crack Commandments."

5. "The 85 Most Disruptive Ideas in Our History," Bloomberg BusinessWeek, accessed May 23, 2018, https://www.bloomberg.com/businessweek/85ideas/.

6. Craig Timberg, Elizabeth Dwoskin, Brian Fung, "Data of 143 Million Americans Exposed in Hack of Credit Reporting Agency Equifax," WashingtonPost, September 7, 2017, https://www.washingtonpost.com/business/technology/equifax-hack-hits-credit-histories-of-up-to-143-million-americans/2017/09/07/a4ae6f82-941a-11e7-b9bc-b2f7903bab0d_story.html?utm_term=.798412ff9321.

CHAPTER 22
CAPITAL: GOOD, CHEAP OR FAST

1. Karen Gordon Mills, Brayden McCarthy, "Innovation and Technology and the Implications for Regulation," Harvard Business Review, Working Paper 17-042, https://www.hbs.edu/faculty/Publication%20Files/17-042_30393d52-3c61-41cb-a78a-ebbe3e040e55.pdf, 5.

CHAPTER 24
BE ALL IN: COLLATERAL & YOUR PERSONAL GUARANTEE

1. "Small Business Facts," Small SBA Office of Advocacy, accessed May 23, 2018, https://www.sba.gov/sites/default/files/Business-Survival.pdf.

2. Big Daddy Kane, "Ain't No Half-Steppin', Genius, accessed May 23, 2018, https://genius.com/Big-daddy-kane-aint-no-half-steppin-lyrics.

3. Arnold Ziegel, Fundamentals of Credit and Credit Analysis (self-pub.: Mountain Mentors Associates, 2014), 5.

CHAPTER 25
CREDIT WORTHINESS: ARE YOU BANKABLE?

1. Ziegel, Fundamentals of Credit, II.

2. First Connecticut Bancorp, 10-K, December 31, 2016, 10.

CHAPTER 26
INTEREST EXPLAINED: THE COST OF CAPITAL

1. Suzanne Kearns, "Is Your Business Profitable? 3 Reasons a Loan May Make Sense," Intuit Quickbooks, accessed May 23, 2018, https://webcache. googleusercontent.com/search?q=cache:glf8C4M_JvkJ:https://quickbooks. intuit.com/r/loans/is-your-business-profitable-3-reasons-a-loan-may-make-sense+&cd=1&hl=en&ct=clnk&gl=us&client=safari.

2. Rebecca Davis O'Brien, "Kansas City Businessman Gets Nearly 17 Years for Payday Lending Scheme," January 5, 2018, https://www.wsj.com/articles/kansas-city-businessman-gets-nearly-17-years-for-payday-lending-scheme-1515190826.

3. "The Truth About Interest Rates for Term Loans," *Accion*, accessed May 23, 2018, https://us.accion.org/resource/truth-about-interest-rates-term-loans/.

CHAPTER 27
YOU WIN: COMPETE FOR MONEY

1. Kenneth R. Gosselin, "Health Team Takes Top Prize in Hartford's Strong Cities Contest," *Courant*, May 29, 2015, http://www.courant.com/real-estate/property-line/hc-sc2-hartford-connecticut-challenge-20150529-story.html.

2. Gosselin, "Health Team."

CHAPTER 28
BIG CORPORATIONS HAVE LOTS OF MONEY: GET SOME

1. Catherine Clifford, "Founder of Company Doing $1 Billion in Sales: Why Working Long Hours Can be Damaging to Your Business," *CNBC*, June 3, 2017, https://www.cnbc.com/2017/06/02/billion-dollar-company-founder-tory-burch-burnout-is-bad-for-business.html.

2. "The Boston Beer Company Annual Report 2016," Samuel Adams, accessed May 23, 2018, https://www.bostonbeer.com/static-files/1211cdad-a140-4c22-8fa5-29dadc84c794.

3. Jess Baker, "Craft Brewing Growth Statistics for 2016 Released by the Brewers Association," *Craftbeer*, https://www.craftbeer.com/editors-picks/craft-brewing-growth-statistics-2016-ba-report.

4. John Kell. "Kellogg Launches VC Fund to Invest in Food Startups." *Fortune*, June 20, 2016, http://fortune.com/2016/06/20/kellogg-launches-vc-fund/.

CHAPTER 29
PATIENT CAPITAL: FAMILY, FRIENDS – AND FOOLS

1. Dave Berkus, *Raising Money* (self-pub.: The Berkus Press, 2014).

CHAPTER 30
ANGELS: CAPITAL FROM HEAVEN – OR HELL

1. Brad Feld, Jason Mendelson, *Venture Deals*, Second Edition (New Jersey: John Wiley & Son, 2013), 5.

2. David S. Rose, *Angel Investing* (New Jersey: John Wiley & Son, 2014.), 5.

3. Laura Huang Ph.D., Andy Wu Ph.D., Min Ju Lee Ph.D. "The American Angel," November 2017, http://docs.wixstatic.com/ugd/ecd9be_5855a9b21a8c4fc1ab-c89a3293abff96.pdf.

4. Feld and Mendelson, *Venture Deal*, 9.

5. Rose, *Angel Investing*, xvi.

6. Huang, Wu and Lee, "The American Angel,"

7. Marianne Hudson, "Angel Investment in the U.S.—Trends & Best Practices. Angel Capital Association, September 26, 2016, http://angelcapitalassociation.org/data/Documents/ACAatAEBAN09-26-16.pdf.

8. Dave Berkus, *Raising Money*, 11.

CHAPTER 31
INVESTORS: SECURITIES & THE SILICON VALLEY WAY

1. Drew Field, *Direct Public Offerings*. (Illinois: Sourcebooks, 1997), 71.

2. Field, *Direct Public*, 71.

3. James E. Burk and Richard P. Lehmann. Financing Your Small Business. (Illinois: Sphinx Publishing, 006), 84.

4. Berkus, *Raising Money*, 28.

5. Feld and Mendelson, *Venture Deals*, 21.

CHAPTER 32
ASK THE CROWD: MY KICKSTARTER EXPERIENCE

1. Kickstarter, Stats, https://www.kickstarter.com/help/stats?ref=hello.

2. Kickstarter, "Stats."

3. Berkus, *Raising Money*, 14.

CHAPTER 33
START HERE: YOUR CAPITAL SEARCH

1. Kathryn Hennessy, ed., *How Money Works*. (New York: DK Publishers, First Edition, 2017).

2. "What is Moonshot Thinking?" Youtube, February 1, 2013, https://www.youtube.com/watch?v=0uaquGZKx_0.

CHAPTER 38
CREDIT CARDS: PLASTIC RULES

1. John Lanchester, "How America Learned to Live and Thrive with Debt—er, Credit," *Bloomberg BusinessWeek*, December 4, 2014, http://www.bloomberg.com/bw/articles/2014-12-04/credit-debt-made-over-as-opportunity.

CHAPTER 40
COMMUNITY DEVELOPMENT FINANCIAL INSTITUTIONS: COMMITTED TO THE MISSION

1. "Community Development Financial Institutions Program, Fact Sheet," U.S. Treasury Department, accessed May 23, 2018, https://www.cdfifund.gov/Documents/CDFI7205_FS_CDFI_updatedDec2017.pdf.

CHAPTER 41
ECONOMIC DEVELOPMENT FUNDS & GRANTS: CHEAP MONEY

1. Neil Vigdor, "Florida's Gov. Scott Returns to Connecticut to Woo Companies South," New NHRegister.com, June 19, 2017, https://www.nhregister.com/business/article/Florida-s-Gov-Scott-returns-to-Connecticut-to- 11311980.php.

CHAPTER 42
COMMUNITY BANKS: EMBEDDED IN THE COMMUNITY

1. "Community Banks Build Communities," ICBA, accessed May 23, 2018, http://www.icba.org/about/community-banking.

CHAPTER 43
CREDIT UNIONS: CREDIT FROM MEMBER-OWNED FINANCIAL COOPERATIVES

1. "Credit Unions," *Investopedia*, accessed May 23, 2018, https://www.investopedia.com/terms/c/creditunion.asp.

2. Andrew Latham, "Top 50 Credit Unions in The US," *Supermoney*, accessed May 23, 2018, https://www.supermoney.com/2015/08/top-50-credit-unions-us/.

3. Amanda Dixon, "America's Top 15 Largest Banks," *Bankrate*, February 21, 2018, https://www.bankrate.com/banking/americas-top-10-biggest- banks/#slide=1.

4. Rohit Arora, "Raising The Credit Union Lending Cap Would Benefit Small Businesses," Forbes, January 25, 2017, https://www.forbes.com/sites/rohitarora/2017/01/25/raising-the-credit-union-lending-cap-would-benefit-small-businesses/#2948607d1328.

CHAPTER 50
CROWDFUNDING: SMALL DOLLARS FROM MANY

1. "About Us," GoFundMe, accessed May 23, 2018, https://www.gofundme.com/about-us.

2. "Risks," *Wefunder*, accessed May 23, 2018, https://wefunder.com/faq/investors

3. Wefunder, "Risks."

CHAPTER 51
ACCREDITED INVESTORS: PROS WITH MONEY SEEKING A RETURN

1. Press Release, "Record Unicorn Financing Drove 2017 Total Venture Capital Investments to $84 Billion, the Largest Amount Since the Dot-Come Ear," National Venture Capital Association/Pitchbook, January 9, 20018, https://nvca.org/pressreleases/record-unicorn-financings-drove-2017-total-venture-capital-investments-84-billion-largest-amount-since-dot-com-era/.

2. "Bloomberg Markets' Annual Ranking of the Richest Family Offices", Bloomberg, accessed May 23, 2018, https://www.bloomberg.com/graphics/infographics/ranking-richest--family-offices.html.

3. Press Release, "Global Assets Under Management Set to Rise to $145.4 Trillion by 2025," PWC, October 30, 2017, https://press.pwc.com/News-releases/global-assets-under-management-set-to-rise-to--145.4-trillion-by-2025/s/e236a113-5115-4421-9c75-77191733f15f.

CHAPTER 52
ACCELERATORS & INCUBATORS: JUMPSTART YOUR IDEA OR BUSINESS

1. Conner Forrest, "Accelerators vs. Incubators: What Startups Need to Know," *TechRepublic*, November 17, 2014, https://www.techrepublic.com/article/accelerators-vs-incubators-what-startups-need-to-know/.

2. *Idealab*, http://www.idealab.com.

CHAPTER 53
SMALL BUSINESS INVESTMENT COMPANIES: GOVERNMENT-FUNDED VCs

1. "SBA SBIC Program," U.S. Small Business Administration, accessed May 23, 2018, https://www.sba.gov/sites/default/files/articles/Early_Stage-SBIC-Program_One- Pager-2016_April.pdf.

CHAPTER 55
MEZZANINE FINANCING: THE CAPITAL MIX

1. Jordan Wathen. "Mezzanine Debt: What It Is and How It Works—With Examples," *The Mootley Fool*, May 22, 2015, https://www.fool.com/investing/general/2015/05/22/mezzanine-debt-what-it-is-and-how-it-works.aspx.

CHAPTER 57
INITIAL PUBLIC OFFERING: WELCOME TO WALL STREET

1. Dave Michaels,"Companies Could Get More Flexability to Launch IPOs," *WSJ*, February 22, 2018. https://www.wsj.com/articles/companies-could-get-more-flexibility-to-start-ipos-1519295400.

2. Steven Davidoff Solomon, "A Dearth of I.P.O.s, but It's Not the Fault of Red Tape," *New York Times*, March 28, 2017, https://www.nytimes.com/2017/03/28/business/ dealbook/fewer-ipos-regulation-stock-market.html.

3. Maureen Farrell and Anne Steele, "Spotify Kicks Off Its Unusual IPO," *WSJ*, February 28, 2018, https://www.wsj.com/articles/spotify-kicks-off-its-unusual-ipo-1519847272.

CHAPTER 58
INITIAL COIN OFFERING: IS THIS THE FUTURE OF MONEY?

1. Paul Krugman, "Bubble, Bubble, Fraud and Trouble," *New York Times*, January 29, 2018, https://www.nytimes.com/2018/01/29/opinion/bitcoin-bubble- fraud. html.

2. Huw Jones, "Gibraltar Moves Ahead with World's First Initial Coin Offering Rules," *Reuters*, February 9, 2018, https://www.reuters.com/article/us-gibraltar-markets-cryptocurrencies/gibraltar-moves-ahead-with-worlds-first-initial-coin-offering-rules-idUSKBN1FT1YN

3. Jones, "Gibraltar Moves."

CHAPTER 59
REVERSE MERGER: IT'S COMPLICATED

1. Bill Meagher, "Reverse Mergers Losing Out to Lower-Cost Offerings," *TheStreet*, January 8, 2016, https://www.thestreet.com/story/13417591/1/reverse- mergers-losing-out-to-lower-cost-offerings.html.

2. Investor Bulletin: Reverse Mergers. SEC Office of Investor Education and Advocacy, accessed May 23, 2018, https://www.sec.gov/investor/alerts/ reversemergers.pdf.

3. Marvin Dumon, "Reverse Mergers: The Pros and Cons of Reverse IPOs," Investopedia, March 16, 2018, https://www.investopedia.com/articles/stocks/09/ introduction-reverse-mergers.asp.

CHAPTER 60
PRIVATE PLACEMENT OFFERING: WEALTHY INVESTORS WANTED

1. "Private Placement," *CuttingEdgeCapital*, accessed May 23, 2018, https://www. cuttingedgecapital.com/private-placements/.

2. "Private Placement," *Investopedia*, accessed May 23, 2018, https://www. investopedia.com/terms/p/privateplacement.asp.

3. "Private Placements, Explained," *FINRA*, July 1, 2015, http://www.finra.org/ investors/private-placements-explained.

BONUS CHAPTER: CHAPTER 61
CAN'T STOP, WON'T STOP: MORE CAPITAL OPTIONS

1. "Home Equity Line of Credit–HELOC," *Investopedia*, accessed May 23,2018, https://www.investopedia.com/terms/h/homeequitylineofcredit.asp.

2. Ben Taylor, "How to Borrow Against Private Equity Stock," *PocketSense*, July 27, 2017, https://pocketsense.com/borrow-against-private-equity-stock-10022397.html.

3. Carolyn Said, "How S.F. Companies Turn Stock Options Into Cash—without an IPO," *San Francisco Chronicle*, September 4, 2015, https://www.sfchronicle.com/business/article/How-S-F-companies-turn-stock-options-into-cash-6485919.php.

4. Kathryn Hennessy, ed., *How Money Works*. (DK Publishers: New York, First Edition, 2017), 70.

5. Libby Kane, "Here's How Rich People Are Using High-End Pawn Shops," *Business Insider,* September 11, 2014, http://www.businessinsider.com/rich-people-use-pawn-shops-borro-2014-9.

6. "Investor Relations," LendingClub, accessed May 23, 2018, http://ir.lendingclub.com/corporateprofile.aspx?iid=4213397.

7. "LendingClub Reports Third Quarter 2017 Results." LendingClub, http://ir.lendingclub.com/Cache/1500105145.PDF?Y=&O=PDF&D=&FID=1500105145&T=&IID=4213397.

8. BJ Lackland, "Beyond VC: Funding Options for Early-Stage Startups," *Gust*, December 18, 2017, http://blog.gust.com/beyond-vc-funding-options-for-startups/.

9. Andy Sack, "Revenue Based Financing," AVC, MBA Mondays, October 17, 2001, https://avc.com/2011/10/revenue-based-financing/.

10. Marco Vangelisti, "A New Funding Structure for Slow Money Projects,", January 16, 2012, http://slowmoneynorcal.org/royalty-financing/?from=@.

APPENDIX

1. Safian, "Why Apple."

2. Safian, "Why Apple."

INDEX

ANTHONY PRICE is the founder and CEO of LootScout, which counsels small businesses how to raise capital. LootScout is a platform for business to access capital, information and must-have services to build the best businesses on the planet. The company seeks to eliminate failure by creating products that make a business better, leading to 100,000 jobs with an economic impact of $1 billion. Price is a trusted advisor to growing businesses throughout the country.

Price is a former economic development executive and the founder of the LootScout Capital Summit, an annual event where thought leaders from across the country convene in Hartford, Connecticut to educate entrepreneurs about capital. His company has partnered with businesses and organizations to produce live and online events about capital.

He has written for the *Federal Reserve Bank of Boston, Hartford Business Journal,* HuffPost, Innovation Hartford, New York Business Journal and *Worcester Business Journal.* Price has appeared on popular TV programs, radio, and social media platforms. His research assistance on small business was acknowledged by Michael Shuman in his book, *The Local Economy Solution: How Innovative, Self-Financing "Pollinator" Enterprises Can Grow Jobs and Prosperity.*

Price has delivered speeches and served as a judge and mentor for business competitions. He is often asked to be a panelist for discussions about small-business capital formation. Price serves on several nonprofit boards in Connecticut; he is also currently on a for-profit board.

26207037R00224

Made in the USA
Columbia, SC
07 September 2018